# The Internationalisation of Stockmarkets

**GOWER STUDIES IN FINANCE AND INVESTMENT**
General Editor: Paul Stonham, EAP European School of Management Studies, Oxford

1 **The Internationalisation of Stock Markets**
David Ayling

2 **Financial Conglomerates: The New Phenomenon**
James Maycock

3 **Pension Funds: Investment and Performance**
Sylvio Prodano

# The Internationalisation of Stockmarkets

## The Trend towards Greater Foreign Borrowing and Investment

D.E. Ayling

Gower Studies in Finance and Investment, 1
Gower

Published by
Gower Publishing Company Limited,
Gower House,
Croft Road,
Aldershot,
Hants GU11 3HR,
England

Gower Publishing Company
Old Post Road
Brookfield
Vermont 05036
USA



British Library Cataloguing in Publication Data

Ayling, D.E.
The internationalisation of stock markets: the trend towards greater foreign borrowing and investment.——(Gower studies in finance and investment; 1)
1. International finance
I. Title
332 HG3881

ISBN 0-566-00825-4

Printed in Great Britain at the University Press, Cambridge

# Contents

**List of figures and tables** **xiii**

**About the author** **xv**

**Acknowledgements** **xvi**

**Preface** **xvii**

**1 Background to the internationalisation of stockmarkets** **1**
An overview 3
The trend towards deregulation and firmer linkages between capital markets 5
Innovation in financial markets 8
The world's largest markets 9
Summary 9
Reference 11

**2 Links between markets** **12**
Domestic versus world financial markets 13
The world as a financial marketplace 16
Domestic financial markets 17
Euromarkets 18
The foreign exchange market 19
International links 21
Summary 21

**3 Restricted versus free international financial flows** **23**
The demand for cross-border borrowing and investment 24
An economist's view 24
An investor's view 25
A borrower's view 27
Gains from diversification 27
Multinationals and world markets 28
Market characteristics that encourage international capital flows 28
Market characteristics that discourage international capital flows 31
Restrictions on securities markets 32
Restrictions via the banking system 34
Open market operations by central banks 34
Regulation of capital flows through commercial banks 35
Restrictions on currency market activities 36
Controls on offshore securities markets 37
Arguments for and against controls on international financial flows 37
Arguments for restrictions 38
Arguments against restrictions 38
The case of developing countries 40
Summary 41
Reference 42

**4 A historical perspective** **43**
Early days 44

The nineteenth century 45
The years 1900 to 1930 45
The depression of the 1930s 46
Thc years 1940 to 1960 47
The years 1960 to 1970 48
The years 1970 to 1980 50
Developments in the Euromarkets 52
Developments in national financial markets 53
The deregulation explosion of the 1980s 54
Summary 56
Further reading on the deregulatory trend of the 1980s 57
Appendix: Selected dates in the development of international financial markets 58

**5 Institutional aspects: The banks and the international institutions 68**
The International Monetary Fund (IMF) 70
The IMF and the evolution of the international monetary system 70
Special Drawing Rights (SDRs) at the IMF 74
The current role of the IMF 75
The World Bank (IBRD, IDA and IFC) 76
The IBRD 76
The IDA 77
The IFC 77
Other international institutions 78
The European Investment Bank (EIB) 78
The Agency for International Development (AID) 79
The Organisation for Economic Cooperation and Development (OECD) 79
The Bank for International Settlements (BIS) 79
Regional development banks 80
The Organisation for Petroleum Exporting Countries (OPEC) 80

International and multinational banking activities 80
Developments in international banking 81
Developments in multinational banking 82
Institutional developments in LDCs 85
Summary 86
Further reading 87
The IMF and the international monetary system 87
International development institutions 88
International and multinational banking 89
The debt crisis 90

**6 Borrowing in international markets** **92**
The Eurocurrency market 93
Eurodollars and other Eurocurrencies 93
Eurocurrency financing 95
The international bond market 97
The foreign bond market 98
The Eurobond market 100
Eurobond issue procedure 102
Recent developments in the Eurobond market 104
International bond instruments 106
Floating Rate Notes (FRNs) 106
Multiple currency Eurobonds 107
Zero coupon/original discount bonds 107
Eurobonds with warrants 108
Convertible Eurobonds 108
Droplock bonds 108
Parallel bonds 109
Swaps 109
The interest rate swap 110
The currency swap 111
The swap market 111
Summary 112

Further reading 113
The Euromarkets 113
Swaps 114

**7 World stockmarkets 115**
European stockmarkets (in general) 116
United Kingdom 117
West Germany 118
France 119
Belgium 120
Netherlands 121
Switzerland 121
Italy 122
Luxembourg 123
The US and Canadian markets 123
The USA 123
Canada 124
The Asian–Pacific region (in general) 125
Australia 125
Hong Kong 126
Singapore 127
Japan 128
Summary 130
Further reading on moves towards internationalisation of financial centres in the 1980s 131
Appendix: Sources of information on world stockmarkets 132
USA and Canada 132
Europe 133
Asia–Pacific region 135

**8 The foreign exchange markets 137**
Floating versus fixed exchange rates 138
Fixed exchange rates 138
Pegged exchange rates 139
Floating exchange rates 140
The nature of foreign exchange markets 141

The forward market for foreign exchange 141
The futures markets for foreign exchange 142
Currency options markets 142
The interbank market 143
Central banks' activities in the foreign exchange markets 145
Types of currency in foreign exchange markets 145
The (incredible) ECU 146
The new markets 148
The International Money Market (IMM), Chicago 149
The London International Financial Futures Exchange (LIFFE) 150
The Philadelphia Stock Exchange (PSE) for currency options 150
The Singapore International Monetary Exchange (SIMEX) 151
The future development of currency options and futures markets 151
Summary 152
Further reading 152
Foreign exchange markets in various countries 152
Options and futures 153

**9 Techniques for the international financial manager 154**
International diversification 155
Gains from international diversification 156
Evidence from the pension fund industry 158
Remaining restrictions on international diversification 159
The cost of capital for international firms 160
Multi-currency capital budgeting 163
Political risk 164
Managing exchange risk 165
Forecasting 167

What determines exchange rates? 167
Trading techniques 170
Hedging 171
Hedging examples using the forward market 171
Hedging using the futures markets 172
Arbitrage opportunities in foreign exchange markets 173
Speculating in modern markets 174
Speculating with foreign exchange options 175
Speculating with stockmarket index options 177
Summary 177
References 178
Further reading on techniques for financial managers 179

**10 Informational and technological aspects 181**
Market intelligence: The need to keep up-to-date 182
The new information technology industry 183
Information technology for the banks 184
Information technology for the markets 187
SICOVAM 187
NASDAQ 188
INSTINET 188
Euroclear 189
Cedel 189
TALISMAN 190
EPIC and Topic 190
SEAQ 190
CORES 191
INTEX 191
Electronic information services for fund managers 192
Personal finance computer links 192
Secrecy laws – the final barrier? 193
Summary 193
Further reading on market technology and financial information systems 194

**11 Summary, conclusions and potential future developments** **196**
The internationalisation of money and capital markets: A review of the process to date 197
Erosion of barriers between markets 197
Increased exposure to international economic forces 197
Movement towards freer markets 198
Harmonisation and improvement of professional standards 198
Wider access to markets 198
Increased flexibility of intermediation techniques 199
Changing roles for the international institutions 200
The nature of money is changing 200
Versatility and new techniques for financial managers 200
The future? 201
The future for the Eurobond market 201
The future for the developing countries 202
The future for money and the monetary system 205
The future for capital mobility and the integration of capital markets 208
Summary 210

**Bibliography** **212**
Books 212
Journals 213
Newspapers 218

Index 219

# List of figures and tables


| **Figures** | | *page* |
|---|---|---|
| 1.1 | The main influences leading to the internationalisation of stockmarkets | 10 |
| 2.1 | The pattern of financial intermediation | 14 |
| 2.2 | The pattern of domestic and world money and capital flows | 15 |
| 2.3 | Domestic markets, foreign exchange markets and Euromarkets | 16 |
| 2.4 | The foreign exchange market as a link between domestic and world markets | 20 |
| 3.1 | Levels of risk and return in domestic financial markets before and after market integration | 26 |
| 5.1 | Links between commercial banks, central banks and the international institutions | 69 |
| 5.2 | Exchange rates of major currencies against the dollar | 72 |
| 6.1 | The swap principle | 110 |
| 8.1 | Financial flows in the foreign exchange market | 144 |
| 9.1 | The relationship between currency options values and spot prices | 176 |

**Tables**

| | | *page* |
|---|---|---|
| 5.1 | Leading multinational banks by country | 83 |
| 6.1 | Eurobond and traditional foreign issues of bonds | 99 |
| 8.1 | Calculation of the ECU currency basket | 147 |

# About the author

David Ayling graduated from the University of Aston in Birmingham with a BSc in Administrative Science in 1976. In 1982 he was awarded a PhD for research into reinsurance under the University of Aston's Interdisciplinary Higher Degrees Scheme (IHD). He has worked in South African manufacturing industry, in the City of London's insurance community and as a university research officer. His previously published work includes various articles on insurance and banking topics and a book entitled *Underwriting Decisions Under Uncertainty: The Catastrophe Market* (Gower Publishing Company). He is currently employed as a Lecturer in Finance at the University College of North Wales, where he is also a member of the Institute of European Finance.

# Acknowledgements

Thanks to Jack Revell, Ted Gardener, Christine Owen and the team at the Institute of European Finance, UCNW, Bangor; to Paul Stonham for the title and editorial skills; to Christine MacKay, Esmé Voller, Tonia Kemp and Sue Potter for secretarial services; and to Caroline Bentley. Any errors or omissions in the text remain the responsibility of the author.

# Preface

The internationalisation of stockmarkets is a twentieth century phenomenon that threatens to change the face of world finance. Its implications extend from the financial marketplaces to industry, commerce, government and the general public. In a nutshell, the internationalisation of stockmarkets involves four main issues: deregulation of financial markets on a global scale; financial innovation faster than ever before; space-age technology for linking marketeers and transferring money and capital across national frontiers; and progress towards integrated world financial markets. These issues combine to provide both an interesting story and an important chapter in the history of mankind. Never before has change swept so quickly through the world's financial markets.

The aim of this book is to extract the main ingredients of the internationalisation process and set them into context within the history of financial change and the growing body of theoretical and professional financial knowledge. The approach taken is to combine descriptive and analytical material to provide an overall picture of the evolving markets. A large proportion of the information for this book came from the shelves of the Institute of European Finance at UCNW, Bangor, North Wales – a unique and growing collection of textbooks, journals, research papers and financial reports. It was also necessary, because of the speed at which the world's financial system is changing, to keep tracks of developments via press reports, TV and radio in order to catch them as they occurred and set them into wider perspective.

The result, hopefully, is a worthwhile and readable book, which will be appreciated by a wide range of finance professionals, economics students and the interested layman. Students of economics, particulary of finance and banking, should find the book invaluable for setting their more specific areas of study into a wider perspective. Professionals involved in financial processes in corporations or in the markets should also find the book useful for setting their own operations into context in a world of rapid financial change. Members of the general public may also find it of assistance as a guide to how international financial developments bring about changes in everyday life.

The internationalisation of stockmarkets is an absorbing topic which will continue to attract attention and debate from many sources. As one of the first analyses of the subject I hope that this book will help focus minds in preparation for future developments in the field.

D. E. Ayling

Limitations are troublesome, but they are effective. . . . Limitations are also indispensable in the regulation of world conditions. . . . But in limitation we must observe due measure. If a man seeks to impose galling limitations upon his own nature, it would be injurious. And if he should go too far in imposing limitations on others, they would rebel. Therefore it is necessary to set limits even upon limitations.

Wilhelm, Richard, *The Book of Changes* (*c*2000–1000BC), translated into English by Baynes, Cary F., London, Routledge & Kegan Paul, 1983, pp 231–2.

# 1 Background to the internationalisation of stockmarkets

The world's financial markets provide meeting places for the needs of borrowers and lenders of many nationalities. Huge volumes of money, capital and securities pass daily through the markets, which allow operation of the basic economic law that no-one enters into a transaction unless they expect to gain from it. The three main types of participants required for the successful working of the markets are lenders, financial intermediaries and borrowers. These may be subdivided into private individuals, businesses, governments, and other public bodies.

On a global scale, the main international lenders are the industrially advanced countries such as the US and those in Western Europe. In these countries (and also in some less industrialised countries) highly developed marketplaces have grown up, which provide links to overseas productive opportunities and channels for foreign-destined business and portfolio capital. The world's main borrowers include rapidly expanding countries with fast developing industries and ample natural resources (such as Canada, Australia and New Zealand), and low-income countries (such as South America and Asia) that have plentiful natural resources but require overseas capital for industrial development.

The final category of borrower includes India and Africa, where the economies benefit from few natural resources and where overpopulation and poverty is rife. These less developed countries (LDCs), historically, have not proved attractive places for overseas private capital. They acquire their development funds through official channels and through international organisations such as the World Bank, which provide a link with the international capital markets.

Traditionally, investors and borrowers have tended to look, first, at domestic financial opportunities and, second, at overseas possibilities. Nowadays, however, there are increasingly strong motives that lead lenders and borrowers to consider overseas opportunities more seriously. These motives may be divided into four main categories.

1 With the trend towards conglomeration and multinational enterprises, large international corporations often engage in international financial transactions to support their direct foreign investments. Their operations may be inspired by political considerations or simply because they find dealing in foreign markets either cheaper or less risky.
2 Investors in portfolios of securities, large and small, have a natural desire to reduce portfolio risk and increase portfolio return and liquidity. The key to balanced portfolio performance is diversification. By diversifying internationally a new dimension is added to domestic portfolio construction because it allows the setting off of characteristics of securities from one country against characteristics of securities in another.
3 The domestic market may be inadequate to supply the needs and speculative motives of the domestic financial community. Borrowers and investors may be forced, or simply prefer, to use foreign markets where the range of new issues, secondary markets, financial assets and instruments is much wider than in the home country.
4 Governmental sectors of economies can act as either lenders or borrowers in the world's financial markets depending on the size of their budgetary positions. The aim of governments in their transactions is to increase or protect the economic welfare of their respective countries. The motives behind these transactions could foreseeably cut across the previous categorisations. Owing to the large amounts of funds involved, government borrowing and lending can exert significant influence on supply, demand, and hence prices in financial markets worldwide.

As a result of these basic needs, the world's capital markets have become increasingly attuned to international financial transactions. The needs, aspirations and fears of investors and borrowers across the world have become entangled in a complex international financial system. Conflicting and complementary interests are becoming increasingly difficult to distinguish as the financial markets respond rapidly to the needs for fluidity and security of overseas financial transactions. The pace of the process now looks set to transform the scale of overseas financing and the nature of the world financial system.

**An overview**

The world's capital markets have become increasingly internationalised since the Second World War. Previously, in many cases, national capital markets either did not exist or were hemmed in by protective regulations and exchange controls. Any cross-border transfers of funds that did occur were largely under government control and the price allocation system of the free market (as we know it) had little opportunity to operate. Over the next 40 years, confidence in the international monetary system and facilities for foreign investment have led (gradually at first, but now significantly faster) to a relaxation of controls over foreign money and capital. As a result, nowadays, albeit with teething troubles, lenders and borrowers in developing and industrial countries alike have access to a broad range of sources and uses of funds outside their national boundaries (although restrictions are far from being totally extinct).

Historically, the pioneers of international money and capital flows were small countries that removed restrictions on overseas transactions in order to access the wider range of opportunities to be found in foreign markets. Switzerland and the Netherlands provide examples of countries where small local markets have benefited from internationalisation. Today, however, even countries with highly developed and vast financial markets (such as the US and, increasingly, Japan) have opened up their markets to the world despite the wide range of choice already available in their domestic markets.

Examples of large international capital flows are not hard to find. For example, in 1984 the US economy intended to draw over 70 per cent of its projected $110 billion of new savings in dollars from external markets. Dollar savings and funds from other major industrial countries are used extensively to finance the current debts of Third World countries. In the banking sector, international lending over the past two decades has increased at an average rate of 20 per cent a year supplying the needs of governments and public enterprises alike. Private international capital flows have funded countries with government deficits for short-term adjustments to external economic disturbances and also for medium- and long-term investment activities. In stockmarkets, the concept of the multi-country equity issue has arrived, recent examples of which include Reuters (floated in London and New York at the same time in May 1984), and British Telecom (floated in the UK, US, Canada, Japan and some west European countries simultaneously in December 1984). Even Japan, the second largest domestic market in the world (next to the US) has pursued a policy of slow but purposeful liberation since 1963 when it joined the Organisation for Economic Cooperation and Development (OECD). Already, Japanese investors are major buyers of dollar-denominated bonds and, with the Japanese authorities currently scrutinising remaining restrictions (such as those on inward direct investment, issue of securities, and purchase of real estate in Japan), it is likely that the liberalisation moves will lead to even more overseas financial transactions by Japanese citizens, corporations and institutions.

Besides moves by governments to open up national markets, there is the Euromarket phenomenon. The Euromarket has developed from its origins as a historical accident into a vast bond market devoid of national boundaries. As an offshore, unregulated market the Euromarket now extends to centres such as the UK, Bahrain, France, Luxembourg, Singapore, Hong Kong, Bahamas, Panama and the Cayman Islands. These markets, more than any other sectors of the world's financial system, draw closely to the concept of a free marketplace. Prices established in these truly international markets tend to reflect objective valuations of financial assets and respond to the interplay of supply and demand more than in smaller, regulated, domestic financial markets. The Euromarkets may thus be considered as impersonal allocators of productive resources and loanable funds across national frontiers. As a source of competition they also provide a powerful incentive for increased internationalisation of domestic capital markets.

The internationalisation process has led to increased substitution of domestic and foreign assets and brought about increased interdependence of financial market conditions and interest rates between the world's capital markets. Unrestrained, the process would lead to what, in effect, would be a single, universal capital market accessible to all the world's individual nations. Provided that capital was invested in projects and securities with the highest rate of expected return for any level of riskiness, the relationship between risk-taking and likely returns would then become equalised across national boundaries. Paradoxically, in theory at least, by removing all restrictions on overseas financial transactions, market users would then have little incentive to look outside their domestic markets because the risk and return opportunities to be found there would be the same as at home.

This day is not yet here, however, and may, indeed, never arrive. Nevertheless, until such extreme conditions do prevail, the international markets and the underlying securities remain highly responsive and ready to adapt to any moves that attempt to curtail the process of internationalisation. When regulatory barriers are erected the markets respond with alternative routes and new facilities for overseas financial operations. Hand in hand with modern technology, the innovations occurring in the financial markets are leading to a situation whereby lenders, borrowers and investors can, more than ever before, treat the whole world as their marketplace.

## The trend towards deregulation and firmer linkages between capital markets

Regulations can both create and destroy financial markets. On the one hand, a government may impose regulations on financial markets in order to protect the interests of the domestic economy as a whole to the detriment of individual market users. On the other hand, regulations are also used to protect markets and investors by ensuring adequate disclosure of information and freedom safely to convey funds across national boundaries. A reduction in the former type of regulation leads to greater internationalisation of markets – as does an increase in the latter. It would be untrue, however, to say that every governmental move to limit or increase cross-border financing via regulations has the desired effect. Governments are not infallible and must contend with the laws and idiosyncrasies of chance, which can send the best laid plans awry. For example, regulations intended to isolate a particular market can have exactly the opposite effect. Alternatively, new markets may spring up to the detriment of the old one in response to rules that attempt to control the essentially fluid free-movement of international capital. Some commentators (for example, Wise 1984) put forward a view whereby regulations prove to be only artificial and temporary restrictions in an essentially universal capital marketplace. Governments imposing restrictions aimed at restricting capital movements in this picture of global financial change can be envisaged as performing a similar role to Peter, the proverbial Dutch boy with his finger plugged into a hole in the wall of a dam. This vision of governmental predicament is not entirely unrealistic. Excessive regulation at the national level has proved to be one of the main causes of international markets. The now vast Euromarkets are living proof of the process.

Now that Euromarkets are here, largely in response to excessive domestic regulation, governments are left with several alternative courses of action. They might consider removing restrictions on the domestic market to emulate the external one. Alternatively, they could seek control over the external market by entering into negotiation with other governments – in which case their voice would be only one of many. A third possibility would be to offer some sort of premium to coax market users back into the domestic marketplace, which could prove as expensive as the original problem that the restrictions were brought in to correct. The final alternative, which is the one that appears to have been followed as far as the Euromarkets are concerned, is to accept the continued existence of the external market. There are political and economic benefits to be derived from living next-door (or even on top of) a Euromarket. It is certainly more simple to deal with than an international financial market system linked by a patchwork of national regulatory frameworks.

Looking back (which is so much easier than looking forward) it can be seen that, overall, there have been significant moves towards deregulating the financial markets and creating closer financial and political links between countries. The 1970s, for example, marked the recognition of the need to redistribute the capital surpluses of rich countries amongst other countries of the world. Between the major industrial nations, the trend has been towards greater cooperation on financial matters of mutual concern and benefit, and many international organisations have grown up to protect international harmony for both trade and capital movements. Particularly influential organisations in this respect include the International Monetary Fund (IMF), the Bank for International Settlements (BIS), the General Agreement on Tarrifs and Trade (GATT), the World Bank (IBRD), and the Organisation for Economic Cooperation and Development (OECD). The influence and activities of these organisations has helped towards the ten-fold increase in the volume of world trade since the Second World War and led to enormous growth of the international money and capital markets. Another example of progress towards international cooperation (within Europe) is provided by the EEC's Code of Liberalisation adopted in 1961 'to progressively abolish . . . restrictions on movements of capital, to the extent necessary for effective economic cooperation'. Since that date further wheels have been set into motion to align the financial markets and conventions of west European countries to their mutual advantage.

Besides agreements entered into at governmental level, structural and institutional changes have occurred, particularly since the 1970s (and increasingly in the 1980s), which have brought about closer links between individual national financial marketplaces. Whether the mood of the period has been towards re-regulation or deregulation, the services available from private institutions and intermediaries have greatly increased. As shall be seen, the degree of adaptability and quality of innovation shown by financial institutions and intermediaries in response to the challenge of internationalisation has been impressive.

It would be unfair to give the impression that the world's financial markets are now almost completely interlinked and unregulated and that everything in the garden is rosy. This is not true. The markets are undergoing a period of transition for which some participants are better equipped and more eager than others. The increased freedom and mobility of capital brought by deregulatory moves and firmer linkages between capital markets has had certain economic advantages but has also led to problems – many of which have yet to be solved. Problems caused by increased sensitivity of funds to interest rate differentials and exchange rate fluctuations are common and governments still find it necessary to intervene or impose restrictions on occasions to provide at least temporary protection to home economies.

A current example of the type of problem that can arise through internationalisation is provided by the developing countries which, with large balance of payments deficits, have fared extremely badly from significant real interest rate spreads between major financial markets. Dialogue between industrial and developing nations aimed at improving this situation is currently in progress but, meanwhile, developing countries can hardly be blamed for imposing capital restrictions and exchange controls while they strive for economic growth and stability. Such developments fall far short of the conceptual idea that increased links between the world's capital markets will operate to the benefit of all parties. In the long run, the ideal may be realistic but, in the short run, for some it is a new and hard road.

## Innovation in financial markets

Recent history has witnessed many economic problems on both domestic and international fronts. Global experience in the last three decades includes periods of rising and falling inflation, increasing unemployment, and rising and falling rates of economic growth. Proposals for dealing with the problems have been put forward from many levels of economic activity. From a macroeconomic perspective governments have had to find new policies aimed at reconciling the needs of individual countries with the needs of the international economy. From the point of view of individual operators in the financial system, however, the need has been to devise new techniques to cope with or circumvent problems of dealing in marketplaces across frontiers. Where deregulation has not gone far enough, offshore markets have sprung up to enjoy a competitive edge owing to their relative absence of regulation. Meanwhile, domestic markets have had to provide more effective services to maintain their own clients. Intermediation techniques in domestic markets have had to improve to satisfy customer needs in some alternative way to the more attractive rates of interest offered by the offshore markets. Hand in hand, the interplay of deregulation and innovation can be seen to be responsible for the dismantling of credit and interest rate ceilings, barriers to entry, and other obstructions to international linkages.

Perhaps the most powerful incentive to innovation in financial markets in the recent past was the move from fixed to floating exchange rates in the 1970s. The abandonment of exchange controls brought simplicity to the field of regulation but, at the same time, increased the need for innovation in the financial markets. Following the introduction of generalised exchange rate floating, new techniques such as multi-country diversification and hedging to cover foreign exchange exposure have become increasingly necessary. Meanwhile, many of the markets and the underlying securities in which they deal have become increasingly international in character. Futures markets and options markets have arrived, and so have multi-currency assets and a host of new internationally-traded contracts.

The final force to be mentioned as contributing to increased innovation in world financial markets is the relentless march of technology and modern facilities for data processing and communication. Financial information, money and capital, has never been so quickly transferable across the world. The result has been increased market efficiency and increased competition between domestic and foreign marketplaces. The facilities for round-the-clock, instantaneous trading are already here.

## Thc world's largest markets

The USA currently has the world's largest financial market, which includes many facilities for foreign borrowers and investors. The Eurodollar and closely linked Canadian Eurodollar markets are also extremely important across the world. As the traditional home of capitalism, the USA provides an experimental ground for new facilities and techniques for international capital and money transfers. For example, the influence of the US system is clearly apparent in recent Japanese market developments. (It would be untrue to say, however, that the US provided the sole source of financial innovation.)

The second most important markets offering facilities for foreign borrowers and investors are those in Western Europe such as the UK, West Germany, Switzerland and the Netherlands. The enormous Euromarkets owe their origins to European markets but now extend to cover the four corners of the globe. The offshore markets often run in parallel with the domestic markets but are relatively free from domestic market rules and regulations.

The third (and potentially second) most important market is that of Japan. From a state of claustrophobic over-regulation, gradual liberalisation is likely to lead to the Japanese markets becoming equally as important on the world financial scene as those of other industrially-advanced countries.

This brief synopsis of the world's financial markets would not be complete without mention of the predicament of the less developed countries (LDCs). Many developing countries, whilst hungry for capital for building up their industries, are currently caught up in the trap of extensive borrowings in the past. For many, economic growth has not been fast enough to pay off their massive debts. Exchange rates have also worked against the interests of the LDCs, which must now negotiate debt restructuring schemes with the lending countries. The LDCs desperately need their own capital markets but, out of necessity, must continue to rely mainly on those of the industrial nations.

## Summary

The process of internationalisation of world stockmarkets appears to be the result of four main forces. The four forces are: (a)

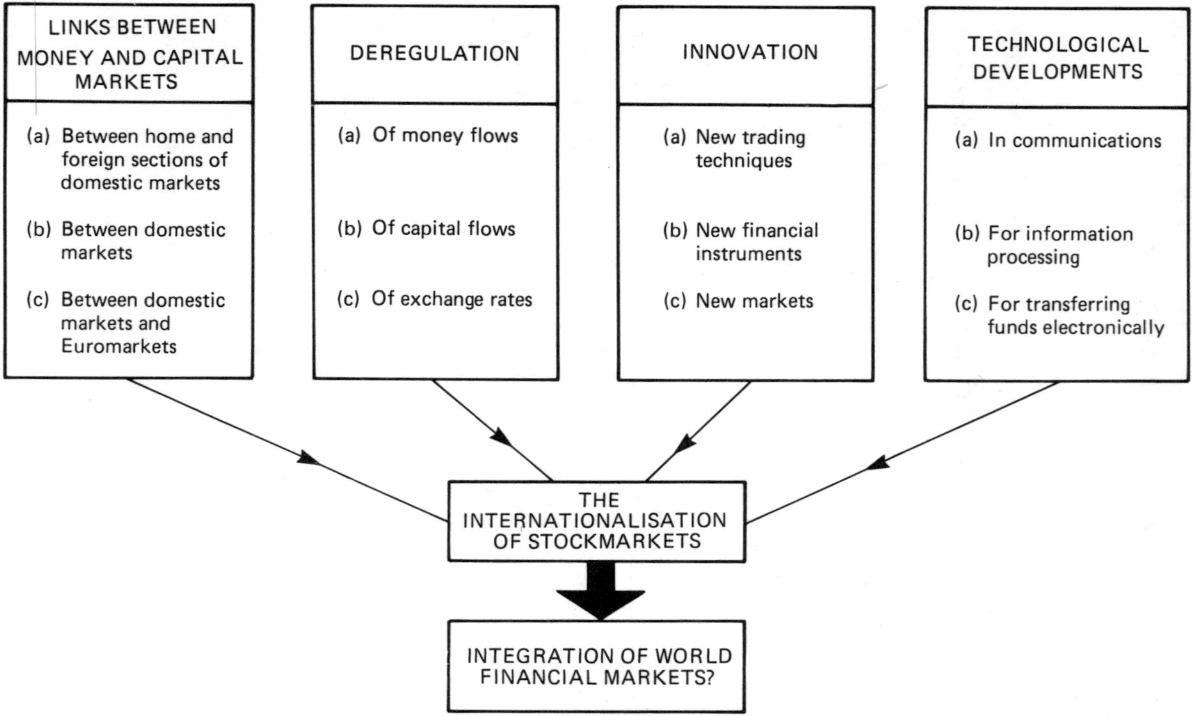


**Figure 1.1 The main influences leading to the internationalisation of stockmarkets.**

increased links between money and capital markets; (b) moves towards deregulation; (c) innovation in financial markets; and (d) breakthroughs in information and communications technology (as illustrated in Figure 1.1).

Increased links between domestic markets create channels through which international funds may flow. Deregulation encourages a freer and faster flow of funds through the established channels. Innovation is occurring at both a macrolevel (for example, in the Euromarkets) and at a microlevel (for example, new techniques and financial instruments). Integration of financial markets (or, if you like, a universal world capital market) is the logical but not necessarily the inevitable result of the internationalisation process. Just what integration of capital markets means, the implications of having a world capital market (should it ever arrive) and the process that led up to the current period of rapid transition are dealt with in the rest of this book.

## Reference

Wise, W., 'The Mending Wall: The Rise of the Universal Financial Market', *The World of Banking*, March–April 1984, pp 16–19.

# 2 Links between markets

Currently, those markets that are not subject to governmental legislation are leading the movement towards the internationalisation of stockmarkets. In the absence of imposed restrictions, unregulated markets are already free to transfer large amounts of money and capital across the world. Many regulated markets are also permitted to deal in foreign funds and securities. The aims of this chapter are to provide a general picture of the links between financial markets both within a single economy and across the world, and to draw a distinction between markets that fall under the jurisdiction of governments and those that do not. The text is mainly descriptive so readers who already have an understanding of world money and capital movements may prefer to proceed to chapter 3 which deals with the cases for and against freedom of international financial flows of funds.

For descriptive purposes, world markets in this chapter are divided into domestic markets, Euromarkets and foreign exchange markets. This is a rather simplified view of the situation but is suitable for present purposes to explain the nature of links between markets. More detailed information follows in the remainder of the text.

## Domestic versus world financial markets

There are many similarities between domestic and world financial markets, the main one being that both provide channels through which funds can flow between ultimate borrowers and ultimate savers. This process is illustrated in Figure 2.1, which shows that surplus funds may take a variety of different routes to eventual users. Returns, in the form of dividends or interest, go in the opposite direction to the arrows in the diagram. Governments, businesses and private individuals can take on the roles of either funds users or funds providers according to their financial needs and preferences. Financial institutions, dealers, brokers and other intermediaries stimulate the flows of funds and allow the markets to work. Forces of supply and demand operate in both domestic and world markets to influence the prices of a wide range of financial opportunities.

Another resemblance between domestic and world financial markets is that both provide facilities for dealing with risk. Financial risks can either be taken on or be transferred in markets for appropriate premiums. In highly developed financial markets, risks can be traded separately from the financial claim and assets from which they arise.

A third similarity between domestic and world financial markets is the provision of organisation for structuring funds flows according to perceived needs. One way of envisaging the structure of financial marketplaces is to distinguish between primary markets (for raising capital in the first instance), secondary markets (for trading in existing securities) and derived markets (markets that have grown up to trade in instruments derived from activities in primary and secondary markets – options markets for example). Another way that markets may be classified is into long- and short-term segments, according to the type of instruments in which they deal. The degree of organisation varies between markets but is of particular importance in the long-term market segments. Competent market organisation, besides providing for efficient transactions, allows for anonymity of buyers and sellers. Anonymity in organised markets increases the marketability of traded securities and also the likelihood that their prices reflect objective evaluations of their true worth. The most organised short-term markets are those for monetary instruments. Organised long-term markets include those for fixed interest debt (bonds) and those for equity (shares).

The markets of individual countries (financial and non-financial) are, to some degree, linked with markets abroad. This holds true,

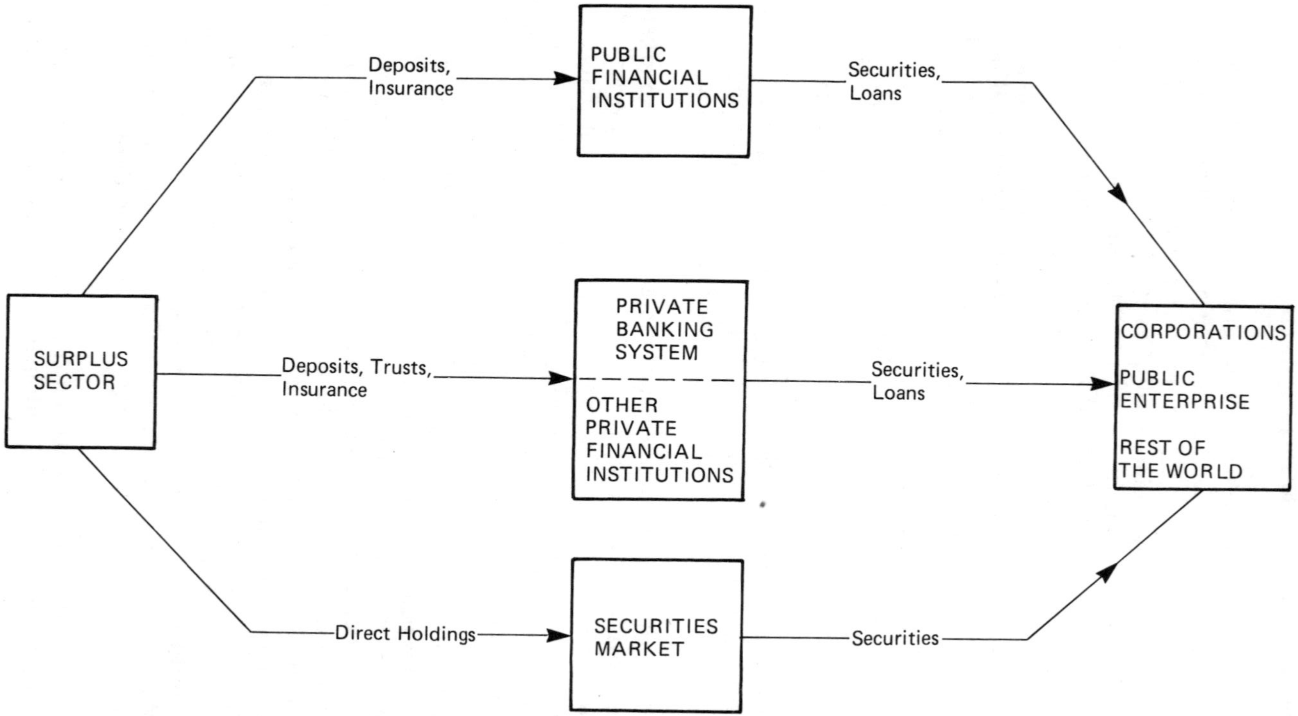


**Figure 2.1 The pattern of financial intermediation.**

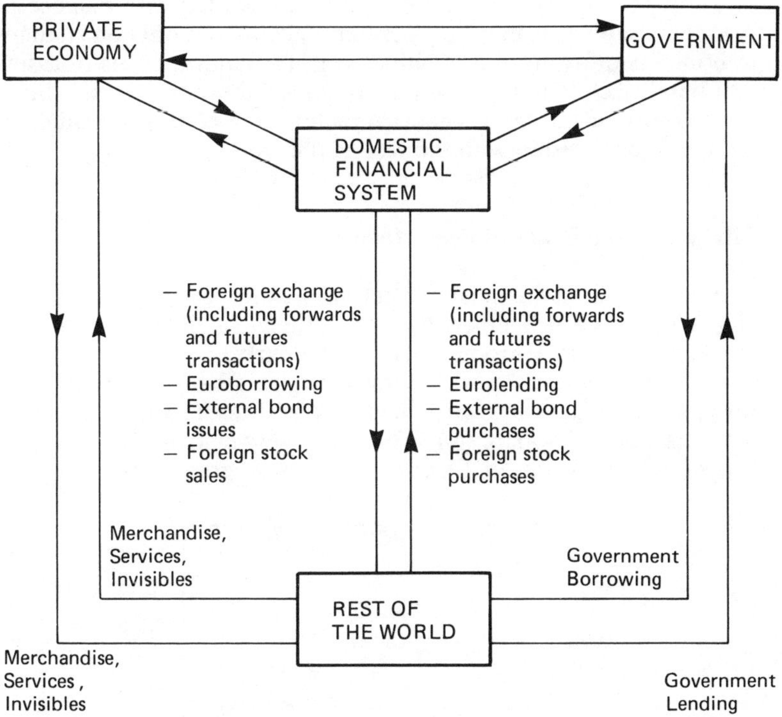


**Figure 2.2 The pattern of domestic and world money and capital flows.**

at least for trading purposes, even for communist countries. The degree to which these channels are open or restricted, of course, depends on the political and economic situations in each individual country. Links between the economy of a single country and the rest of the world are illustrated in Figure 2.2. This shows that the main international funds flows are those arising from trade (payments for imports and exports), for private loans and portfolio investment, and bilateral inter-governmental loans. Some of these activities are difficult to measure for some countries without extensive data collection. An overview of the situation will, however, be available from reports (such as those provided by central banks) on countries' balances of payments. In particular, balance of payments reports usually contain information on direct investment flows, changes in foreign bank lending, non-residents' new bond issues and money market transactions, and trading in government and company securities. The limitation of dealing with balance of payments reports is that they contain information only on changes in holdings of assets and liabilities (rather than on levels of assets and liabilities). The information contained therein is useful, however, to provide at least a general picture of a country's trade and financial relationship with the rest of the world.

### The world as a financial marketplace

The international financial marketplace comprises domestic financial markets (which link with each other, the foreign exchange markets and the Euromarkets), Euromarkets (which link with each other, domestic markets and foreign exchange markets) and foreign exchange markets (which link with each other, domestic markets and Euromarkets). The links between the markets are shown schematically in Figure 2.3. The diagram represents the

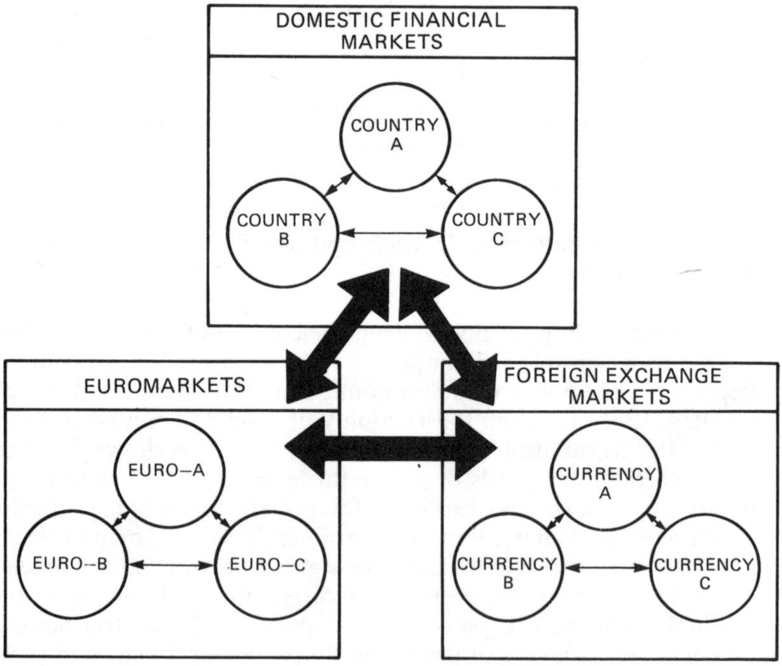


**Figure 2.3 Domestic markets, foreign exchange markets and Euromarkets.**

world as comprising three countries, each with an associated Euromarket and currency market. Each of the three countries and their associated currencies are represented in each of the three types of market in a unified fashion. The illustration is highly simplified because the world consists of many countries and each country may not yet have forged all the links shown in the diagram. The situation has also not yet been reached where each country has both a regular currency and a Eurocurrency.

Despite these shortcomings, the figure does show that there are basically two ways whereby financial transactions between national boundaries can take place. Either they can occur directly between different national markets, or they can be routed via the external Euromarkets. The exchange markets provide the link between domestic and Euromarkets by providing facilities for the exchange of currency, thus making foreign currency denominated instruments acceptable to nationals of many different countries.

Each of the different types of market is now considered in further detail.

## Domestic financial markets

Domestic financial markets provide facilities for dealing in short-term monetary instruments and long-term markets for dealing in stocks, bonds, mortgages and other forms of long-term credit. In some cases, individuals and businesses access the markets through brokers or 'over-the-counter' facilities. Alternatively, access to the markets may be gained indirectly through institutions such as banks, insurance companies, building societies, loan societies, investment companies or unit trusts.

To provide a link with overseas markets, there is likely to be a foreign section of each domestic marketplace to provide domestic investors with the opportunity to purchase foreign securities and/or to allow foreigners access to the domestic market. The size and stage of development of the foreign segment of each domestic market varies between countries of the world depending on attitudes towards protectionism or freedom of markets. Both domestic and overseas users of the domestic market's foreign section must abide by any regulations introduced to protect national economic interests.

Besides the (regulated) foreign segment of the domestic market there is likely to be a part of the market specialising in links with the external Euromarkets. The external segment has its own rules and regulations, which will be of a far more liberal nature. The relative absence of regulation in this section of the market stems from the fact that external financial operations come under a different political jurisdiction to the domestic market. The external segments of each of the world's domestic capital markets are very similar with regard to rules and regulations. The Euromarket therefore provides an alternative, fairly unrestricted market, which operates parallel to the domestic financial markets of its host countries.

**Euromarkets**

Euromarkets (often called offshore markets or external markets) provide marketplaces for assets dominated in currencies other than the one normally used by the host economy. Since the financial instruments and securities contracts traded in the Euromarkets are denominated in one or more foreign currencies, there is an obvious need for links with the foreign exchange markets. Linkages between Euromarkets and foreign exchange markets are outside the jurisdiction of national governments and monetary authorities so they, too, tend to be fairly unregulated.

The Euromarkets have grown up to serve banks, security firms and underwriting groups whose business interests transcend national origins and connections. The independence of the Euromarkets permits trading in multinational money and capital flows that remain apart from national monetary and fiscal policies. Access to the Euromarkets can, however, still be controlled by national authorities. Once access has been granted, users of the Euromarkets enjoy a great deal of flexibility and mobility of funds.

Prices of securities in the international markets are almost completely free from taxes, currency controls and other restrictions. The result is that prices in Euromarkets tend to reflect world factors rather than national factors. Similarly, the structure and level of interest rates in Euromarkets cannot be directly influenced by government policies – although governments are able to exert indirect influences. Indirectly, external interest rates can be influenced by national regulations and restrictions, local taxes and other factors. The relationship between national and international rates is fairly straightforward. For example, if a 4 per cent reserve requirement is placed on a particular instrument in the national market, the rate in the Euromarket would differ by 4 per cent. The Euro-rate would be determined by the free working of supply and demand for the instrument unlike the regulated domestic rate.

The Euromarkets both complement and compete with national

markets. Whether the existence of the external market is good or bad for national interests is difficult to decide because, like many other economic phenomena, Euromarkets can work for or against the interests of particular nations. Perhaps their continued existence alone offers the answer to this question. They do, after all, provide a useful safety valve in the world economic system and aid international equilibrium. The Euromarkets also provide a more efficient mechanism for international borrowing and lending than the alternative – a network of loosely linked national markets. Finally, if it were not for the Euromarkets, borrowers (or lenders) seeking external sources (or uses) of funds would have to patronise the financial markets of another nation.

## The foreign exchange market

The foreign exchange market ties in closely with the other financial markets. It consists of a worldwide network of buyers and sellers of currencies. Supply and demand, and hence prices, are determined for currencies by activities of exporters, importers, shippers, banks, multinational companies, foreign investors and lenders, tourists, and other users of foreign currencies worldwide. Foreign exchange markets in each particular nation are linked by sophisticated lines of communication with foreign exchange markets in the rest of the world. This global communications network allows a high uniformity of prices to prevail in all the currency markets across the world at any one time. Market dealers tend to specialise in a small number of currencies – even just one. They rarely see each other or the actual currencies in which they deal but operate through the vast foreign exchange market communications system, transferring currencies electronically from one account to another. The importance and size of the market can be gauged if one considers that foreign exchange constitutes the largest segment of official reserves held by industrial nations (up to 30 per cent of total official reserves in some European countries). The market's state of development shapes the world's opportunities for foreign trade, investment, borrowing and lending. Functions of the foreign exchange market include maintaining par values between different currencies, providing exchange facilities for holders of currencies, providing facilities for reducing exchange risk, and financing short-run swings in national trade payments. The links between capital markets, money markets, trade, the foreign exchange market and the rest of the world are shown diagrammatically in Figure 2.4. The exchange rate for any particular currency at any one time is determined by the direction and flow of funds around the channels shown.

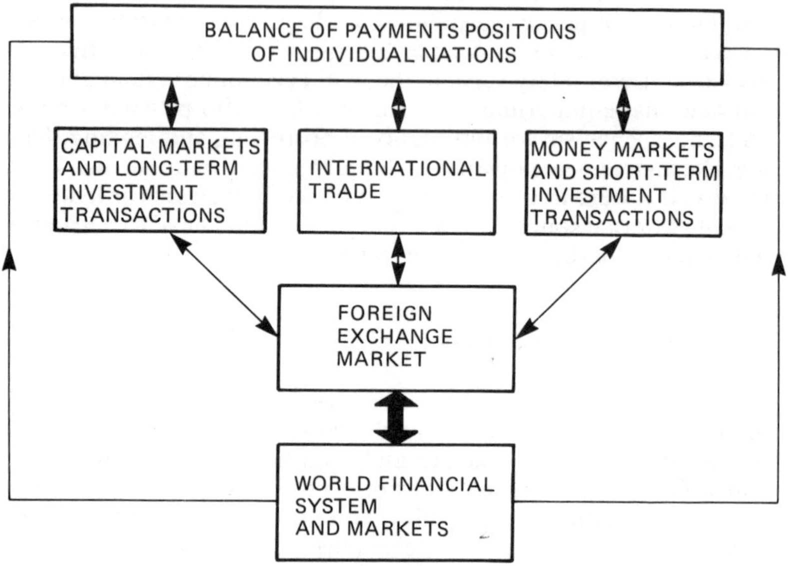


**Figure 2.4 The foreign exchange market as a link between domestic and world markets**

At the core of the foreign exchange market is the interbank market, where the commercial banks deal continuously between each other. They are the marketmakers who stand ready to buy and sell currencies. Foreign exchange brokers are often used as middlemen. The speed and efficiency of the market is enhanced by the fact that commitments between dealers are usually by word of mouth. Most market users are content to deal through the banks for their foreign exchange transactions, although there are signs of change – with some multinationals, for example, finding it worthwhile to seek direct access to the market.

Activities of banks in the foreign exchange markets come under two main headings: commercial and regulatory. Commercially, banks operate both at a national level (to provide services to customers) and at a wholesale level (for dealing between themselves in the interbank market). Regulatory activities in the market are undertaken by countries' central banks which attempt to influence the market favourably in response to governmental policies. As their government's bankers, the central banks also play an important role by providing exchange facilities for governmental flows of funds and also for those of the public sector.

The foreign exchange markets are probably the most important markets in the world financial system since they provide the link between the multitude of separate domestic financial systems and an independent system for supporting international transactions. They work to the benefit of both suppliers and users of capital, opening up doors to individual domestic financial systems and allowing movements of funds denominated in different currencies.

## International links

At one time there were no organised facilities for financial flows between countries. Now there are many in response to the need and willingness for people and institutions all over the world to indulge in international trade and finance. For the future, the more linkages forged between markets, the more efficiently will money and capital be able to flow around the world in response to economic forces of supply and demand. Links between markets either take the form of institutional linkages (which require government authorisation) or arise through the process of free enterprise (for example, the services provided by securities firms and underwriters). Other influences that speed up the linking up of financial markets across the world include the activities of multinational companies, expertise provided by commercial banks with international interests, technical advances in communications and the influence of internationally-minded private and public pressure groups.

The most influential remaining restrictions on the internationalisation process are those provided by the walls of legislation introduced by governments to protect and distinguish between individual domestic markets. Distance and geographical position are no longer a barrier due to technical advances in financial systems, which now operate over wires, over the airwaves or via satellite.

## Summary

All financial markets, small or large, domestic or universal, offer facilities for exchange or transfer of money, capital and risk for traders, investors and borrowers. The ability of markets to perform this role is determined by the range and quality of services offered by intermediaries and the extent of restrictive measures (or absence thereof) imposed by government authorities.

The world as a financial marketplace comprises domestic markets, Euromarkets and foreign exchange markets. Links between the markets include those paved by intermediaries with government approval and those that have grown up outside the jurisdiction of governments. Already the international system of financial markets has become complex, each national market having the potential of becoming a microcosm of the greater world financial system. The state of technology is no longer a constraint on the complete link-up of financial markets across the world.

If technology is no longer a barrier, then the only remaining constraints on the complete internationalisation of stockmarkets are those of an economic and political nature. With the current state of technology and world communications we know that links between markets *can* exist – but this does not help answer the question of whether they *should* exist. The question of whether or not trade and financial flows should be free or restricted has attracted a great deal of attention and debate at government level and in academic circles over the years with, as yet, no universally agreed solution. This topic, taken from the viewpoints of market organisers, market users and governments is examined in the next chapter.

# 3 Restricted versus free international financial flows

The three aspects of world stockmarkets examined in this chapter are: why there is a demand for cross-border financing; how the flow of funds answering this demand can be encouraged or stemmed; and the cases for and against restrictions on international financial flows.

An overall view of the world economy with and without international capital movements is presented and is followed by an examination of how the situation is perceived by investors and lenders. The concept and potential benefits of international diversification are introduced to illustrate how individuals and institutions might improve their investment opportunities. Diversification provides the link with another aspect of the internationalisation process – namely the diversified activities of today's multinational companies, which both need and fuel the trend towards internationalisation of stockmarkets.

The stockmarkets and currency markets themselves are examined next. Various aspects of these marketplaces are considered for whether they encourage or discourage foreign investment. As an important aspect of the financial environment, the role of central banks is also taken into account in this section because of their control over domestic money and foreign exchange.

Restrictions on domestic markets contrast markedly with controls (or rather the lack of them) on offshore markets, which are also examined in this chapter for their advantages and disadvantages to the international investor.

The final part of the chapter tackles the controversial cases for and against restrictions on international financial flows. Rather than put forward a hard view on the matter, the aim here is to put forward both sides of the argument. Key points are presented to allow readers to make up their own minds on the topic. Finally, to put the cases for and against restrictions into a more practical context, the situation of today's developing countries is outlined in order to demonstrate the advantages and disadvantages of government-imposed restrictions at various stages of a nation's economic development.

## The demand for cross-border borrowing and investment

The demand for international borrowing and investment can be approached from a number of angles. Taking a macroeconomic view, demand for international capital movements can be approached by asking the question, 'Does foreign investment and borrowing increase world welfare?' In the absence of a universally agreed definition of 'welfare', this is a difficult question to answer. At a microlevel, taking into account the needs of individual borrowers and lenders, a more pressing and more easily answered question is 'Can I benefit from using overseas markets?' Both of these questions are now considered to provide an overall picture of the demand for international lending and borrowing.

### *An economist's view*

One explanation behind foreign investment (and trade) from economic theory is that of 'comparative advantage'. This is a concept that holds that total world output increases above what would otherwise be the case if productive assets – which include capital – can proceed to places and uses for which they are most suited. The concept of comparative advantage has often been put forward to support the case for free trade – but it applies to capital markets too. It means that suppliers and users of capital should constantly seek out the most profitable opportunities no matter what their geographical location. Since the nature of capital varies in terms of price, riskiness and other characteristics, the world's financial markets should perform the function of bringing together suppliers of capital with particular characteristics with potential users of capital, who find those characteristics suitable for their needs. Looked at in this light, domestic regulations restricting foreign movements of funds can be compared with barriers to entry imposed by governments to restrict free trade. In the absence of restrictive legislation, savings would be allowed to be transferred from countries where they are plentiful, cheap and lacking investment opportunities to countries where savings are scarce, expensive and where there may be profitable opportunities. Savers in the cheap-capital countries would then be able to postpone present consumption into the future and savers in the expensive-capital countries could shift future consumption into the present. This exchange would allow total production and welfare to increase. According to the theory of comparative advantage, this state of affairs would still prevail even if all countries had identical investment opportunities and time preferences for consumption – so long as preferences for liquidity still differed. Given differing liquidity preferences, the financial markets would still provide a channel for long-term capital from countries with low-liquidity preferences to pass to countries with high-liquidity preferences whilst short-term capital moved in the opposite direction.

Consider the wind, which constantly moves from areas of high pressure to areas of low pressure, and you have a fairly good analogy of how capital would move around the world in the absence of restrictive legislation and with many links between markets. It is worth noting, however, that attempts to control financial flows (and the wind for that matter) can work to man's advantage. Governments may have good reasons for introducing restrictive legislation on international capital movements.

### *An investor's view*

Investors have two good reasons for looking towards overseas markets for investment opportunities. The first reason is that the type of investment opportunity sought may not be available in the domestic market. The second reason is that overseas markets may, due to anomalies in world markets, offer higher rates of return for similar levels of risk-taking. Investors are more likely to try to invest abroad for the first of these reasons if their domestic market in underdeveloped with only a narrow range of securities and financial instruments available. The likelihood of foreign investment by investors seeking preferable return and risk characteristics for their investments is determined by differences in supply and demand conditions between domestic and overseas markets. Figure 3.1 illustrates the demand for cross-border financing and investment by considering the case of a two-market world economy. Figures 3.1(a) and (b) show the equilibrium relationship between risk-taking and expected returns within each of the financial markets of countries A and B. The line drawn on each graph

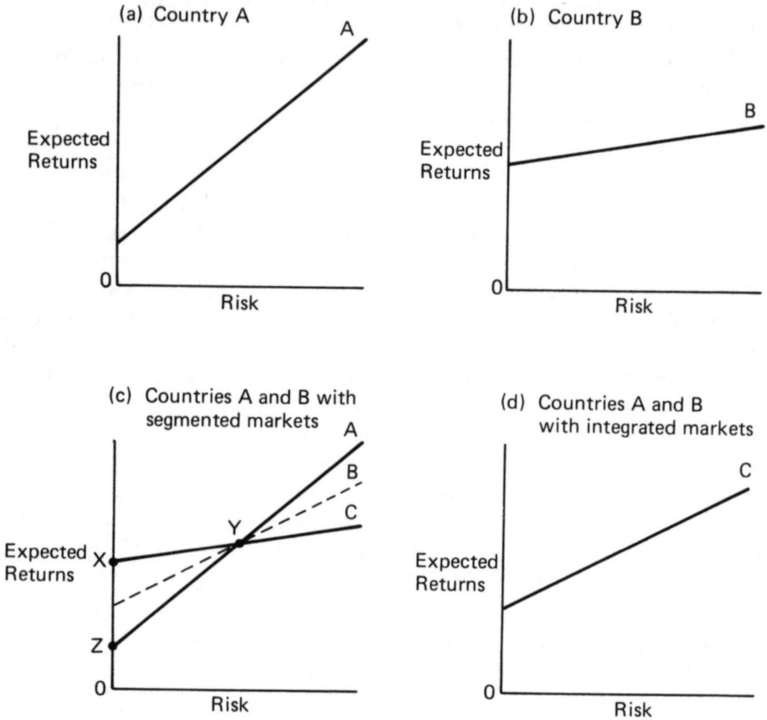


**Figure 3.1 Levels of risk and return in domestic financial markets before and after market integration.**

represents the cost of capital for capital users and also the expected returns for investors – two sides of the same coin. Higher levels of risk are associated with higher expected returns and costs of capital. The line is usually referred to as the Capital Market Line (CML) in financial and economic literature. The slopes and intercepts of the CMLs in countries A and B are different because of different market conditions in the two countries. Figure 3.1(c) illustrates the situation if markets A and B are segmented. Lines X–Y and Y–A represent the locus of superior investments available to investors if they have access to the markets in both country

A and country B. Between points X and Y investors would prefer to invest in country B because, for given levels of risk-taking, returns are higher than in country A. Between points Y and A, investors would prefer to invest in country A for the same reason. By investing in foreign markets, investors would therefore be able to maximise their investment opportunities. Figure 3.1(d) represents the new equilibrium if completely free capital movements were permitted and investors were free to invest in either country A or B. Countries A and B would thereby constitute a single, integrated market.

The example works equally well if the titles of the axes are changed from 'expected returns' and 'risk' to 'yield' and 'maturity' respectively. Having relabelled the axes, the diagrams would illustrate how markets combine with regard to interest rates for the range of maturity dates available on risk-free securities (for example, on high-class bonds). A time dimension would thereby be added to the model.

*A borrower's view*

Figure 3.1 can also be used to illustrate how borrowers can minimise their costs of capital by using foreign markets. With segmented markets, borrowers would choose to raise funds in market A between points Z and Y in Figure 3.1(c) and in market B past point Y. Again the new equilibrium position if complete freedom of international borrowing is permitted is represented by line C in Figure 3.1(d).

*Gains from diversification*

Investors (and borrowers using variable rate instruments) can gain from diversification which, in its simplest form, can be described as taking many small chances rather than one large one in pursuit of economic objectives. For example, by investing in many different securities, overall, losses on individual securities would offset against gains on others and the probability of achieving an expected rate of return would be much higher than if all hopes for gain were contained in a single security. This particular way of dealing with risk is usually called 'naive diversification'.

A more sophisticated form of diversification (called Markowitz diversification after its inventor [Markowitz, 1952]) involves searching for investment opportunities with risky characteristics that counterbalance each other in a more precise fashion. (If there was no zero on a roulette table, a simultaneous bet on both 'rouge' and 'noir' would illustrate how this technique can be used to achieve expected outcomes – although, in investment situations, the expected outcome would, hopefully, be superior to the one in the roulette example.) In theory at least, Markowitz diversification can be used to reduce risk to zero by investing in only two (perfectly-negatively-correlated) securities.

Techniques for international diversification are dealt with in more detail in Chapter 9. For present purposes it should be noted that if investors are free to use overseas markets, opportunities for risk reduction increase. Opportunities for naive diversification increase with the number of securities accessible in world markets. More opportunities for using Markowitz diversification arise in a world situation where some financial markets are booming and others declining at any one time.

### *Multinationals and world markets*

Multinational corporations are yet another manifestation of the concept of diversification. They diversify between countries, product markets, financial markets and in many other ways. Since these giant enterprises have business interests in many areas of the world they, too, are a driving force behind the demand for cross-border financing. They need both national and international financial markets to finance projects and handle the various currencies in which they do business. Multinationals make particular use of Euromarkets and foreign bond markets to satisfy their long-term borrowing needs. Owing to their size and spread of interests, multinationals also use foreign markets, either directly or indirectly, through foreign-located subsidiaries via bilateral payments between subsidiary and parent companies. Indirect use of foreign markets is, of course, sometimes frowned upon by regulatory authorities because multinationals can syphon off funds from the countries where they do business. Such unsavoury characteristics of multinationals must be weighed up against their advantages – such as transferring capital and technology to undeveloped countries and boosting worldwide employment levels.

## Market characteristics that encourage international capital flows

Market forces and government regulations influence the world's supply of stock exchanges and the nature of the securities traded therein. Consequently, stock exchanges range from those that are highly regulated to those that are largely unregulated and from those that are highly organised to those that are unorganised. Some modern markets are so well organised that securities can be purchased 'over-the-counter' or from financial 'supermarkets' offering a wide range of investment opportunities. In organised markets, lenders and borrowers need never meet and there are likely to be other facilities available – such as margin trading whereby investors need only place a deposit to cover potential losses when making their investments (rather than suffer the inconvenience of having to buy stock now and sell it again later). A high level of sophistication is therefore the first important characteristic for a stockmarket that wishes to attract both foreign and domestic investors.

A second characteristic that is useful for stockmarkets wishing to attract business of an international nature is that of fairness. The degree of fairness is closely linked with the degree of market sophistication because both these characteristics affect the objectivity of market prices. That is to say, prices in highly developed markets are more likely to reflect the underlying or intrinsic nature of the securities to which they apply. There is another side to the concept of fairness, which applies particularly to the foreign investor. Foreign investors may feel a sense of isolation from domestic markets if news affecting prices takes longer to reach them than it does domestic investors. Overseas investors are unlikely to consider such a situation as 'fair', so it is in the interests of foreign-orientated stockmarkets to be well-placed on lines of international communications

Accesibility is a third desirable characteristic for stockmarkets offering services to foreigners. The degree of accessibility can be increased by choosing appropriate geographical locations, maintaining up-to-date communications and funds transfer systems, and avoiding excessive governmental restrictions.

Sophistication, fairness and accessibility, then, are the keys to success for international financial centres. Let us now look at some of the measures taken in practice to secure these qualities.

*Encouragement of high auditing, accounting, disclosure and reporting standards by listed companies* The existence of high standard of information disclosure allows investors to make informed judgements about the intrinsic values of listed securities. Foreigners investing in a market where standards of disclosure are high will have less to fear that the price paid for a stock is a poor reflection of its worth than if information reporting standards are low.

*High standards for listing requirements* Listing requirements for companies seeking a marketplace for their stock may be used to increase the objectivity of market prices. For example, minimum capital requirements or minimum number of shareholders' requirements ensure that a large proportion of companies' equity capital is placed in the market. The alternative is to allow excessive control by issuing corporations, since they would still own a large proportion of their own stock. Separation of ownership from control is but one aspect of listing requirements, which can make markets more attractive to foreign investors.

*Controls on insider trading* Insider trading involves directors and other representatives of a firm profiteering from inside knowledge which is likely to affect share prices. It is illegal in most countries but is, in many cases, difficult to prove. Effective controls over insider trading increase the efficiency of stockmarkets to the benefit of both domestic and foreign investors.

*Trading floor supervision* Market supervision may be exercised through legislation or internal regulations. Procedures for trading (such as specified maximum daily price movements) increase investors' confidence – especially for small investors. Foreign investors' confidence increases in the knowledge that the trading floor procedure helps safeguard their interests – at least temporarily – despite the physical distance separating them from the market.

*Safe underwriting procedures* Underwriters, for their commission, guarantee new listings that all new stock coming onto the market will be taken up at a specific price. If market demand is low, the underwriters agree to buy up any remaining shares at a previously agreed price. To ensure safe stock issues, it is important that underwriters act in syndicates of sufficient number to ensure against the possibility of default. Market stability is less endangered if many underwriters share the placement risk rather than would be the case if a single underwriter kept all of it for his own account.

*Well developed information and communication systems* Information comes in many forms – in newspapers, on computer screens, in regular reports and accounts, through advertising in journals and trade publications, by radio or on television. The greater is public awareness of events as they happen, the more in touch investors are and the more efficient is the market. Without adequate dispersion of information between countries, foreign investors would require additional premiums to offset their additional uncertainty.

*A professional, highly developed securities industry* Developed securities industries offer the services of a large number of underwriters, dealers, brokers, analysts, money managers, mutual funds, unit trusts, investment trusts, information services and other services for market users. The size, complexity and professionalism of the securities industry determines the range of services available to attract domestic and foreign borrowers and lenders to the stockmarkets.

*Stable political environment* Political risk can discourage foreign (and domestic) investment. Instability in a country's political system may lead to blockage or expropriation of foreign investors' funds so it is desirable for stockmarkets to be located where the political system is fairly stable. Currently, most highly developed stock exchanges are situated in politically stable areas.

*A substantial supply of stocks* Stockmarkets grow in response to demand for services by capital users. Economies of scale may be reaped by stockmarkets if the supply of stocks is high. The overall supply of stocks is determined by factors that include the number and size of productive organisations, free market activity, expectations for growth and development, and political attitudes – domestically and worldwide. Governments are, of course, in a strong position to influence the supply of stocks coming onto the stockmarket through measures such as tax concessions or tax impositions. The degree to which foreign funds are represented on stockmarkets therefore varies between countries.

**Market characteristics that discourage international capital flows**

Having described means by which stockmarkets (and their governments) might go about increasing the degree of foreign stockmarket participation it would seem appropriate to look at the other side of the coin and consider how international funds flows can be discouraged. Factors that reduce the amount of foreign investment and borrowing include protective restrictions on movements of funds and taxes on earnings. These factors are usually under the control of governments and their overall effect is to increase segmentation and cause differences in risk and return relationships between capital markets.

The degree to which governments introduce measures to inhibit capital movements across national borders varies. The US stockmarkets, for example, with the exception of the period between

1963 and 1974 (during which an Interest Equalisation Tax was levied on foreign investments) have generally remained open to the world. UK markets, too, have been generally free from restrictions since 1979. France, on the other hand, provides an example of a country that has maintained many restrictions on currency and capital transactions to inhibit the inward and outward flow of funds.

The methods available to governments for restricting international funds flows fall under four main headings: restrictions on security markets; restrictions enforced via the banking system; restrictions on currency markets; and restrictions on access to the Euromarkets. Restrictive measures that fall under each of these headings, which are currently in force or which have been used in the past, are now described. Governments may use the methods either individually or as a package to bring about the required degree of isolation between domestic and external financial markets.

**Restrictions on securities markets**

These include:

*Ceilings on non-residents' purchases of domestic securities* Restrictions on foreign stockholdings may take the form of quantitative restrictions on either the whole or selected parts of the market. They may apply to primary or secondary markets (or both) and be temporary or permanent. The period immediately preceding a move from fixed exchange to a system of variable exchange rates (the early 1970s) witnessed many such restrictions on foreign capital flows in a number of domestic markets.

*Ceilings on residents' purchases of foreign securities* These, again, may be temporary or permanent and aimed at influencing all or selective types of securities. They can also apply to all or selective classes of individuals or institutions. Countries that have imposed such restrictions, at least temporarily, in the 1980s include Australia, Greece, Iceland, New Zealand, Portugal, Spain, Sweden and Turkey. Ceilings placed on the foreign investment activities of institutions such as investment trusts, unit trust and pension funds have a particularly significant impact on the volume of international funds flows since these institutions account for a large proportion of stockmarket activity.

*Deposit requirements on purchases of domestic securities by non-residents and/or purchases of foreign securities by residents* By requiring a deposit from domestic or foreign investors engaging in cross-border securities purchases, the authorities can effectively increase the real costs of foreign investment. The deposits are usually held by authorised banks in accounts that pay no interest. Investors are thus prevented from receiving returns from the time value of their funds.

*Controls on new issues* Governments or authorised public bodies may exercise control over new issues of foreign securities in domestic markets. Belgium, France, Italy, Scandinavia, West Germany, Switzerland, Netherlands and Japan are among the countries that have exercised such controls to date. The aim of the controls need not necessarily be to discourage foreign investment, however, but merely to maintain orderly market conditions via a new issue calendar.

*Withholding taxes* Withholding taxes is the most common tax hazard for international investors. The general idea is that foreigners making gains within a country should also pay taxes in that country. In practice the burden of the tax often falls on the borrower who must pay interest payments gross to foreign investors. Current rates of withholding tax around the world range up to as much as 50 per cent (but 15 per cent is most common) and constitute a significant discouragement to international investment. Some countries do not impose the tax. Others enter into agreements with other countries to reduce withholding taxes or allow them to be recovered or offset against domestic income taxes.

*Interest Equalisation Tax (IET)* This tax was imposed on the New York capital market between 1963 and 1974. US residents' purchases of foreign securities were taxed on a graduated scale to discourage the purchasing of foreign securities on the New York Stock Exchange (NYSE). While the tax was in force, the after-tax cost of borrowing on the NYSE became aligned with costs of borrowing in west European domestic markets. This of course discouraged international borrowing between Western Europe and the USA but gave an enormous boost to the Euromarkets which, by comparison, were a cheap source of funds.

*Other practices* The range of possible restrictions on foreign use of stockmarkets is endless. Some of the more common measures have been described. Other measures include the use of trustees to separate foreign earnings from voting rights, enforcement of a minimum period of investment before earnings can be delivered and restrictions on foreign investments by local authorities.

## Restrictions via the banking system

The banking system in most countries can be divided into two main sections: the commercial banking system, and the government's banking operations via the central bank. The government's bank has significant influence over the financial markets, particularly the currency market, either from its own operations or via its control over the commercial banks. If the central bank can influence market prices, a significant influence can be exerted over the amount of foreign investment into and out of the country. Since foreign investments usually require the conversion of one currency into another at some time during the investment process, the banks are in the key position to influence the real rate of return once the conversions have taken place. An investor from country A, for example, investing in country B may be discouraged from further overseas investment if his returns paid to him in the currency of country B are falling in real value simply because the exchange rate for converting country B's currency into country A's currency is falling.

Foreign investment can be discouraged or restricted via the banks in the following ways.

### *Open market operations by central banks*

Central banks may intervene in spot or forward currency markets to change equilibrium levels of supply and demand. If successful, a central bank's intervention will result in a price shift for its currency in a direction that benefits the domestic economy. Currency price shifts of this kind will influence foreign investors whose returns are denominated in the particular currency. The intervention is also likely to influence many other economic variables – possibly to the detriment of the economy. Complex economic reactions are set in motion when currency prices are changed from what they would normally be in a free market. Nevertheless, interventions by central banks are often successfully undertaken temporarily to maintain a weak currency or to reduce currency price fluctuations.

In order to achieve desired currency price changes it is common for central banks to operate as unobtrusively as possible. If intentions are widely advertised, opinions can be formulated on matters such as the bank's ability to defend its position for any duration of time. As a result (particularly, in the present financial climate), the bank's intended price change might not occur. On the other hand, as an alternative to actual intervention, the announcement of potential intervention alone might have the desired effect on currency prices without an actual intervention becoming necessary. January 1985 witnessed an example of this strategy when chancellors of several European countries announced that joint action would be taken if their currencies continued to depreciate against the dollar. The announcement alone was enough to move exchange rates (temporarily) in the desired direction. The dollar continued to appreciate in the currency markets, however, and eventually an actual intervention became necessary.

*Regulation of capital flows through commercial banks*

Controls on the flow of currencies into and out of a country are possible via the domestic banking system through which the majority of capital passes. The three main types of control that regulatory authorities might impose on the banks to restrict financial flows are: deposit requirements; quantitative restrictions; and indirect cost-based controls.

*Deposit requirements* Capital inflows (outflows) can be discouraged by requiring non-residents (residents) to lodge deposits with domestic banks. The deposits may be in either the domestic or a foreign currency. Deposits in the domestic currency can be used for making loans to residents. Deposits in foreign currencies can be lent to foreigners or exchanged for domestic currency in the foreign exchange market. Where deposit requirements are in force currency buyers must wait longer and sellers sell earlier than if the requirements did not exist.

*Quantitative restrictions* Quantitative restrictions can be placed on banks' permissible net liabilities (liabilities minus assets) denominated in foreign currencies. The effect of the restriction is to limit (or prohibit) banks' opportunities for bidding for deposits from non-residents.

*Indirect cost-based controls* Rather than specifying fixed limits on banks' net liabilities, the regulatory authorities might introduce a minimum reserve requirement on banks' currency liabilities to non-residents. The effect of the measure is, again, to discourage banks from bidding for non-residents' deposits.

*Other methods* Other restrictions aimed at limiting the size of or return on non-resident funds located in the domestic banking system may be enforced. Tourists, too, may find themselves subject to restrictions on the amount of domestic currency that they are allowed to take into or out of the country or on the amount of foreign currency that they can legally purchase.

**Restrictions on currency market activities**

Restrictions on currency markets are aimed at insulating foreign exchange reserves and the domestic currency from speculative and other forces in other parts of the world economy. Regulatory authorities' attempts to control foreign capital flows through the exchange markets have in general met with less success than those that operate via the banking system. Some of the methods that have been tried in the past are, nevertheless, included below.

*Two-tiered markets* Under a two-tiered market system, the aim is to create two currency markets, one of which is controlled (via the banks) while the other is free to respond to open market forces. The controlled and uncontrolled markets are sometimes called the 'convertible' and 'financial' markets, respectively. The convertible market is usually used only for commercial transactions or by users who have the necessary official documentation. Although the Belgian, French, Italian, South African and Spanish governments have tried running a two-tiered system in the past, only the Belgians have considered it viable for any length of time.

*Investment currency pools* Under an investment currency pool system, a limit is placed on the amount of currency available for investments into and out of the country. Those wishing to purchase foreign currency for making foreign investments must therefore wait until existing resident foreign investors sell off some of their investments. That is to say, sales and purchases of foreign investments by residents must be matched. Governments that have tried the system (for example, the UK from 1939 to 1979 and France from 1969 to 1971 and again in 1981) have found it problematic because prices in the currency investment pool are pushed above prices in the free market by forces of supply and demand. It also fails to stem the outflow of securities purchased by non-residents.

*Closed circuit markets* Closed circuit markets (as tried by

Netherlands from 1971 to 1974) are similar to investment currency pools but restrict the currency supply to non-resident investors.

**Controls on offshore securities markets**

Although the Euromarkets are subject to very little regulation there are some restrictions that apply to securities denominated in some currencies. For example, domestic authorities can control authorisation of public and private issues. Other powers may be exercised via banks leading the underwriting syndicate in the country of issue. Investors may also find themselves subject to tax by their domestic authorities on interest earned in offshore markets.

The lack of regulation of offshore markets, once domestic requirements have been met, may be interpreted in two ways. On the one hand it allows capital to flow freely around the world. On the other, it means that there is no final line of support (such as central bank acting as a lender as a last resort) for the market. The Euromarkets could therefore be described as more risky than a regulated domestic market (although the author is unaware of any defaults). This additional risk element could (in theory) lead investors in Euromarkets to require a higher rate of return to compensate for their increased sense of insecurity. Professional competence on the part of market organisers is therefore an essential requirement for the stability of the Euromarkets in the absence of supervision by a strong regulatory authority.

**Arguments for and against controls on international financial flows**

The cases for and against restrictions on international capital flows are difficult to put forward without touching on some sensitive moral and political issues. Basic to the argument is the question of whether freedom of governments to protect national interests should be allowed to interfere with the freedom of corporations and individuals to exchange, borrow and invest to their best advantage. Most would agree that the ideal solution lies somewhere between the two extremes of complete freedom and complete isolation of capital markets. History has shown that the best use of restrictions has been for short periods aimed at correcting temporary economic imbalances. In the long run it is difficult to maintain walls around national financial markets – the penalty for success being the emergence of new markets, which serve more adequately the needs of international borrowers and investors.

Whether or not controls should be introduced to restrict flows of foreign capital depends on the degree to which governments feel the need to isolate their markets from the influence of the world economy. The higher the vulnerability of the domestic economy to adverse world economic conditions, the stronger is the case for restrictions. Most common of all motives for giving up the advantages of free international capital movements is the need to protect a deteriorating balance of payments position. Indeed, there is a noticeable trend amongst developed countries in the last thirty years that during periods of economic downturn more countries impose restrictions than in periods of growth. The implication is clear: economic strength leads to a desire to open up capital markets whilst economic weakness creates a case for a more isolationary policy until the problems are sorted out.

*Arguments for restrictions*

Reasons why protectionist measures are imposed on international financial flows by individual governments include the following.

- To isolate the domestic money and capital markets from large movements of international funds.
- For monetary management when objectives of credit or exchange rate policies are threatened by capital inflows.
- To maintain ownership of enterprise by limiting or prohibiting the sale of shares of domestic companies to overseas buyers.
- To limit or stop the flow of the domestic currency into the international markets. The aim is to prevent adverse affects on interest rates and exchange rates caused by sudden price changes occurring in the international markets.
- To attempt to reduce costs of long-term foreign borrowing by reducing the private sector's supply of foreign debt.
- To protect against (or in retaliation to) regulations and restrictions imposed by foreign markets. The potential introduction or removal of restrictions provides governments with a powerful bargaining tool.

*Arguments against restrictions*

There are two main arguments against restrictions. One view often put forward is that controls introduced to protect one segment of the economy either may not work or may have inconvenient side-effects on another segment. A second line of argument simply points out that any benefits of protectionism could be outweighed by lost benefits of political and economic integration with the rest of the world via an open-door policy. Following the first line of argument, some of the possibly unforeseen problems of introducing restrictions include:

- *Uncertainty* Investors' and borrowers' uncertainty might increase if governments introduce and frequently revise short-term restrictions. The effect may dampen economic progress.
- *Costs* Regulations often prove costly for both market users and market administrators. It may be necessary to incur the expense of new bureaucratic organisations or government departments.
- *Difficulty of implementation* Efforts to restrain free market forces are more effective in the short run than in the long run. Black markets may grow up in response to excessive restrictions. Even without black markets, individuals can be very ingenious in finding ways around restrictions if there are advantages to be gained.

Under the second line of argument, lost benefits from not allowing free international financial flows include:

- Fewer opportunities for international portfolio diversification.
- A narrower range of risk, liquidity and maturity options for borrowers and lenders.
- Lost opportunities for financial gains from investment in developing countries.
- Decreased opportunities for internationally-oriented domestic financial institutions.
- Loss of political benefits, such as links with foreign countries that are also engaged in international finance and trade.
- Slower world economic growth. (If markets are isolated, subsections of the economy can only borrow from each other to the detriment of economic growth.)
- Movement away from a more stable world financial system. The effects of sudden economic changes can be spread over time and across the world, provided that links between the world's marketplaces are open. Rather than heralding the beginning of the Third World War, for example, the 1973 and 1979 oil price rises instigated by OPEC eventually benefited the world because a large proportion of OPEC's additional profits became reinvested in productive opportunities in non-OPEC countries.
- The non-availability of funds for rebuilding the economy after a natural disaster such as an earthquake or prolonged drought.

The listed advantages and disadvantages of markets open to

foreign capital flows clearly make the point that restrictions on foreign capital movements are a two-edged sword.

## The case of developing countries

In the preceding section the point was made that restrictions on foreign capital flows were more common in periods of recession than in periods of economic growth. To illustrate the point more clearly it is useful to examine the situation of less developed nations in their struggle to bring their weak economies up to the levels of their industrialised counterparts. Consider, therefore, the case of a developing country that successfully uses non-domestic funds to improve its economy. The stages of development through which the economy would pass would, if all went well, be as follows:

Stage 1 *Depressed economy* At the beginning of the process the economy is in a bad situation and running a balance of trade deficit because of heavy borrowing from abroad. There is therefore a good case for quantitative controls in order to maintain the value of the domestic currency and cope with the high demand for foreign exchange.

Stage 2 *Progress* The use of foreign capital is successful and investments become profitable. Imports are outstripped by exports thus generating profits to pay off the initial debts. Across-the-board quantitative restrictions could now give way to more specific controls. There might also be a need to devalue the domestic currency.

Stage 3 *Further progress* Profits continue to be made. Devaluation moves are successful, lower unit costs of exports leading to higher overall earnings. Initial debts can be paid off and the continued accumulation of wealth raises the level of prosperity.

Stage 4 *Boom economy* The developing country becomes a developed economy. Only a few controls need remain in order to maintain the balance of payments.

Through stages 1 to 4, as the credit-worthiness of the nation increases, the sources of funds change from those coming mainly from the public sector (international institutions) to those coming mainly from the private sector. Stringent political regulations eventually give way to free market forces for determining the allocation of capital. Needless to say, the four stage process described does not operate smoothly in every case. The current world debt crisis provides evidence enough of some severe practical problems. The main problems tend to arise around stage 3 where the onus is on the developing country to pay off its foreign debt. A considerable time can lapse between arrangements for debt being entered into and when the debt must be paid off, and this lapse may lead to additional costs for loan repayment. A country that borrowed $1 billion ten years ago to be repaid in local currency would, if the local currency decreased in value against the dollar at around 10 per cent per year, be faced with the prospect of paying back the equivalent of around $2.6 billion – in addition to the periodic interest payments. If growth financed by foreign debt is not high or fast enough, then repayment problems arise – as indeed they have for many developing countries (and their creditors) caught up in the current debt crisis. Paradoxically, free international movements of capital give weak economies the opportunity for development – but it also opens the door to dangers from the world economy. Despite such problems there is still a strong demand for capital in developing countries, both for development purposes and for dealing with repayment problems from past borrowing should they arise.

## Summary

The demand for cross-border financial flows arises naturally from the desires of investors and borrowers to broaden their range of opportunities for investments and sources of funds. Investors seek gains from international diversification and from exploitation of international anomalies whilst borrowers seek cheaper sources of funds in world markets. Multinational corporations already have an advantage in their international financial operations because of the geographical spread of their business interests.

Stockmarkets can increase the international flow of money and capital by becoming more accessible, fair and attractive to foreigners. Moves towards increasing market efficiency, extending the range of securities handled, forging links with overseas markets and improving the level of professionalism and service for overseas customers increase the international status of stock exchanges. Governments, too, can influence the volume and rate of flow of money and capital passing through the economy via the tax system, the banks, or the imposition or removal of restrictions on market activities. Offshore markets, however, remain outside the reach of government controls and offer many opportunities for those who are able to circumvent internal restrictions.

Whether or not a government should follow an open-door or protectionist policy with regard to international financial flows requires careful consideration of complex economic and political issues. Advantages and disadvantages arise from both types of policy. In addition, short-term and long-term objectives and interests may conflict. Ultimately, the answer lies in the state of development and strength of the economy. To suggest that weak economies should impose restrictions on international capital flows whilst developed economies should abandon them is, however, too simplified. In theory, such a view can be used to explain how a less developed country can be raised to developed country status but, in practice, matters are far more complex. International borrowing and lending can lead to difficulties such as those currently evidenced by the debt crisis, where the lesson to be learned is that overseas-financed industrial development can only run smoothly if growth prospects are high enough to enable repayment of foreign debt.

**Reference**

Markowitz, H. M., 'Portfolio Selection', *Journal of Finance*, 1952, pp 71–91.

# 4 A historical perspective

In this historical perspective to the events that are currently occurring in the financial markets, key facts and dates are presented in historical order to give a picture of the developing international financial markets as they respond to economic and political events. Readers will notice that the number of events recorded as relevant to the internationalisation process increase over the years at an exponential rate. This is partly because events that happened many years ago are more difficult to trace than those that happened recently – but mainly because most of the important events have occurred within the last decade or so. Although the key events themselves may have happened only recently, the pressures leading up to them go back much further in time. It is therefore hoped that the following historical account will not only report what happened but also provide an insight into why it happened. An appendix listing key dates in the development of the world's financial markets is provided at the end of the chapter for readers who would like to put their own interpretation on events.

## Early days

The origins of modern international markets are rooted in ancient history and man's natural desire to explore and trade with neighbouring communities. This desire has remained constant over the centuries but the facilities and arrangements for satisfying it have changed considerably. For financing of enterprise it is known that, as early as 2000BC, Babylonian merchants financed their activities from funds provided by the rich. The funds were deposited in temples, which could thus provide a very basic banking service. By 400BC the Greeks had their equivalent of the modern joint-stock company and markets for handling currencies and interest-bearing securities. Each following civilisation was accompanied by further contributions towards business life. Roman law, for example, a powerful influence on modern legal systems, spread with the Roman conquests and brought with it a code of behaviour for financial markets in the Roman Empire. The Romans also used bills of exchange to finance international trade. From these early days (with the exception of the feudal periods in the middle ages) man's propensity to trade, lend and borrow internationally has increased and the facilities for doing so have become more refined.

England has been a safe and popular place for traders since the thirteenth century and, in the fourteenth century, exchange booths were common across Europe to serve the needs of international traders. These early exchange markets were the origins of many of today's modern stockmarkets. The early exchange booths in Frankfurt, for example, became an official market for bills of exchange in the sixteenth century and a predecessor of the modern Frankfurt stock exchange. Holland, which, like Great Britain, has always demonstrated a natural aptitude for seafaring and trade, played an active role in early markets and had established banks and a stockmarket by the end of the seventeenth century. Another important development in the seventeenth century was the establishment of the Lombard banks in Italy, which provided venture capital and other services for overseas enterprise. Banking activities, including the establishment of the Bank of England, were also largely responsible for the growth of British influence around the world at this time. Undertakings such as the East India Company, which operated in distant lands, could not have gone ahead without a sound financial system to provide the required capital. By the end of the eighteenth century the seeds of the modern international financial system were firmly planted. The number of banks, security exchanges and international lending houses (including Rothschilds) had grown enormously. The stage was set for providing the capital needs of the industrial revolution of the nineteenth century.

### The nineteenth century

The industrial revolution of the first half of the nineteenth century saw the rise of Great Britain as an industrial power. London became a major centre for finance houses and merchant bankers offering export and import credit facilities and other financial services. Britain invested vast sums of money in the USA and the colonies in the form of low risk loans. International brokers' services were used to move funds between the domestic and overseas banking systems. Free movement of capital became a distinctive feature of the nineteenth century (and, indeed, of the period leading up to the First World War). The colonial system relied on free movement of capital for establishing and trading with markets for primary goods all over the globe. The relatively stable political environment during this period provided security and encouraged international flows of private capital. By the end of the nineteenth century the political environment was also conducive to international agreements on financial matters at government level. International cooperation reached a peak when Britain, West Germany, USA, Russia and other countries agreed in 1897 to fix the values of their currencies to gold. This improved the stability of the international markets and provided a basis for coordinating domestic economic policies. The nineteenth century also witnessed the establishment of many new stock exchanges, including those at Geneva (1850), Tokyo (1858) and Hong Kong (1891).

### The years 1900 to 1930

The industrial revolution of the nineteenth century, nurtured by the growing international financial system and interest in joint-stock companies, developed into the technical revolution of the early twentieth century. New York became a leading financial centre with an enormous capital market facility for financing innovative new industries. The early technical companies involved in electricity projects, communications and transport had accepted the need for separation of ownership from control with the consequence that, at this time, around 90 per cent of all international capital movements was in the form of portfolio investment. The First World War temporarily discouraged international funds flows but gave a further boost to innovations in the technical industries following the war effort. After the war, capital was urgently required by many countries in Europe for reconstruction and stabilisation programmes. The USA, fast becoming the world's richest country, became the main supplier of non-resident capital in the 1920s. By 1930, US involvement abroad was over $6.5 million, with Germany as the largest borrower.

Besides the needs of post-war Europe, the income-creating activities of countries engaged in the production of primary goods also required overseas financing at this time. As the needs for overseas finance and financial expertise increased, Britain, having lost ground to the USA markets at the beginning of the century owing to a weakening pound, regained its status as a major international financial centre. The USA continued to develop its financial system with the establishment of the Federal Reserve System in 1914, which boosted confidence in the banks and was followed by moves to improve the stockmarkets. Interest in improving and maintaining standards in the securities industry spread to Canada where, in 1916, the Investment Dealers Association (IDA) was founded to improve professionalism in the market. Increased stockmarket facilities in North America encouraged investors' preferences to change increasingly away from safe, fixed interest securities such as bonds towards shares, which offered ownership rights and the prospect of higher earnings. In 1929, demand for equity capital on the New York stockmarket reached a new high – only to be followed by the disastrous Wall Street Crash. This event led to a sudden loss of confidence in equity markets and had repercussions that lasted well into the 1930s.

## The depression of the 1930s

In 1931 the world's economy collapsed, thus leading to the depression of the 1930s. All major countries abandoned the gold standard. Regulations wrapped around entire financial systems led to a substantial reduction in the volume of international trade and finance. Wholesale defaults on the parts of debtor countries caused lenders to be distrustful of debtors and borrowers to fear the possibility of being unable to repay instalments on loans. The amount of international portfolio capital fell drastically. When international investment did pick up again, most funds were directed into the USA. This development had unfortunate repercussions for the future of international capital mobility. Many governments and economists saw the movement of funds into the

USA as unjust because the US economy was already rich in domestic savings. Government restrictions were consequently imposed to counteract movements in the free market. Domestic policies aimed at finding a way out of the depression held priority over the free market concept. It was at this time, for example, that Japan began its slow climb to its present international status by combining its several stockmarkets into the Japanese Securities Exchange under government control in 1934.

Inside US markets the memory of the Wall Street Crash lingered on and gave rise to acknowledgement of the need to improve regulation of the system. The US Securities Exchange Commission (SEC) was set up in 1934 to raise information disclosure standards by firms issuing stock on the market. Investors and analysts, also concerned with security, became interested in techniques for analysing market movements and for assessing the worth of stocks. Eventually, this interest would give rise to powerful analytical tools, such as technical analysis, fundamental analysis and modern portfolio theory.

### The years 1940 to 1960

The 1940s and 1950s saw more moves towards agreements at government level on financial matters of common international interest. Financial institutions enjoyed a resurgence to cope with provision and control of the large volumes of government loans and private equity capital financing new industries in the wake of the Second World War. Industrial countries became increasingly aware of the capital needs of the developing nations and the need for a stable international monetary system. In 1944, following the fall of the gold standard, a conference at Bretton Woods, New Hampshire, led to the introduction of a fixed exchange rate system for the currency markets. Under the new system, rather than being fixed against gold, currency values were fixed in relation to the dollar. The setting up of the International Monetary Fund (IMF) and the International Bank for Reconstruction and Development (IBRD) followed on from the agreement at Bretton Woods to provide a safety valve in the international monetary system and a source of capital for countries in financial difficulties.

Within Europe the post-war reconstruction process forged further international links. Funds appropriated under the US Marshall Plan (1948) helped Europe rebuild its industry and led, in 1950, to the European Payments Union (EPU), which was set up by recipients of the Marshall Plan to provide an international payments system within Europe. Within the next decade a revival of interest in international markets occurred, spurred on by the advent of the European Economic Community (EEC) in 1958. This union led to the restoration of convertibility of European currencies for non-residents and the EPU was eliminated. Other moves towards unification were of a more *ad hoc* and defensive nature. For example, in 1960, a run on gold in the US pushed the price up to $40 per ounce and Swiss banks intervened in the London market to hold down the price. The central banks of other major countries joined together in forming the London gold pool to support gold prices.

Around this time the volume of international capital movements was increasing faster than the volume of world trade – a trend that continued into the 1960s. The US stock exchange system became a model for the new stock exchanges being inaugurated in many other countries. Despite the increasing volume of international capital and political moves toward union, however, the world's markets were still extremely fragmented with only the USA in the position of being able to raise money for use anywhere in the world.

## The years 1960 to 1970

North America and Western Europe had now reached a comfortable level of industrialisation and were keen to maintain friendly links across the Atlantic. Needs for development capital in a third major area of the globe, the Asia–Pacific region, led to an extension of the infrastructure of the international financial markets in the 1960s. The number of financial centres in less industrialised continents (Latin America, Asia and Africa) increased to handle the faster flows of development capital. For example, the Malayan Stock Exchange was set up in 1960, along the lines of the Sydney Stock Exchange, to serve the interests of both Singapore and Malaya. The increased needs for capital by the developing countries led to the establishment of the International Development Association (IDA) in 1960 which, since that date, has played an important role in routing capital to needy areas. Some of the world's poorest countries borrowed heavily in the hope that economic growth would enable eventual repayment of the loans. From 1959 to 1968 West Europe recorded a fourfold increase in foreign bond issues for supplying capital for the industrialisation of the developing countries.

From 1963 onwards, following the introduction of the Interest Equalisation Tax (IET) in the USA, the Euromarkets became extremely important sources of international finance. Eurodollar bond issues of 1963 were closely followed by Euro Deutsche-mark issues and bonds denominated in Eurofrancs and Euroguilders in 1964. Bonds denominated in the Eurocurrencies of other countries followed. Increased use of the Euromarkets led to increased needs for professionalism and organisation in the market. As a result, the Euromarket introduced its own Association of International Bond Dealers (AIBD) to provide rules for market-makers and generally improve standards and security. International trading in Eurobonds was also facilitated by services such as Euroclear (set up in Brussels by Morgan Guaranty Trust Co.) and Cedel (set up in Luxembourg), which provided clearing facilities for the increasing number of market users.

The degree and desirability of internationalised European capital markets came in for scrutiny from a number of sources in the 1960s. For example, the Organisation for Economic Cooperation and Development (OECD), which came into existence in 1961, published a report in 1966 on balance of payments adjustments including a section on the usefulness of an international capital market. In the same year the EEC's general report, *Ninth General Report on the Activities of the Community (April 1965–March 1966)* European Economic Community Commission, Brussels, June 1966, referred to the need to coordinate company law and various financial activities (including the issue of stocks and shares) within Europe. A further report, *The Development of a European Capital Market (Report of a Group of Experts Appointed by the EEC Commission)*, Brussels, November 1966, examined the effectiveness of national capital markets, their accessibility to foreigners and the need for more links between them. A section of the EEC's general report of 1967, *The Tenth General Report on the Activities of the Community (April–March 1967)*, European Economic Community, Brussels, July 1967, suggested movement towards abolition of exchange controls, wider scope for institutional investors in foreign markets, and coordination of markets' organisational and legislative frameworks within Europe.

Despite the studies into the possibility of increased cross-border financial activity at this time, there was ample evidence that progress in this direction should not be rushed without careful deliberation. Towards the end of the 1960s balance of payments disturbances occurred in many countries because of increasingly large international capital flows. Countries began to become increasingly protectionist. Maintenance of fixed exchange rates, in particular, became problematic with currency revaluations by West Germany and Netherlands in 1961 and devaluations by Britain in 1967 and France in 1969. Meanwhile, although the USA had lost some of its financial leadership to the Euromarkets, the dollar remained an important cohesive factor in the foreign exchange markets.

## The years 1970 to 1980

The 1970s saw rapid developments in foreign markets and in international institutional arrangements for maintaining monetary stability. OPEC oil price increases in 1973 and 1979 demonstrated how the world economy could be rocked by events occurring in one section of the globe. Many countries also experienced currency problems caused by a weakening dollar, which necessitated frequent adjustments to exchange rates. The dollar's rough ride through the 1970s included devaluations in 1971 and 1973 and a dollar crisis between 1977 and 1978, during which the dollar declined around 10 per cent against other leading currencies. The consequences of the dollar's variability included an increased popularity for other currencies (such as the Deutsche-mark and Swiss franc) and a changed attitude towards fixed exchange rates. The resultant movement away from mainly fixed towards mainly floating or managed exchange rates left governments with more freedom to follow domestic objectives such as redistribution of income or maintaining employment levels – but at the cost of variability of their currencies. Developments leading up to this relatively swift change in the international financial scene proceeded as follows.

On 15 August 1971, the USA closed the 'gold window' (the convertibility of dollars into gold) and introduced an import surcharge. This move followed the first US trade deficit of the twentieth century. The effect of closing the gold window was to change the Bretton Woods exchange rate system from a system based on gold to one based on the dollar. The Smithsonian Agreement of 17 December (between France, West Germany, Italy, Netherlands, Belgium, UK, USA, Sweden, Canada and Japan) went some way towards easing the situation by introducing a replacement system which, although not reinstating the convertibility of dollars into gold, introduced an element of flexibility and allowed currencies to fluctuate between +2.5 per cent and −2.5 per cent of the fixed dollar exchange rate.

In 1972, in Europe, further agreements were entered into at government level. Eight European countries (the original six EEC countries plus the UK and Denmark) agreed on a new system whereby fluctuations between currency values of members of the pact were minimised relative to each other – yet could still fluctuate against the dollar according to requirements of the Smithsonian Agreement. Thus, whilst maintaining the 2.25 per cent fluctuation allowance with the dollar, the group of European countries agreed to keep fluctuations between themselves down to between +1.125 per cent and −1.125 per cent. The narrower range of fluctuation became known as 'the (EEC) snake', the larger fluctuation range became known as 'the (Smithsonian) tunnel', and the whole arrangement was known as 'the snake in the tunnel'. The advantage of the system within Europe was stability of currencies between European trading partners. A problem of the system, however, was the need for frequent intervention by national monetary authorities that wished to support weaker currencies. Some countries (including France, Denmark and the UK) found it necessary, occasionally, to let their currencies float for a period in order to find new currency equilibrium values as determined by free market forces.

By the beginning of 1973 the Bretton Woods system began to break down. Free movement of capital began to impinge too closely on needs for domestic economic control. In particular, large volumes of dollars flowing out of the USA strained the system to breaking point. At the same time rapidly rising oil prices were also exerting pressure on exchange rates. The pressures of maintaining currency values according to the Bretton Woods system became too severe and, on 2 March 1973, the situation became so bad that the foreign exchange markets were forced to close down for two weeks. The Bretton Woods era had come to an end.

The stamp of approval for floating exchange rates came in 1977 after an IMF meeting in Jamaica at which it was decided that, as long as it was formally agreed, any exchange rate system was permissible. The new arrangements became part of the IMF Articles of Agreement in 1978. Which exchange rate system is actually the best (fixed, managed or floating) has remained a popular topic for debate at both government and academic levels ever since.

The system that replaced the Bretton Woods arrangement is hardly a system at all. It is, rather, a variety of agreed arrangements whereby countries have considerable flexibility in deciding to have fixed, floating or managed exchange rates. One important survivor of the Bretton Woods system is the IMF, which served to introduce order into the new exchange rate arrangements by acting both as a lender in times of difficulty and as a forum for organising the international monetary system. For its lending activities, the IMF introduced a new unit of account – the SDR (Special Drawing Right). Originally, in 1970, the SDR was equal to one dollar but, following the changes in monetary arrangements in 1974, the value of the SDR was redefined in terms of the weighted value of 16 major currencies.

A further development in exchange rates, in Europe, came in 1979 when representatives of European countries met to find a replacement for the 'snake in the tunnel'. Following the discussions the European Monetary System was set up with objectives similar to those of the IMF – but with particular reference to European affairs. Belgium, Denmark, Ireland, Italy, Luxembourg, France, Netherlands and West Germany contributed to the scheme. With the new system came a new unit of account – the European Currency Unit (ECU). This new currency unit was a 'cocktail' of member countries' currencies, its role being, at that time, similar to that of the IMF's SDR (namely as a supplement to national reserves). Eventually, however, the ECU would take on a much wider role in the financial markets.

The improved control over domestic matters by governments achieved by switching to floating exchange rates in the 1970s was won at the expense of increased risks for businesses involved in international dealings. Previously, currency values over time could be predicted with reasonable accuracy; now they could not. The demand for reducing uncertainty of financial flows denominated in different currencies led to rapid innovation in the foreign exchange markets. Before the change to floating exchange rates, currency markets were used mainly to provide the basic service of exchanging one currency for another. With the advent of floating exchange rates, a myriad of new types of foreign exchange market arrived to serve the needs of those engaged in international financial transactions.

### *Developments in the Euromarkets*

At the beginning of the 1970s the Euromarket had already grown to substantial size as a channel for capital flows that avoided the US Interest Equalisation Tax (IET). In 1974 the IET was removed leading to massive foreign lending by the US. The removal of IET was too late, however, to halt the march of the Euromarkets, which were to receive further boosts before the end of the decade. The oil shocks of 1973 and 1979, although unpopular amongst non-OPEC countries in the short-run, gave rise to large capital flows from OPEC countries to European and US banks, where they became known as 'petrodollars'. These funds became popular short-term financial assets in the US markets and Euromarkets because of the low prevailing interest and inflation rates. In retrospect it is possible that the low interest rates were a little too attractive because the oil-importing countries used large amounts of petrodollars for funding budget deficits, thus starting a chain of events that led up to the debt crisis of the eighties. Increased size of the Euromarkets was accompanied by further types of investment becoming available for investors. For example, the first dollar denominated FRN (Floating Rate Note) was issued during a period of high interest rates in 1970. Many more innovations in the Euromarkets followed. Euro issues denominated in Canadian dollars became popular. The first SDR currency cocktail Eurobond was issued in 1975 and was followed by the first Japanese yen Eurobond in 1977.

*Developments in national financial markets*

Outside the Euromarkets there was also movement towards internationalisation of domestic capital markets. It became common for equity (particularly stocks of multinationals) to be traded simultaneously in different countries. There were also developments in investment banking, underwriting and security distribution methods worldwide with an emphasis on consortia activity. New types of market began to operate – such as the International Money Market (IMM), which opened in Chicago in 1972 to provide international investors with a wider range of speculation and hedging alternatives for their foreign trading activities and investments. Meanwhile, at an institutional level, more attention was paid to encouraging and coordinating international financial flows. In 1977 the EEC produced a non-binding framework for regulating securities – the Code of Conduct Relating to Transactions in Transferrable Securities – which aimed, eventually, to lead to similar treatment of securities in all EEC countries. Even France's highly restricted markets came under scrutiny when the Perouse Commission made its report in 1979 and suggested ways of improving methods for quoting, trading and clearing securities on the Paris stockmarket. On the other side of the world further changes in Japanese law were leading to creeping liberalisation of the Tokyo stockmarkets. The most sweeping liberalisation move during the period, however, occurred in the UK on 23 October 1979, when Margaret Thatcher's Conservative Government removed all UK exchange restrictions. This move heralded the arrival of a new movement towards freedom of international money and capital transactions.

## The deregulation explosion of the 1980s

Developments in the 1980s, so far, have included a slide into world recession, a technical revolution in the financial markets, and a general movement towards deregulation of financial markets and institutions. The developing countries, because of their heavy borrowing in the previous decade, have fared worst from the world recession. When exchange rates and interest rates turned against them the amounts to be repaid by the LDCs had grown substantially in real terms. In addition, demand for raw materials during the recession fell making it difficult for the LDCs to earn the foreign exchange which they urgently required. The recession led to a decrease in the demand for oil and, in 1983, it became necessary for OPEC members to lower the price of oil despite shortages in the supply caused by the war between Iran and Iraq. The cheaper oil went some way towards ending the recession but further problems, in the shape of a high valued dollar in world currency markets from 1983 to 1985, were yet to come. To many, the high-valued dollar during this period appeared to be boosting economic growth and welfare in the USA at the expense of reduced growth prospects in other areas of the world and leading to uneven world economic development.

Uneven economic development is both a cause and an effect of exchange rate fluctuations in the currency markets and hence the early 1980s saw many moves at government level to remove immediate pressures from events occurring in the international financial system. In December 1982, for example, it was necessary for the IMF to lend SDR 3.6 billion to Mexico after Mexican exchange markets were forced to close down because of difficulties in meeting debt service payments. Brazil also received an IMF loan (SDR 4.96 billion) in 1983. The financing requirements of developing countries with debt-repayment difficulties led to a need for larger sums in international money pools. The IMF increased its quotas to SDR 19 billion in February 1981 and, in January 1983, EEC countries raised their aggregate commitments under the General Agreement to Borrow (GAB) to SDR 90 billion. A Special Action Program was set up by the World Bank in 1983 to provide further help to developing countries in financial difficulties. Meanwhile, to many bankers and lenders of sovereign debt, the situation looked decidedly gloomy. The alternatives for the large international lenders appeared to be either to cut their losses by writing off the bad debts or to risk sending more good money after bad in the hope that growth prospects in the second half of the eighties would allow eventual repayment of the loans. The world's lenders sought strength in numbers to share problems and provide mutually acceptable solutions. The international dialogues and agreements entered into at this time were inevitable because international capital movements now dwarfed the economic activities of most individual nations. Only consortia activity could produce the required economic muscle to bring about desired changes. The ineffectualness of actions against external economic pressures by individual governments became apparent in exchange markets in the shape of failures to fix exchange rates. In the wake of a steadily building Euromarket and an information and technological revolution, the only course left open to governments that had failed to stem the flowing tide was to persuade other governments to free their markets too – hence the deregulation explosion of the mid–1980s.

The deregulation trend began in the UK in 1979 with the abandonment of exchange controls. In 1980 Switzerland lifted exchange restrictions on Swiss franc denominated deposits of non-residents. As the 1980s progressed further changes occurred to allow more individuals, corporations and institutions access to foreign markets. Taiwan and South Korea passed laws to permit ownership of equity by foreigners through investment funds. Sweden and Finland allowed free trading by foreigners in domestic equities. Australia introduced a programme for deregulation. The USA removed many restrictions on banks' international trading activities in 1981 and, in 1984, removed the withholding tax on US bonds held by non-residents. Almost all European countries now permit entry of foreign banks to domestic markets. Even Arabic countries such as Egypt, Turkey and Saudi Arabia have begun to experience pressures for lowering restrictions aimed at isolating financial markets. Perhaps the most important deregulatory changes of all, however, have taken place in Japan. Although the liberalisation of Japanese markets has not been as fast nor yet gone as far as in other countries of the world, its significance is great because of the vast sums of capital involved. Japan is set to become the second largest capital market in the world because of the vast sums held by the Japanese Post Office Bank, the largest institutional investor in the world. If Japanese regulations changed to permit the Japanese Post Office Bank to invest some of its $350 billion in the international markets the shape of world financing would change overnight. It is not surprising that the US President brought the Japanese 'liberalisation package' personally to Tokyo in November 1984.

What happens next in the international markets is difficult to say. The extreme possibilities leading on from the deregulation explosion are, on the one hand, the prospect of highly efficient, integrated world financial markets but, on the other hand, a drastic, forced return to isolationism and protectionism. Meanwhile, the deregulatory trend is continuing and governments are finding it increasingly difficult to resist the financial markets' new freedom. There is, without doubt, some cause for uneasiness, particularly in the short-term, for individual segments of the markets caught up in the process of structural change and for individual governments that are losing effective control over private market forces. Political concern is aroused because only joint actions involving several governments can influence the markets in any significant way. It is natural for some feelings of uneasiness to precede change, however, and such a response can only be regarded as healthy. Foresight, lessons from the history of the financial markets and a deeper understanding of the implications of greater capital mobility would help reduce the possibility of any major economic disaster.

For business and the private financial institutions the current needs are for greater flexibility in the design of new markets and new financial instruments to cope with the fluctuating exchange rates of the freeing international financial system. For governments and the public institutions the needs are for greater co-operation and agreement on matters of mutual concern – in particular with regard to the future stability of the world economy.

**Summary**

The internationalisation of stockmarkets began as soon as man entered into trade with his neighbours. Facilities such as the early depository institutions and foreign exchange booths grew up to develop over the centuries into today's modern stockmarkets. Man's objectives over the centuries have hardly changed, but the technology, techniques and facilities for achieving them have done so dramatically. There has always been a conflict between the freedom of the individual and the freedom of governments to act on behalf of society as a whole. This conflict can be seen today in the financial markets, where attitudes between protectionism and freedom of capital movements still vary.

The engines of change in the financial markets are: firstly, the expanding Euromarkets; secondly, advances in market technology; and thirdly, the host of innovations in the markets. History has seen fit to allow the external markets to grow to such proportions that individual governments and their central banks can no longer defend their economies against free market forces. For maintaining control and stability of the financial markets the responsibility and power for intervention is passing from individual governments to groups of governments operating through the international institutions that serve their mutual interest. Meanwhile, whilst the variable exchange rates persist, innovations are occurring rapidly in the financial markets to provide risk reduction services for the world's traders, lenders and borrowers.

### Further reading on the deregulatory trend of the 1980s


Altschul, T. S., 'Relaxing the Rules in Japan', *Asiabanking* (Hong Kong), no 48, March 1984, pp 108–9.

Altschul, T. S., 'Deregulation Versus Reregulation', *International Financial Law Review* (UK), vol 3, no 12, December 1984, pp 11–16.

Conover, C. T., 'Quest for Powers: The Changing World of Financial Services', *Comptroller of the Currency Quarterly Journal* (USA), vol 3, no 2, June 1984, pp 9–11 (also pp 24–32).

Fallon, P., Adam, N. and Ollard, W., 'The Great Deregulatory Explosion', *Euromoney* (UK), October 1984, pp 51–61.

Fautz, W., 'Deregulating the Yen Financial Markets', *Swiss Bank Corporation Economic and Financial Prospects*, no 4, August/September 1984, pp 1–4.

Field, P. *et al*, 'How Deregulation Swept Australia', *Euromoney* (UK), August 1984.

Hamilton, A. D., 'Financial Decontrol in Japan: A Case of When not Whether', *The Banker* (UK), vol 134, no 72, August, pp 29–33.

Keiko, Atsumi, 'Changing Cautiously and Independently', *Asiabanking* (Hong Kong), no 52, July 1984, pp 45–6.

Kure, B., 'Orderly Liberalisation of Financial Markets', *Japan Institute of Social and Economic Affairs Economic Eye*, vol 5, no 1, March 1984, pp 4–7.

'Liberalisation of Currency Control', *Norwegian Bankers' Association Financial Review*, vol 58, no 2, June 1984 p 7.

National Australia Bank, 'Stock Exchange: The Stockbroking Industry', *National Australia Bank Monthly Summary*, September 1984, pp 9–11.

Okomura, H., 'Financial Liberalisation Gathers Pace', *The Banker* (UK), vol 133, no 692, October 1983, pp 27–33.
Osborn, N., 'Canada Gets to Grips with Deregulation', *Euromoney* (UK), November 1984, pp 26–36.
Rampton, C. B., 'Exchange Control – History, Policy and Practice', *Bankers Institute of New Zealand Bankers Review*, vol 3, no 4, May 1984, pp 30–4.
Smith, B. W., 'Shaping a Better World for Financial Services', *Comptroller of the Currency Quarterly Journal* (USA), vol 3, no 2, June 1984, pp 13–17.
Sullivan, B., 'Down with Protectionism', *Euromoney* (UK), October 1983, pp 41–4.
'The Rush to Deregulation', *Westpac Banking Corporation Review* (Australia), no 14, May 1984, pp 3–4.
Toon-woong, K., 'Financial Policy in Transition', *Korea Newsletter* (UK), no 18, July 1984, pp 5–6.
Tourret, R., 'New Rules Help Liberate System', *Asia Banking and Corporate Finance* (Hong Kong), no 46, January 1984, pp 66–71.
'United States Lifts Interest Withholding Tax for Foreigners', *Union Bank of Switzerland Business Facts and Figures*, August/September 1984, pp 10–11.
Yoshitomi, M., 'Japan's Path to Financial Market Liberalization', *Japan Institute for Social and Economic Affairs Economic Eye*, vol 5, no 3, September 1984, pp 4–8.

## Appendix: Selected dates in the development of international financial markets

| | |
|---|---|
| c2000BC | Babylonian temples are used as deposit facilities for the rich. Funds are used by merchants for international trade. |
| 500–300BC | Greeks finance commercial ventures with joint-stock capital. Facilities are available for dealing with foreign currency payments. |
| Roman Empire | Bills of exchange are used to finance international trade. The Romans provide the first code of law for financial markets. |
| Middle Ages | Feudal system of government reduces the volume of cross-border transactions. |
| 1215AD | In England, the Magna Carta hails the arrival of a new period of mercantilism. |
| 14th century | England becomes a haven for free traders. |

| | |
|---|---|
| 15th century | Foreign exchange booths are set up in Western Europe (e.g. at Frankfurt in 1402). |
| 16th century | The Frankfurt stock exchange is founded, trading mainly in bills of exchange. |
| 17th century | Holland establishes banks and a securities exchange. |
| | The Lombard bankers of Italy boost trade and industry. |
| | Many banks and securities exchanges are founded to meet the needs of international traders. |
| 18th century | Rothschilds international banking houses are established. |
| | Further establishment of banks, securities exchanges and international banking houses. |
| 19th century | Britain exports large volumes of capital – mainly to the USA. |
| | Joint-stock companies pave the way for the industrial revolution. |
| 1850 | Swiss stock exchange founded in Geneva. |
| 1878 | Japanese stock exchange set up in Tokyo. |
| 1891 | Stock exchange set up in Hong Kong. |
| 1897 | Many countries, including Russia, fix their currency values in relation to gold – the gold standard. |
| 20th century | London becomes leading international centre for bill-brokers and bond issuers. |
| 1912 | Britain's foreign lending exceeds £300 millions. |
| | A consortium of foreign banks helps finance the Canton Hankow Railroad in China. |
| 1914 | Outbreak of First World War. |
| | Federal Reserve System established in USA. |
| | 90 per cent of international capital movements are in the form of portfolio investments. |
| | USA has a strong export position and enormous capital market facilities. |
| 1916 | Investment Dealers Association (IDA) is founded in Canada to maintain professionalism in the stockmarket. |
| 1919 | USA has $6.5 billions invested abroad (excluding war loans to the Allies). |
| | West Germany and the Allies sign the Versailles Treaty. |
| 1920 | West Germany is the world's largest international borrower. |
| | The first meeting of the League of Nations is held in Paris. |

| | |
|---|---|
| 1921 | West Germany and America sign the Peace Treaty in Berlin. |
| 1920s | USA is main supplier of non-resident capital. |
| | Large capital movements aid stabilisation and reconstruction programmes in Europe. |
| 1929 | Wall Street Crash. |
| | Total international debt is back to pre-war levels. |
| 1930 | Bank for International Settlements is established. |
| 1931 | World economic collapse leads into the depression of the 1930s. |
| | All major countries abandon the gold standard. |
| 1933 | The Glass-Steagall Act is passed in the USA to create a distinction between commercial and investment banking. |
| 1934 | The Securities and Exchange Commission is set up in the USA to control and regulate the stock exchange. |
| | Japanese stockmarkets merge to form the Japanese Securities Exchange under government control. |
| 1936 | The Tripartite Agreement (between Britain, France and the USA) encourages movement towards international monetary cooperation. |
| 1938 | Liquidations and depreciation of portfolio investments reduce the value of US gross overseas investment to below 1930 values. |
| 1939 | Outbreak of the Second World War. |
| 1930s | Many restrictions on international trade and financial markets. |
| | Wholesale defaults on loans by debtor countries. |
| | Total collapse of international financial markets. |
| 1944 | The International Monetary Fund (IMF) is set up after the conference at Bretton Woods, New Hampshire. |
| 1945 | The World Bank (IBRD) is set up. |
| | Following the Second World War, international capital movements occur at a faster pace. |
| 1946–50 | Foreign exchange markets are exposed to post-war inflationary pressures and controls. |
| 1948 | The Japanese stock exchange reorganises itself along the lines of the New York stock exchange. |
| 1949 | Many countries devalue their currencies as the US gold stock reaches $25 billions. |
| | Stockmarkets are inaugurated at Tokyo, Osaka and Nagoya (Japan). |

| | |
|---|---|
| 1950 | The European Payments Union (EPU) is established by recipients of the European Recovery Plan (The Marshall Plan) to facilitate multilateral payments within Europe. |
| 1951 | The OEEC (Organisation for European Economic Cooperation) adopts a Code of Liberalisation under which member countries pledge to abolish restrictions on agreed transactions and payments. |
| 1954 | Kenya sets up a stock exchange in Nairobi. |
| 1956 | The World Bank sets up the International Financial Corporation (IFC). |
| 1958 | The European Payments Union (EPU) is established with the advent of the European Economic Community (EEC). |
| | Financial markets in Europe revive. |
| | Prevention of Fraud (Investments) Act passed in the UK. |
| 1960 | Gold prices reach $40 per ounce. Central banks of major countries intervene in the London market to hold down gold prices. The London gold pool is set up. |
| | The International Development Association (IDA) is set up by the World Bank. |
| | 19 firms (ten from Singapore) set up the Malayan stock exchange along the lines of the Sydney stock exchange. |
| 1961 | The Organisation for Economic Cooperation and Development (OECD) comes into existence. |
| | OECD member countries adopt a Code of Liberalisation of Capital Movements to 'progressively abolish ... restrictions on movements of capital, to the extent necessary for effective economic co-operation' (does not apply to capital transactions with maturities of less than one year). |
| | West Germany and Netherlands revalue their currencies. |
| 1962 | IMF emergency fund set up ($6 billion) under the General Agreement to Borrow (GAB). |
| 1963 | The US levies an Interest Equalisation Tax (IET) on foreign borrowing. |
| | The first Eurodollar bond is issued. |
| | Japan joins the OECD. |
| 1964 | West Germany announces the Kuponsteur tax to be paid by foreign holders of German internal bonds. |
| | The first Euro Deutsche-mark bond is issued. |

| | |
|---|---|
| 1966 | An OECD working party report draws attention to the usefulness of an international capital market. |
| | The EEC's Ninth General Report on the Activities of the Community refers to the possibility of harmonising European company law and certain financial standards. |
| 1967 | An EEC report (*The Development of a European Capital Market*) emphasises the need for links between national financial markets. |
| | The EEC's *Tenth General Report on Activities of the Community* suggests movement towards a freer European capital market with harmonised institutional and legal standards. |
| | IMF outlines a plan for establishing Special Drawing Rights (SDRs). |
| | Britain devalues the pound sterling on 18 November, heralding a one-year monetary crisis. |
| 1968 | The Association of International Bond Dealers (AIBD) is established to increase order in the international bond markets. |
| | Foreign bond issues in Europe and the US are ten times the level of 1958 issues. |
| | The Euroclear system is set up in Brussels for clearing Eurobonds. |
| | A two-tier gold market replaces the London gold pool. |
| 1969 | Many countries experience balance of payments disturbances and monetary crises. |
| | The Deutsche-mark is floated on 30 June and revalued on 26 October. |
| | IMF establishes a buffer stock financing facility and the first Amendment to the Articles of Agreement goes into effect. |
| | France devalues the franc (10 August). |
| 1960s | The dollar is the main stabilising factor in foreign exchange markets. |
| | The productive capacities of many countries are reestablished. |
| 1970 | Cedel is set up in Luxembourg to provide a similar service to Euroclear. |
| | The Canadian dollar is floated (1 June). |
| | The Securities Investor Protection Act is passed in the USA. |

The IMF opens up its Special Drawing Rights (SDR) department. SDRs are used to supplement gold and dollars for national reserves on the basis of 1 SDR =$1.

The first dollar-denominated floating rate note (FRN) is issued in the international bond market.

1971 The Deutsche-mark and Dutch guilder are floated. Swiss franc is revalued (9 May).

A major US dollar devaluation.

Convertibility of dollars into gold is suspended (15 August).

Under the Smithsonian Agreement, foreign currencies are permitted to vary 2.25 per cent either side of agreed rates against the dollar (17 December).

Certain restrictions preventing Japanese investors from investing abroad are lifted.

The yen, Deutsche-mark and other currencies are revalued (18 December).

1972 EEC countries introduce the 'snake in the tunnel' whereby foreign exchange fluctuations between members' currencies are minimised.

The International Money Market (IMM) opens in Chicago (16 May).

The pound sterling is floated for a short period from 23 June when British international reserves are at a peak.

Denmark withdraws from the European Monetary Agreement but rejoins later in the year.

1973 Swiss franc floated (23 January).

Another US dollar devaluation (13 February). Yen and Italian lira are floated.

The foreign exchange markets close down (2 March) for two weeks.

Deutsche-mark revalued. (Joint Float, 19 March.)

Deutsche-mark revalued (29 June).

Dutch guilder revalued (17 September).

OPEC countries quadruple the price of oil.

The external debt of non-oil developing countries reaches $130 billion.

1974 The USA removes the Interest Equalisation Tax and relaxes controls on capital exports.

The Committee of Twenty puts forward a programme for the evolution of the international monetary system.

| | |
|---|---|
| | France withdraws from the European System of joint-floating exchange rates (10 July). |
| | Many banks experience losses on foreign exchange. Some banks fail. |
| | The IMF redefines the value of the SDR. The new SDR reflects the value of 16 major currencies rather than just the dollar. |
| 1975 | The first Eurobond denominated in SDRs is issued. |
| | The French franc rejoins the joint-float (10 July). |
| 1976 | The French franc leaves the joint-float (15 July). |
| | The Deutsche-mark revalues (mid-October). |
| | IMF members meet in Jamaica and agree to let market forces determine exchange rates. |
| 1977 | EEC produces the Code of Conduct Relating to Transactions in Transferable Securities. |
| 1977–78 | US dollar exchange rates experience a sharp decrease. |
| 1978 | The IMF's Articles of Agreement are amended (The Second Amendment). |
| | The Deutsche-mark revalues (mid-October). |
| | Following its fall, the dollar recovers after dealings with the IMF and in the international financial markets. |
| | Floating rate notes (FRNs) which depend on LIBOR (the London Inter-Bank Offered Rate) are introduced in the Euromarkets. |
| | The EEC defines the European Currency Unit (ECU) based on the values of nine currencies. |
| 1979 | The 'snake in the tunnel' joint-float is replaced by the European Monetary System (EMS). |
| | The European Monetary Fund is set up (March) with objectives similar to those of the IMF. Members are Belgium, Denmark, West Germany, France, Netherlands, Italy, Ireland and Luxembourg. |
| | The first EMS realignment. Deutsche-mark revalues (late September). |
| | The OPEC countries double oil prices triggering off a world recession. |
| | The International Banking Act is passed in the USA eliminating many differences between regulations on US and foreign banks operating in the USA. |
| | The UK removes all exchange restrictions (23 October). |

| | |
|---|---|
| | The National Association of Security Dealers and Investment Managers (NASDIM) is set up in the UK to encourage high standards of professional behaviour in the financial markets and provide a forum for discussion on matters concerning the securities industry. |
| | The Perouse Commission examines methods to improve the Paris stockmarket. |
| 1970s | Equity markets become increasingly internationalised. |
| | Most countries move to a system of floating or managed foreign exchange rates. |
| | West German, Swiss, and other currencies become competitive *vis-à-vis* the US dollar. |
| 1980 | Switzerland lifts all exchange restrictions on Swiss franc denominated deposits of non-residents. |
| | Gold prices escalate dramatically. |
| | In the USA, the Depository Institutions Deregulation and Monetary Control Act is passed – phasing out interest rate ceilings. |
| | IMF emergency fund is increased to $7.1 billion (SDR 6.4 billion). |
| | Japan passes the New Foreign Exchange Law. |
| | Non-OPEC countries record massive trade deficits. |
| | Foreign currency assets of banks in the European Eurocurrency market exceed $750 billion. |
| | Gross volume of international banking flows exceeds $1,300 billion. |
| 1981 | The method for calculating the SDR is changed. The new SDR is based on the currencies of the five countries with the largest export performances from 1975 to 1979 (US$, DM, yen, £ sterling and French franc). |
| | The IMF enters into a borrowing agreement with the Saudi Arabian Monetary Agency (SAMA). |
| | Greece joins the EEC. |
| | EMS realignment. Deutsche-mark and guilder revalued, French franc and lira devalued (October). |
| | EEC establishes a pool for financing member countries through their balance of payments difficulties. |
| | The first 'droplock' bond is issued in the Euromarket. |

International Banking Facilities are authorised in the USA, which allow banks to conduct approved international transactions without being subject to interest rate and reserve requirements.

1982 Belgium, Denmark and Luxembourg devalue their currencies against other EMS currencies.

Brazil and Argentina are unable to meet their foreign debt obligations.

Mexico is unable to maintain debt servicing payments and closes its foreign exchange markets. The IMF lends Mexico SDR 3.6 billion to rectify the situation.

The London International Financial Futures Exchange (LIFFE) opens to provide a service similar to that of the IMM in Chicago.

EMS realignment. West Germany and Netherlands revalue their currencies. France and Italy devalue (June).

1983 OPEC members lower the price of oil from $34 per barrel to $29 per barrel.

Australia and New Zealand devalue their currencies (7 and 8 March).

The external debt of non-oil producing developing countries reaches above US $650 billion. Total outstanding debt of the LDCs reaches $750 billion.

The IMF emergency fund is increased to $19 billion (SDR 17 billion).

The IMF increases its funds quotas from around SDR 60 billion to SDR 90 billion.

The World Bank sets up a Special Action Program to aid less developed countries.

The IMF lends Brazil the equivalent of SDR 4.96 billion.

EMS realignment: West Germany, Netherlands and Belgium revalue their currencies. France, Italy and Ireland devalue (late March).

Japan. President Regan visits Tokyo with a 'liberalisation package' (November).

Japan (December). Many restrictions on Euroyen bonds are lifted. Japanese banks are allowed to issue Euroyen loans to domestic or foreign borrowers. Foreign banks are allowed to provide trust banking services. Foreign financial institutions are allowed to lead-manage Euroyen bond issues. Japanese authorities consider lifting withholding taxes.

| | |
|---|---|
| 1984 | The US repeals the withholding tax on US bonds held by non-residents. |
| | The method for calculating the ECU currency basket is revised (2 July). |
| | Norway devalues the krone by 2 per cent. |
| | Australia introduces a deregulation programme to allow entry to foreign banks and remove certain exchange controls. |
| | UK agrees that the London stock exchange will eventually abolish fixed commissions and allows banks to buy into stockbroking firms. |
| | London stock exchange begins trading in currency options. |
| | In Europe, 23 (of 24) OECD countries allow entry of foreign banks to domestic markets. Sweden, the remaining OECD country intends to allow foreign banks entry in 1986. |
| | Japan invests over $20 billion per year in foreign securities. |
| 1985 | Portugal and Spain join the EEC. |
| | Bank of Korea takes steps to equalise the treatment of foreign and domestic banks in Korea. |
| | In France, liberalisation leads to the emergence of a Eurofranc market. |
| | Portugal and Norway allow entry of foreign banks. |
| 1980s | Governments with low reserves find it increasingly difficult to counter currency market forces. |
| | Technical developments allow money to be transferred across national frontiers at the speed of light. |
| | Fast growing Asian economies (Taiwan and South Korea) permit ownership of equity by foreigners via investment funds for non-residents. |
| | Stockmarkets in Egypt and Turkey begin to revive. |
| | Pressure increases for Saudi Arabia to remove restrictions on equity investment. |
| | In Japan, pressure mounts for further deregulation of markets. |
| | Sweden and Finland set up free share registers to allow free trading by foreigners in domestic equities. |

# 5 Institutional aspects: The banks and the international institutions

Financial institutions have always played an important role in the financial system both as avenues for funds and as guardians of financial stability. Their main purposes have been to develop natural resources, transfer capital and technology, develop financial markets, and educate investors. These functions are still important for both national and international institutions. Now, however, there are additional pressing problems to be dealt with. Central banks, for example, are beginning to lose the fight against international market forces and are seeking solution to their problems within channels provided by the international institutions. There is a growing need for increased communications between developed countries and LDCs to deal with the flows of capital and technology across the globe. There is also an awareness of a possible world economic crisis and the need to avoid it. Attention is therefore directed from all over the world on matters related to increased financial flows, mounting external debts and the volume of international trade. This chapter describes the institutional framework that has grown up over the years to deal with these problems.

The main channels for funds are shown in Figure 5.1, which

illustrates the relationships between the private financial institutions (the commercial banks and the merchant banks) and the public or government institutions (the central banks and the international institutions). The structure for channelling funds from the surplus sector to the user sector can be envisaged as comprising three tiers. Firstly, there is the commercial section, where the banks compete for business in the private markets, taking deposits and lending them out at the best attainable rates.

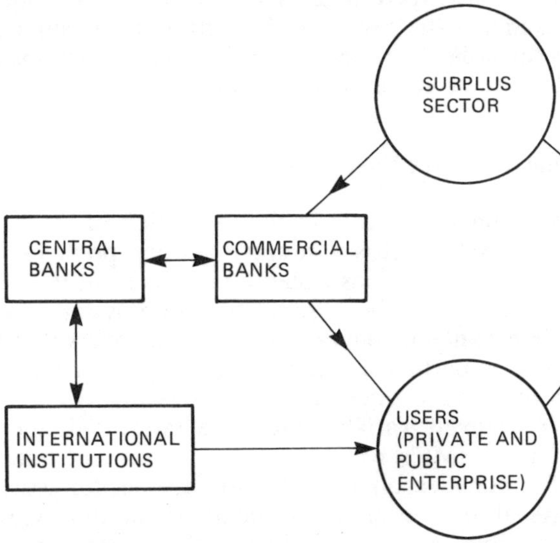


**Figure 5.1 Links between commercial banks, central banks and the international institutions.**

Secondly, there are the central banks whose interests lie not only in the operations of the free market but also in the wider monetary and economic policies of the governments that they serve. The central banks are able to influence the behaviour of the commercial banks either through statutory powers or in return for providing security for the commercial sector as a lender at the last resort. Lastly, there are the international institutions whose relationship with the central banks can in some ways be compared with that which exists between the central and commercial banks. That is to say, in return for cooperation on matters of international importance, the international institutions (for example, the IMF) can offer emergency funds for coping with difficult economic circumstances. The flows of funds running through the three-tier structure are those seeking profitable opportunities, those directed towards achieving and maintaining market stability and those channelled towards economic and social objectives on a world scale.

The first part of this chapter examines the IMF, the World Bank and other institutions that aid international cooperation. Profit-seeking activities of international institutions, namely those undertaken by the growing population of international and multinational banks, are described in the second part of the chapter. The final part examines the situation of the developing countries, where progress towards highly sophisticated financial systems has not progressed as fast as in the industrial countries.

## The International Monetary Fund (IMF)

The IMF plays an important role in the regulation of the international monetary system. It is a suitable starting point for examining international institutions because of its current influence on international matters and because its evolution over the years illustrates how international cooperation can help cope with freeing world markets. In particular, the IMF has helped the financial system through the fundamental change from relatively fixed exchange rates to relatively variable exchange rates. This section deals firstly with the IMF's role during the movement towards exchange rate flexibility; secondly, with IMF facilities for assisting member countries through economic difficulties; and thirdly, with the Fund's current role and relationship with the World Bank.

### *The IMF and the evolution of the international monetary system*

The IMF was created in 1944 under the Bretton Woods regulations. The original objective in establishing the Fund was to cope with the international problems of the 1940s and bring an end to the recession and unnecessary protectionism. Under the IMF's original Articles of Agreement the aim was to limit activities of individual nations, which could adversely affect the common good. This aim is set out clearly in Article 1 of the IMF's original Articles of Agreement, which sets out the objectives of the fund as follows:

1 To promote international cooperation through a permanent institution which provides the machinery for consultation and collaboration on international monetary problems.
2 To facilitate the expansion and balanced growth of international trade, and to contribute thereby to the promotion and

maintenance of high levels of employment and real income and to the development of the productive resources of all members as primary objectives of economic policy.

3 To promote exchange stability, to maintain orderly exchange agreements among members and to avoid competitive exchange depreciation.

4 To assist in the establishment of a multilateral system of payments in respect of current transactions between members and in the elimination of foreign exchange restrictions, which hamper the growth of world trade.

5 To give confidence to members by making the general resources of the Fund temporarily available to them under adequate safeguards, thus providing them with the opportunity to correct maladjustments in their balance of payments without resorting to measures destructive of national or international prosperity.

6 In accordance with the above, to shorten the duration and lessen the degree of disequilibrium in the international balance of payments of members.

Under the Bretton Woods system fluctuations in currency values were to remain within 1 per cent of agreed rates and be maintained by the currency buying and selling activities of central banks. Within this system the IMF's role was to act as overseer and source of agreement if individual countries wished to revalue or devalue their currency by more than 10 per cent.

The system worked well for two decades until needs for greater flexibility began to show in the 1960s. Currency realignments became common; the British pound devalued in 1967, the French franc devalued and the Deutsche-mark revalued in 1969, the Canadian dollar was floated in 1970, the Deutsche-mark and Dutch guilder were floated and the Swiss franc revalued in 1971. The crisis came at the end of 1971 when the dollar devalued and the US suspended the convertibility of dollars into gold. The move marked the end of the gold standard and the beginning of the movement towards floating (sometimes wildly) exchange rates. The effect of the changing attitudes towards exchange rates can be seen clearly in Figure 5.2, which shows the values of leading currencies against the dollar from 1967 to 1984. The horizontal lines between 1967 and 1972 are due to the currency realignments which took place during the period (under the Smithsonian and 'snake-in-the-tunnel' arrangements). By 1973 the horizontal lines give way to a far more variable pattern of exchange rates.

The IMF took the initiative to hold a special meeting in Jamaica

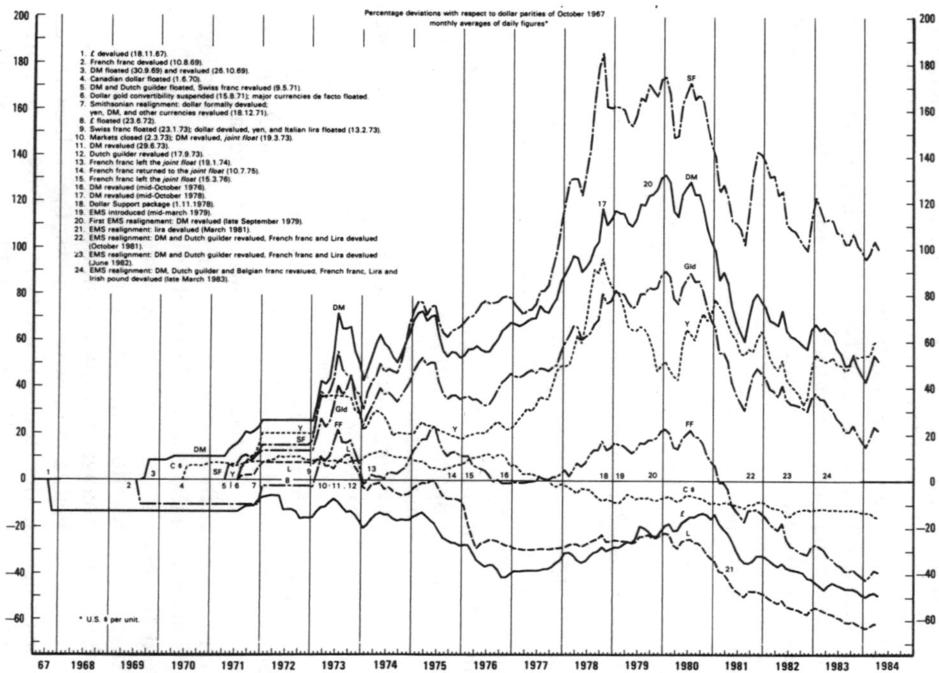


Figure 5.2 Exchange rates of major currencies against the dollar.

in 1976 to find a better way to deal with control (or non-control) in the currency markets. At the meeting it was resolved that floating rates should stay and, if necessary, fixed fluctuation bands should be abandoned. The new, extremely flexible arrangement was drawn up by which IMF members could choose between a range of alternatives, which spanned from pegged exchange rates to completely floating exchange rates.

Under the new system the IMF Articles of Agreement were amended so that members could choose to follow either the arrangements under the new Article 8 or those under the new Article 14. Members who chose to abide by Article 8 agreed not to impose restrictions on payments and transfers for international transactions without prior approval of the Fund. Members choosing to abide by Article 14 could, if they wished, maintain restrictions on payments transfers for current international transactions and adapt to changing circumstances. Those choosing Article 8 became the 'floaters' and those choosing Article 14 became the 'peggers'. For the peggers the IMF allowed the fixing of currency values to a single currency or to a group of currencies and also provided for fluctuation limits around centrally agreed rates. The floaters, on the other hand, required far less attention from IMF administrators. To keep order and provide guidance for members and their exchange market activities, the IMF introduced a set of additional principles. These are encaptured in Article 4 of the amended Articles of Agreement, which states:

1 A member shall avoid manipulating exchange rates or the international monetary system in order to prevent effective balance of payments adjustment or to gain unfair competitive advantage over other members.
2 A member should intervene in the exchange market if necessary to counter disorderly conditions, which may be characterised *inter alia* by disruptive short-term movements in the exchange value of its currency.
3 Members should take into account in their intervention policies the interests of other members, including those of countries in whose currencies they intervene.

The overall aim of the new IMF system could therefore be described as that of promoting economic stability and growth through orderly exchange rates whilst remaining flexible enough to allow intervention when circumstances require it. IMF influence is only brought to bear in the event of extreme exchange market activities or the abnormal economic circumstances of member countries.

Corrective action is taken by the Fund only in one or more of the following circumstances:

- If protracted large-scale intervention in the exchange markets by a member country leads to large exchange rate movements in one direction.
- In the event of unsuitable levels of borrowing or lending by members for balance of payments purposes.
- If exchange rate movements that cannot be justified in relation to underlying financial and economic conditions occur.
- If the domestic policies of member countries are aimed at encouraging abnormal capital flows. (The IMF will not intervene, however, if capital movements across national borders do not interfere with current account transactions.)

*Special Drawing Rights (SDRs) at the IMF*

The IMF has arranged facilities for assisting member countries with economic difficulties. The funds that furnish this facility are provided by member countries under the General Agreement to Borrow (GAB) and are called Special Drawing Rights (SDRs). SDRs are, essentially, a credit facility available to IMF members through the creation of a reserve asset parallel to gold and the US dollar. The amount of SDRs available to individual members varies according to their holdings of quota in the IMF. Member countries can apply for SDRs in any of the following circumstances:

- To overcome short-term balance of payments difficulties.
- To overcome structural balance of payments difficulties.
- For financing temporary export shortfalls due to factors beyond the member country's control.
- To finance contributions to buffer stock agreements (designed to stabilise prices of primary products) by members with payments difficulties.
- To provide additional financing for serious balance of payments difficulties.

The history of the SDR goes back to 1967 when the SDR system was devised at an IMF meeting in Rio de Janeiro, Brazil. In 1968 the IMF Articles of Agreement were amended to authorise the creation of the SDR which, at this time, was valued at $1 or 0.888671 grams of gold. After the move to floating exchange rates the SDR was redefined in terms of a currency cocktail. Originally the currency cocktail took into account the values of 16 currencies in proportion to their importance in world trade – but this system was too complicated to last. In 1981 the IMF changed the composition of the SDR to reflect the values of the five most important currencies in world trade: US$ (42 per cent), Deutsche-mark (19 per cent), French franc (13 per cent), Japanese yen (13 per cent) and British £ (13 per cent). Members borrowing SDRs must pay interest according to a formula that takes into account the short-term interest rates prevailing in the countries whose currencies comprise the SDR.

The IMF has clearly stated its intention to promote the SDR as the main international reserve asset in the international financial system and has attempted to improve its attractiveness over the years. The move from basing the SDR's value on a fixed dollar/gold price to a weighted value of a basket of currencies in 1974 had the effect of stabilising SDR prices in world markets. Interest rates on SDR have also remained at competitive levels. The range of institutions allowed to hold SDRs has widened and, for the future, plans are underway to allow countries to swap holdings of gold and foreign exchange for SDRs. Thus, besides using SDRs for purchasing foreign currencies, IMF members can use them in forward and swap transactions and even make SDR-denominated loans to member and non-member institutions.

*The current role of the IMF*

The IMF continues to play an important role in the international markets providing surveillance over and guidance of exchange arrangements chosen by member countries. The Fund's lending facilities for assisting member countries with balance of payments problems continue to be required and have been extended. In 1984, the Fund's lending facilities comprised a compensating financing facility, a buffer stock financing facility and an extended financing facility. These and other credit facilities provide a safety valve in the international financial system to cope with events such as sudden oil price changes and, currently, the debt crisis.

At this stage it is useful to consider the IMF in comparison with the World Bank (described in the next section) to show how the operations of the two institutions differ. In some respects the role of the IMF and the World Bank are comparable – they both provide financial assistance to countries with economic problems. Traditionally, however, the main role of the IMF has been to offer temporary, short-term financial support for balance of payment problems, operating mainly through the domestic financial system. The World Bank's operations are geared more specifically to development aid and assisting economies with structural difficulties. The IMF has also lent on a long-term basis to assist with structural economic difficulties but its loans differ from those of the World Bank, which tends to support specific projects rather than governments.

## The World Bank (IBRD, IDA and IFC)

The World Bank plays an important role in the economic development of the less developed countries (LDCs). It provides project and programme finance and technical assistance, acts as a financial catalyst between borrowers and lenders, advises on policy and institutional development, and sponsors consultative groups. The Bank operates jointly with the IMF on many matters in order to promote structural change and improve efficiency in the LDCs but differs in terms of facilities provided. The term World Bank actually describes three institutions – the International Bank for Reconstruction and Development (IBRD), the International Development Association (IDA) and the International Finance Corporation (IFC). The three organisations within the World Bank have the common aim of channelling funds to the LDCs. Their main characteristics are as follows.

### *The IBRD*

The IBRD was set up within the IMF in 1945 in order to provide credit to governments for development purposes in the wake of the Second World War. It is now owned by 144 governments, each of which subscribe agreed amounts of capital. Its lending operations are, however, financed mainly through borrowing in world capital markets. In 1984 the IBRD's liquidity and reserves were larger than ever before (its net income amounting to around $600 million) and its lending operations have increased substantially. Over the forty years since its inception the IBRD's field of interest has changed from post-war redevelopment projects in industrial countries to development projects in the LDCs. By 1984, IBRD loans (up to 20 years to maturity) were in excess of $90,000 million, the main borrowers being Asia, Latin America, Europe and the Middle East. Africa has also borrowed substantial amounts. Most of the funds have been used to sponsor energy, agriculture and rural development, and transport projects. Less than 25 per cent of the loans have gone to industry and development finance companies. Loan costs have been maintained at reasonably low levels by supplementing borrowings in international capital markets with the IBRD's paid-in capital, accumulated earnings and loan repayments. Nevertheless, interest rates for IBRD and its borrowers have increased substantially in recent years from around 7.5 per cent in 1978 to around 11.5 per cent in 1984. The LDC debt crisis, which led on from these interest rate increases, has resulted in an IBRD move towards the idea of encouraging further flows of capital from the private sector to supplement its own lending activities.

### *The IDA*

The IDA was established in 1960 to serve a similar role to the IBRD but with special facilities for the world's poorest countries. The IDA is now an important source of concessionary assistance, policy guidance and institutional support for poor countries. Funds for these purposes are procured mainly from budgetary contributions of developed nations. IDA loans (now in excess of $30,000 million) are interest free with maturities up to 50 years. Most of the loans have been extended to Africa and South Asia. The Sub-Saharan African nations with their terrible drought and famine conditions are the priority for IDA assistance in the mid 1980s.

### *The IFC*

The IFC was set up by the World Bank in 1956 to promote growth in the private sectors of LDCs. As a multilateral investment bank, the IFC acts as a catalyst in the process of mobilising domestic and foreign capital between developed and developing nations. It is instrumental in identifying and strengthening incentives for private investors. Membership of the IFC is currently around 125 countries and its capital stands at around $2 billion. Unlike the IBRD and IDA, the IFC tends to operate independently of IMF operations, although it may draw on the IBRD for certain services (such as administration). In 1985 the IFC considered plans for establishing a new investment fund aimed at attracting up to $500 millions to stockmarkets of semi-industrial nations to promote international portfolio investment. Similar plans were already underway for the South Korean and Mexican stock exchanges. The incentive put out to international investors to encourage them to set aside funds for such purposes is that, given adequate diversification, they would gain from the rapid growth-potential of the developing countries' stockmarkets, which currently produce around 13 per cent of world output but represent only 2 per cent of world stockmarket capitalisation.

To sum up, the activities of the World Bank can be divided into three main sectors: aiding the poorest countries (IDA), financing LDCs (IBRD), and helping the privatisation process following economic development above LDC status (IFC). In 1983 the World Bank initiated a Special Assistance Programme to coordinate its activities and help restore momentum for worldwide economic development. With mounting concern over the debt crisis there are likely to be further moves by the World Bank towards co-financing (collaborating with other sources of financial support) with development banks, commercial banks and export credit agencies. The scale of world borrowing and lending passing through the World Bank is large and growing. From 1947 to 1984 total World Bank net transfers per year increased to $4,500 million and disbursements increased to $10,000 million a year.

## Other international institutions

There are many other international institutions currently operating in the world financial markets either to the common good or for the benefit of smaller numbers of countries with a common interest. To cover all these organisations in this volume would be an impossible task but some of the more important institutions are outlined below.

### *The European Investment Bank (EIB)*

The EIB is an EEC institution that provides a source of finance for industrial activites. It is a large borrower in the international bond markets with total borrowings in 1984 amounting to ECU 4.36 billion (compared with ECU 2.31 billion in 1981). The Bank's function is to tap the various markets when interest rates are favourable and then lend them on to, among others, Denmark, Ireland, Greece and the UK. Examples of the type of borrower attracted to the EIB include British Nuclear Fuels and the South of Scotland Electricity Board. The role of the EIB is, in some respects, similar to that of the World Bank, the main difference being that clients of the World Bank are mainly LDCs, which require minimum interest rates, whilst the EIB serves mainly industrial borrowers. As a result, EIB loans tend to be higher than those from the World Bank, the former being able to pass on higher rates to borrowers with more ease. EIB loans also tend to be negotiated individually and in line with going costs of funds in the financial markets, whereas the World Bank is able to charge its customers a standard rate by operating a currency pooling system.

*Agency for International Development (AID)*

The AID administers the US foreign aid programmes. The organisation considers applications for funds from developing nations if no funds are available from other sources. Interest rates on AID loans are usually heavily subsidised and maturities tend to be long. If ever these preferential rates are too onerous, mechanisms are available for renegotiation of terms with the US Treasury. The main restriction on loans through AID is that the purpose for which the funds are used should not interfere with or go against US economic policies.

*The Organisation for Economic Cooperation and Development (OECD)*

The OECD was established in 1961 as the successor to the Organisation for European Economic Cooperation (OEEC). Members of the Organisation include most of the developed nations of the world. The OECD regularly publishes useful statistics and reports on the world financial situation. Within the OECD a group of countries have combined to form the Development Assistance Committee (DAC) to provide development assistance for LDCs, mainly in the form of project aid. DAC comprises most European countries, Australia, Canada, Japan, New Zealand and the USA.

*The Bank for International Settlements (BIS)*

The BIS began its existence shortly after the First World War to improve procedures for transferring money between countries that had currencies that were not fully convertible. Nowadays most currencies are convertible and the role of the BIS has changed to that of providing a meeting place for discussion on monetary and foreign exchange matters. It is located in Basle, Switzerland, and meetings are often held between governors of the major central banks (European countries plus USA, Canada and Japan). With outstanding foreign assets of Western banks within the BIS area to LDCs currently standing at around $340 billion, there is much to be discussed at BIS meetings. Although proceedings of the meetings are seldom communicated to the rest of the world, the BIS provides regular bulletins and statistics on international banking and international markets.

*Regional development banks*

The objective of regional development banks is to assist the development of capital markets and high-priority industrial sectors in developing countries. Early examples of development banks include the Development Bank of Japan (1892), which helped build up the Japanese shipping and steel industries, and the National Financiera of Mexico (1920). Since the 1960s development banks have been established in Sri Lanka, Turkey, Thailand, Iran, Syria and other developing countries. Current development banking activities include those of the Inter-American Development Bank, the African Development Bank and the Asian Development Bank. Although development banks have been successful in stimulating the economies of developing countries, they have also been criticised for exercising monopolistic powers. For example, they may have the effect of forcing lending rates in domestic markets down so far that they cease to attract funds.

*The Organisation for Petroleum Exporting Countries (OPEC)*

This organisation provides a mechanism for cartel oil-price agreements for countries that include Saudi Arabia, Kuwait, UAE, Quatar and Iraq. OPEC decisions have far-reaching consequences in the international markets because of oil's worldwide use as a major source of energy.

**International and multinational banking activities**

The international institutions described so far operate mainly in the service of governments. The banking activities described in this section are available to governments too, as well as to the multitude of corporations and individuals around the world who require international financial services. The amount of international banking business has increased significantly in the 1980s in the wake of technical advances in banking services and deregulatory changes, which now allow the branches of many more foreign banks to compete alongside domestic banks in national markets. The consequence of this increased competition is that borrowing and lending rates in different markets are becoming more closely aligned. Another consequence of increased competition is a much more flexible attitude towards the design of financial instruments. Bankers' skills at tailoring financial instruments in terms of currency of denomination, maturity, credit quality, repricing periods, cash flow characteristics and other aspects are being tested to the full in the competitive environment of the 1980s. When business operations are contained within a single economy, the domestic banking system can offer a wide range of services. In this book, however, we are more concerned with international and multinational banking operations that offer, in particular, facilities for traders, borrowers and lenders involved in the transfer of money and capital across national boundaries. The nature and development of these foreign banking services are now reviewed.

### *Developments in international banking*

International banking involves financial arrangements for intermediating between countries. Developments in this field have great importance for the internationalisation of stockmarkets and the trend towards greater foreign borrowing and investment. International banking services include the provision of foreign exchange facilities, the collection of savings in an international context, and the provision of international finance. In performing these functions the international banks have, during the 1970s and 1980s, experienced a leap in the amount of business and a transformation in the type of business handled.

Foreign exchange is, perhaps, the most obvious place to look for change. Here, for example, it is noticeable that the number of currencies traded has increased five times in the last 40 years and that the range of services for currency traders has been extended. New developments include Eurocheques, currency options, currency swaps, and opportunities for longer (up to five years) forward transactions. International transfers of funds can now take place at the speed of light either through the traditional, correspondent banking system (whereby the banks maintain foreign currency deposits subject to local banking regulations) or through the Eurosystem (whereby local regulations can be avoided). These services, along with improved counselling and advice, have arisen from clients' needs for risk reduction in the variable exchange rate climate, which has prevailed since the 1970s.

With regard to the second major economic function of the international banks – that of making funds available to foreign countries – the international banks have two main ways of exporting capital. The banks themselves can invest funds at other foreign banks for the purposes of payments or liquidity or by granting foreign credits. Thus banks in one country can work to the mutual benefit of banks in other countries and also assist in promoting capital exports. The second main form of assisting the export of capital is through the banks' dealings in the markets where they may indulge in underwriting and stockmarket trading. Underwriting of international issues has become increasingly performed by banks in line with developments in the Euromarkets. Long-term foreign bonds open to public subscription may be floated by banks operating a consortia or syndicated system. Larger, multinational banks tend to lead the syndicates for public offerings. For privately placed paper, on the other hand, the smaller institutions may deal with the launching themselves in conjunction with other smaller banks. A second type of underwriting activity – issues in foreign currencies – is performed by banks via the Euromarkets. Here, rather than lead the underwriting themselves, banks may enlist the services of specialist underwriting firms with special knowledge of the Euromarkets and a previous record of successful launches. The other link with international financing is via the purchase of sale of shares and bonds in the international stockmarkets. New York, London and Zurich are important centres for Eurobond and international share trading.

The third major function of international banks in the trend towards greater international lending and borrowing is the collection of savings in an international context. In the past the collection of deposits may have seemed an effortless task on the part of the banks because savers automatically looked towards them to provide interest on excess funds. In the competitive environment on the 1980s, however, bank salesmanship may have become much more important to persuade savers to bring their funds to banks rather than other types of financial intermediary. Attraction of foreign funds is now an extremely specialised task and banks must continually be able to offer up-to-date financial services to their foreign clients. Competition between banks in their efforts to attract foreign deposits is currently running high on an international scale. Discretion, know-how, and counselling services are important weapons in the quest for foreign deposits.

### *Developments in multinational banking*

International banking is essentially bilateral whereby banks in one country employ foreign correspondent banks in their overseas operations. Multinational banking is the next stage on from international banking and involves providing credit services to host and third country entities. Thus the multinational banks operate in their own territories and also with their own branches in overseas territories. Major multinational banks, by country, are shown in Table 5.1.

**Table 5.1 Leading multinational banks by country**

| | |
|---|---|
| USA | Citicorp, Chase, Chemical Bank, Mantrust, Morgan, Bank of America, Bankers Trust, First Chicago |
| Canada | Bank of Montreal, Royal Bank, Dominion Bank |
| Japan | Bank of Tokyo, Dai-Ichi Kangyo Bank, Industrial Bank of Japan, Mitsubishi Bank, Sumitomo Bank |
| West Germany | Deutsche Bank, Dresdner Bank, Hypobank, Westdeutsche Landesbank |
| UK | Barclays, Midland, National Westminster, Lloyds Bank |
| France | Banque National de Paris, Credit Lyonnais, Société Général, Credit Commercial de France |
| Netherlands | ABN Bank, Amsterdam-Rotterdam Bank |
| Switzerland | UBS, SBS, Creditsuisse |
| Italy | Comit, BNL, Credito Italiano, Banco di Roma, San Paolo di Torino |

The move towards multinational banking is fairly recent. For example, US multinational banking goes back only as far as the beginning of the 1960s. Recent changes in US banking have been rapid, however, with the passing of the International Banking Act (1979), the Depository Institutions Deregulation and Monetary Control Act (1980) and the authorisation of International Banking Facilities in 1981. West Germany's and Japan's multinational banking did not really get under way until the 1970s. Despite the late start, however, because of their economic power, development of multinational banks has been rapid worldwide. Multinational banks now count among the world's top hundred banks as far as volume of business is concerned. Australia is the latest newcomer to the deregulation of foreign banking and moves in this country are likely to influence further deregulation of banking activities in the Asia–Pacific region. There are currently around 360 foreign banks operating in London and around 260 in New York. In Europe, 23 out of 24 OECD countries now allow entry of foreign banks to domestic markets. Sweden, the remaining OECD country, intends to allow entry to foreign banks in 1986. The result of the increase in foreign banking as far as their clients and the regulatory authorities in each particular country are concerned is that differences between domestic and foreign banks tend to exist 'on paper' only.

Although the preference of multinational banks may lie in international business because of the large profits to be made there, lending to local customers also continues through the foreign banks' branch networks. Where full branches are established in overseas territories, international intermediation activity in foreign exchange and Eurodeposits can take place through links with the interbank market.

Lending services by the multinationals have tended to be characterised by the syndicated loan approach, whereby borrowers' funds are raised from a number of national lenders in a number of different currencies. These syndicated loans have accounted for a significant part of total capital flows to developing countries during the past decade. In the 1970s there were ample funds available in the international markets and little expectation that the developing countries would one day find difficulty in repaying the large sums that they borrowed at the time. There is currently, therefore, a great deal of cooperation between the multinational banks themselves and organisations such as the IMF and the World Bank to secure both the eventual repayment of loans and the continued economic progress of the LDCs. The LDC problem is, essentially, a world banking problem because the syndicated loan technique ensures that risks (and therefore facilities for dealing with problems) are spread between many financial institutions, countries and banking systems. The system has worked fairly well with only major defaulters such as Mexico and Brazil causing undue trouble. The LDC debt crisis is not, however, yet over and, with the continuing world recession, it could last into the 1990s or even beyond.

Growth of the Euromarkets has greatly increased banks' ability to make loans (Eurodollars account for approximately 65 per cent of total multinational banking activity). The banks therefore play an important role in providing Eurocurrency loans for the long periods of time that are required by the long-term investment projects undertaken by the multinational organisations.

An interesting recent development in the field of international lending by banks is a move away from the syndicated loan method, which has proved popular for the last 20 years. The move is largely in response to the tendency for lead banks to leave only slim profit margins for other members of the syndicates. Larger customers, such as Denmark, Sweden, France and Spain, have recently become interested in more subtle methods of international bank lending. The new financing methods, the note-issuing facility (NIF) and the revolving underwriting facility (RUF) (described further in chapter 6) are not loans at all in the traditional sense of the word, but arrangements whereby groups of banks join together in underwriting continuous short-term credit for the customer over a period of years. Rather than lending their own money, the banks thus become guarantors of low-cost credit from the short-term money markets. Their customers therefore have, via the banks, access to the market where the banks themselves compete for funds. In the international capital market the RUF and NIF are having an important effect, because they have brought a wide range of banks into the market as underwriters. Even the Bank of China has participated in RUFs since their inception in 1981. By 1985 the volume of RUFs and NIFs was approaching that of the traditional syndicated Eurocredits.

## Institutional developments in LDCs

Having considered the role and development of the sophisticated international and multinational banking system, it would seem appropriate to look at the other end of the spectrum – banking and institutional developments in the LDCs. Here, the banking system (commercial and central banks) plays an important role in promoting economic progress. In these countries a strong central bank and an efficient money market are prerequisites of financial stability, particularly in times of export booms or slumps. It is common for LDCs' central banks to be fairly small and operate along the lines of and in competition with other commercial banks. Part of the reason for their small size is that, unlike those in developed nations, central banks in developing countries have little incentive to transfer any surplus funds out of the country. Rather, their role is to provide a link with the international financial system to provide an avenue for the flow of funds into the country for financing industrial, commercial and agricultural developments. Links with the World Bank and other sources of development capital are particularly important in this respect.

Banks and stockmarkets provide the required channels for capital and technology from foreign investment in the LDCs. If economic growth is sustained, the LDCs could achieve developed nation status and become a capital exporter. Unfortunately this happy state of affairs has yet to arrive for most of the LDCs caught up in today's debt crisis. The main characteristics of financial markets in today's LDCs are therefore: the absence of a broker-dealer network; the existence of destablising speculative activity; no forward markets; tight government controls on foreign exchange; and unrealistically low interest rates on domestic securities. Economic growth is difficult under these circumstances and foreign investors may be dissuaded from buying local securities because of difficulties in reselling them in the local market. There is also a strong incentive for LDC capital to find its way onto the stockmarkets of developed countries. In semi-industrialised countries (one step up from LDC status) such as Brazil and Singapore, however, there are fast developing financial systems with regional links. Even with financial development, however, care must be taken that the outcome is not a dual economy – with financial centres becoming rich from their international links whilst the urban areas lag behind. In India, for example, where development banks play an important role, it has been necessary to enforce long-term plans to ensure that bank finance is efficiently used to encourage development of priority agricultural and industrial businesses rather than concentrate all lending on city-based enterprises.

In the long-run, only international links with the world's financial markets will provide the capital for economic growth in LDCs. Institutions such as the World Bank have a useful but difficult job persuading private capital to follow the syndicated bank loans of the 1960s and 1970s into the LDCs but a start has at least been made. More moves are afoot, in the form of guidance, expertise; and co-financing to provide the required capital. Currently the number of co-financed projects in LDCs is over 800 and, over the ten years to 1983, during which World Bank projects cost around \$275 billion, \$140 billion was the result of co-financing. Increased provision of information for potential investors by the Bank and improved expertise for appraisal and supervision of projects is likely to increase the amount of co-financing in future years. Banking systems, stockmarkets and other financial institutions should become more sophisticated in the LDCs in response to increased flows of development funds and policies aimed at ensuring their effective use.

## Summary

Public and private international institutions provide channels for financial flows and assistance on economic matters. The roles of the two types of institution are becoming increasingly blurred with public institutions finding it necessary to deal in private markets and private institutions finding it increasingly necessary to play their part in the guidance of international financial flows. The international institutions, in particular the IMF, have demonstrated flexibility and expertise in dealing with changing world financial trends in response to the need for cooperation on matters of international importance. The most pressing problems currently requiring solution are the LDC debt crisis, the need to build up financial markets in developing countries, the rate of growth of the Euromarkets, which is beginning to affect domestic markets, and control of the worldwide trend towards deregulation. Developments in the banking sector of the international financial markets are illustrative of the type of problem to be solved under the trend towards deregulation – governments must now choose between allowing foreign banks to start up business in their countries or cut off their countries from supplies of international funds.

Of all the countries in the world, the LDCs are currently experiencing the most difficulties in expanding their financial systems. With little need to export capital, the financial systems of these countries tend to be small, unsophisticated, highly protected and rely on international institutions for their development capital. The size of financial markets in LDCs is likely to remain small unless economic growth in these countries can catch up with the rest of the world – in which case a more open system of banks and stock exchanges could be promoted to their advantage.

## Further reading

### *The IMF and the international monetary system*

Ainley, Michael, 'The General Arrangements to Borrow', *International Monetary Fund Pamphlet*, no 41, 1984, pp 1–87.

Bird, G., 'Reforming the Fund: The Future Role of the International Monetary Fund and the International Monetary System', *The Three Banks Review* (UK), no 140, December 1983, pp 3–21.

Boyd, J.H., Dahl, D.S. and Line, C.P., 'A Primer on the International Monetary Fund', *Federal Reserve Bank of Minneapolis Quarterly Review*, Summer 1984, pp 6–14.

Comotto, R.D. *et al*, 'The Financial Structure and Operations of the International Monetary Fund', *Bank of England Quarterly Bulletin*, vol 23, no 4, December 1983, pp 546–56.

de Vires, M., '40th Anniversary of Historic Conference Commemorates Birth of the Fund and the Bank', *International Monetary Fund Survery*, 2 July 1984, pp 193–7.

'EMS – Progress Towards More Stability', *Deutsche Bank Bulletin* (West Germany), July 1984, pp 4–8.

Fahy, J.C. 'IMF Conditionality: A Critical Assessment', *OPEC Review* (UK), vol 8, no 3, autumn 1984, pp 229–44.

Higgins, J.W.A., 'Sovereign Lending and the IMF Conditionality', *International Financial Law Review*, vol 3, no 5, May 1984, pp 25–7.
'How Much Longer Can The Floating Exchange Rate System Survive?', *International Currency Review*, vol 16, no 2, September 1984, pp 7–12.
Johnson, C., 'A Better Monetary System', *Lloyds Bank Economic Bulletin* (UK), no 68, August 1984, pp 1–4.
Kleinheyer, N., Simmert, D.B. and Liethard, B., 'The European Monetary System Five Years On: Achievements and Prospects', *Inter Economics* (West Germany), no 3, May/June 1984.
Nowzad, B., 'The Extent of IMF Involvement in Economic Policy-making', *Amex Bank Review Special Papers* (UK), no 7, September 1983, pp 1–23.
Pissula, P., 'The IMF and the Countries of Eastern Europe: Rumania, Hungary and Poland', *Inter Economics* (West Germany), no 2, March/April 1984, pp 65–70.
'Re-Evaluating the Floating Exchange Note System', *Sanwa Bank Sanwa Economic Letter* (Japan), March 1984, pp 3–7.
Scharrer, H., 'The IMF: A Success Story?', *Inter Economics* (West Germany), no 4, July/August 1984, pp 162–6.

*International development institutions*

Abedi, A.H., 'South Bank', *Journal of Institute of Bankers in Pakistan*, vol 50, no 2, June 1984, pp 37–46.
Clausen, A.W., 'New Tasks Ahead for the Financial Institutions', *Credit Suisse Bulletin*, vol 90, autumn 1984, pp 2–4.
Flemming, A.E., 'World Bank Turning to New Borrowing Markets, Innovative Techniques', *International Monetary Fund Survey*, 5 March 1984, pp 1 and 73–7.
Gorman, D. and Radford, P., 'The World Bank: Its Role in Financing Development', *Barclays Review* (UK), vol 41, no 3, August 1984, pp 51–61.
'International Developments', *Central Bank of Ireland Quarterly Bulletin*, no 4, winter 1983, pp 30–45.
Mayer, O.G., 'Development Without Miracles: the World Bank after Forty Years', *Inter Economics* (West Germany), no 4, July/August 1984, pp 167–72.
Mendelsohn, M.S., 'Banking on the World Bank', *The Banker* (UK), vol 134, no 703, September 1984, pp 25–37.
Peagan, N., 'Guiding Asia's Growth', *Euromoney* (UK), April 1984, pp 75–84.

Pijush, M.K., 'A Note on the New International Economic Order', *Monte dei Paschi di Siena Economic Notes* (Italy), no 3, 1984, pp 86–103.
Rice, G., Corr, J. and Fennel, S., 'Maintaining Financing for Adjustment and Development', *Finance and Development* (United Nations), vol 20, no 4, December 1984, pp 44–7.
Snoy, B., 'World Bank Borrowing Strategy: Basic Principles and Innovative Borrowing Techniques in a Changing World Environment', *Société Universitaire Europèene de Recherches Financières Bulletin*, no 42A, 1984, pp 1–12.
'The Asian Development Bank', *Asiabanking* (Hong Kong), no 61, April 1985, pp 40–85.
'The Financial Structure and Operations of the IBRD', *Bank of England Quarterly Bulletin*, vol 25, no 1, March 1985, pp 47–56.
Various authors, 'Asian Development Bank: Sections 1, 2, 3 and 4', *Asiabanking* (Hong Kong), no 49, April 1984.
Wohlmuth, K., 'IMF and World Bank Structural Adjustment Policies, Cooperation or Conflict?', *Inter Economics* (West Germany), no 5, September/October 1984, pp 226–34.
Zulu, J.B. and Nsouli, S.M., 'Adjustment Programmes in Africa', *Finance and Development* (United Nations), vol 21, no 7, March 1984, pp 5–9.

*International and multinational banking*

'Banking Developments', *Bank for International Settlements International Banking Developments*, 1st quarter, 1984, pp 1–12.
Davis, S., 'International Bank Strategies Beyond the Debt Crisis', *The Banker*, vol 134, no 700, June 1984, pp 29–35.
Grubel, H.G., 'The New International Banking', *Banca Nazionale del Lavero Quarterly Review* (Italy), no 146, September 1984, pp 263–79.
Gut, Rainer E., 'Trends in International Banking', *Credit Suisse Bulletin* (Switzerland), vol 91, spring 1985, pp 2–4.
Hakim, J., 'International Banking: A New Awakening. A Survey', *The Economist* (UK), vol 290, no 7334, 24 March 1984, pp 1–26 suppl.
Haslem, J.A., Chistofi, A., Bedingfield, J.P. and Stagliano, A.J., 'The Relative Profitability of International Banking Activities', *World of Banking* (USA), May/June 1985, pp 25–7.
Hutman, C.W. and McGee, L.R., 'International Banking Facilities: The Early Response', *Bankers Magazine* (USA), vol 167, no 3, May/June 1984, pp 82–6.

Jecker, R.A., 'Salient Trends in International Banking', *Swiss Credit Bank Bulletin*, autumn 1983, pp 2–4.
Laasco, J., 'The Internationalisation of Finnish Banking', *Bank of Finland Monthly Bulletin*, vol 58, no 10, October 1984, pp 26–31.
Orsich, A.D., 'Controlling International Banking Operations', *Standard Chartered Review* (UK), October 1984, pp 2–4.
Osborn, N., 'Is International Banking Still in Fashion?', *Euromoney* (UK), October 1984, pp 252–61.
Prussia, L.S., 'Outlook for the World Financial System: A Banker's Perspective', *Contemporary Policy Issues* (USA), no 4, January 1984, pp 64–70.
Quinn, B., 'Supervisory Aspects of Country Risk', *Bank of England Quarterly Bulletin*, vol 24, no 2, June 1984, pp 235–40.
Teeters, N.H. and Terrell, H.S., 'The Role of Banks in the International Financial System', *Federal Reserve Bulletin*, vol 69, no 9, September 1983, pp 663–71.

*The debt crisis*

American Express Bank, 'International Debt. Banks and LDCs. Updating Supplement', *Amex Bank Review Special Papers* (UK), no 10, October 1984, pp 1–52.
Androsch, H., 'Is There a Solution to the Debt Problem?', *Creditanstalt CA Quarterly* (Austria), no 11, 1984, pp 4–6.
Avramoric, D., 'International Financial Cooperation: Problems and Prospects', *Australian Banker*, vol 98, no 2, April 1984, pp 65–70.
Bevan, T., 'International Indebtedness – The Banking Crisis of the 80s?', *Barclays Review* (UK), vol 59, no 2, May 1984, pp 31–7.
Bobb, E., 'The Role of International Banks in the Financing of Economic Development in the Late 1980s and Beyond', *Central Bank of Trinidad and Tobago Quarterly Economic Bulletin*, vol 9, no 7, March 1984, pp 62–72.
Calverly, J., 'Is the Debt Crisis Nearly Over?', *Euromoney* (UK), October 1984, pp 279–88.
'Debt Rescheduling: What Does It Mean?', *Finance and Development* (United Nations), vol 20, no 3, September 1983, pp 26–30.
Killick, T., 'The IMF's Role in Developing Countries', *International Monetary Fund Finance and Development*, vol 21, no 3, September 1984, pp 21–6.
Midland Bank, 'International Lenders and World Debt', *Midland Bank Review* (UK), winter 1984, pp 17–22.

Morgan Guaranty Trust Co, 'The LDC Debt Problem – At the Midpoint?', *World Financial Markets* (NY), October/November 1984, pp 1–11.

Quinn, G., 'The International Debt Crisis', *Irish Banks' Irish Banking Review*, December 1983, pp 36–44.

Robinson, N., 'LDC Debts: The Economic Background', *Business Economist*, vol 16, no 1, winter 1984, pp 5–19.

# 6 Borrowing in international markets

The Euromarket can be loosely divided into a Eurocurrency market for short-term finance and a Eurobond market for longer-term financing. An alternative division would be to separate the Euromarket into a section for credits (short-term Eurocurrency time-deposits) and a section for tradable instruments (the long-term Eurobond section). At one time either of these ways of describing the market would have been a fair reflection of the market's structure, but now there is evidence of change. The distinctions between a credit and a tradable instrument and between short-term and long-term sections of the market are becoming increasingly blurred in responses to changes in the activities of the institutions – mainly the banks – that handle the business. 'Fluidity' is the essential characteristic that sets the emerging Euromarket apart from its previous form. Casting the intermediaries in the role of financial tailors, this means that borrowers in the modern Euromarket are less likely to be offered an 'off-the-peg' financial instrument and more likely to be offered one that has been 'made-to-measure' than they would have been in the Euromarket of ten years ago.

To describe the market, in this chapter a traditional description of the main types of instrument available for raising finance is provided, but this is followed by evidence that supports the view that the Euromarket is becoming more like a melting pot than a collection of separate markets for specific types of instruments. One of the latest catalysts in the process of change is a new, simple concept called the 'swap' – an arrangement whereby individual borrowers can, through an intermediary, exchange responsibilities for each other's costs of borrowing. Swap activities by institutional and private borrowers represent a powerful new form of arbitrage which, besides making the international market as a whole more efficient, also weakens the barriers and case for distinct, separate sub-divisions within the market. The swap principle has yet to bring about the revolution that it threatens, however, and, for this reason, the markets are, initially, described how they are and, then, how they might change in the future.

## The Eurocurrency market

In its wider role the Eurocurrency market provides facilities for interbank and foreign exchange transactions and for domestic and international intermediation. The particular aspect of the Eurocurrency market to be focused on here is, however, facilities for short- and medium-term lending. Loans raised in this section of the market normally have maturities of between zero and six months but, increasingly, facilities for longer-term borrowing (between one and ten years) are becoming available.

### *Eurodollars and other Eurocurrencies*

Within the Eurocurrency market the most important and widely used currency is the Eurodollar. This fact is not just a reflection of the economic importance of the USA in the world economy but also the result of historical progress. The first Eurocurrency was the Eurodollar back in the 1920s when US dollars were deposited in Berlin and Vienna in response to the deteriorating relationship between East and West. At this time the USSR and East European nations feared that their dollar assets would be frozen and, in order to protect their interests, deposited funds in Western Europe. Here they could safely be converted into local currencies and lent out on a short-term basis. Events of 1957, when British banks were prevented from financing trade for non-residents provided the next boost for the international use of the Eurodollar. After the introduction of the restrictions, the dollar became a useful currency because it allowed British banks to extend loans to international customers. Rather than discouraging Eurodollar loans, the UK realised the advantages of having an important centre for dollar financing in the city of London and permitted the new extension of banking business to flourish. Another boost for Eurodollars came a year later in 1958, when the EEC was founded and currency convertibility returned to Western Europe. Commercial banks thereby became able to accept and lend in dollars rather than, as before, when only central banks could deal in dollars. Further development of the Eurodollar market came in the shape of Regulation Q in the USA which, between 1963 and 1974, controlled the export of US funds for corporate investment and encouraged companies wishing to expand abroad to use London's Eurodollar market to acquire the necessary finance. The rush for funds while Regulation Q was in force was so great that Eurodollar interest rates were higher than domestic rates. Following the OPEC oil price rises of the 1970s, when Saudi Arabia and other oil producing countries had around $100 billion from oil sales to be reinvested in international markets, interest rates in the Eurodollar market fell below domestic rates where they have tended to be ever since.

Present-day lenders to the Eurodollar market include commercial banks, central banks, individual investors and non-financial institutions. Borrowers include commercial banks, multinational corporations, securities brokers and dealers, exporters, importers and government agencies. Today the market is no longer confined within Europe but extends to Canada, Bahamas, Singapore, Middle East, Japan and Hong Kong. In fact, the market travels around the world on a daily basis according to market opening hours. When European centres (London, Brussels, Zurich, Hamburg, Luxembourg and so on) close down for the day, North American and Canadian markets are open. The market moves on to Asia (Singapore, Hong Kong and Tokyo), by which time it is opening time the next day in Europe. Millions of dollars worth of funds pass through the market every day.

Although the Eurodollar remains by far the most common Eurocurrency, (around 70 to 80 per cent of the Eurocurrency pool), nowadays the markets also deal in Euromarks, Euroyen, Eurosterling, Euroswiss francs, Euroguilders, Euro French-francs and most other major convertible currencies. The maturity of loans granted in Eurocurrencies has also changed from being solely short-term to longer-term arrangements with some time-deposit arrangements being for up to ten years.

Unfortunately, the size of the Eurocurrency market is difficult to measure because of the nature of Eurocurrencies (that is, external currencies, outside the control of domestic banking regulations, which move around the world at rapid speed). Even if a measure for the size of the market today was available, it would be different from yesterday's and tomorrow's. For anyone wishing to try to estimate the size of the market, perhaps the best way to go about it would be to collect recent balance of payments figures for all the countries in the world and then add together all the amounts of currencies that had left each domestic economy. This total of external currencies would represent the size of the Eurocurrency pool at a moment in time.

### *Eurocurrency financing*

Eurocurrency financing tends to be for clients who need to raise thousands or millions, rather than hundreds, of dollars – or equivalent sums denominated in other currencies. Loans are easy to establish for known names but other borrowers may access the market if they can provide the guarantee of, say, a well-respected parent company. Despite their large size the loans can be arranged quickly with documentation following after verbal arrangements by telephone. An important factor contributing to the ease with which such large amounts can be raised is the banks' willingness to operate as syndicates at a low additional administrative cost to be added to interest costs. Flexibility of arrangements is an additional feature that attracts borrowers to the market. Borrowers may, if they choose, rearrange maturities or the currency of denomination of their loans with minimal administrative inconvenience. Maturities of loans usually fall within the 30 days to seven year range and interest rates charged tend to float at a narrow margin above LIBOR (the London interbank offered rate). For prime borrowers this margin tends to be lower than for non-prime borrowers, who must pay an additional premium to compensate for their perceived riskiness. Loans with longer-term maturities tend to attract higher interest rates than short-term loans – but this is not always the case. It is usual for interest to be repaid at the maturity of the loan rather than through an amortisation process. Of course the actual interest rate charged responds to supply and demand in the market. In recession periods and periods of excessive world liquidity rates tend to fall. Boom periods and liquidity shortages have the effect of increasing borrowing rates. Differences between Eurorates and domestic rates for any particular currency reflect, firstly, any restrictions on the domestic currency (for example, interest rate ceilings and exchange controls) and, secondly, the sovereign risk of the country associated with the currency. If currency restrictions continue to be removed by the authorities of the world's domestic markets at the current rate it is foreseeable that Eurorates and domestic rates will become closer in line. Followed to its logical conclusion, this would imply that the whole world, rather than just the Euromarket, would have become an international market.

The impetus for currency deregulation originates outside the Euromarkets but within the markets themselves the seeds of change in other directions are being sown. Supply and demand for loan funds and economic factors affecting the lending institutions are leading to the removal of two important (but some would say, artificial) distinctions. The first of these changes has already been mentioned – the increased facilities for longer-term borrowing in a sector of the market that has traditionally dealt in short-term finance. The instrument that has eroded the distinction between short- and long-term Eurocurrency financing is the 'rollover credit' by which loans granted now can be renegotiated at a series of future dates – say, every six months. Thus the rollover credit can be viewed either as a series of short-term credit instruments joined end-to-end or as a single long-term instrument with variable terms of repayment.

The second barrier for erosion is the one between a credit and a tradable instrument. The impetus behind this change can be traced to the debt crisis of the 1980s, which had the effect of boosting the development of the short-term Euroloan market. Many banks have become tangled in the web of international long-term lending to the developing countries and now face repayment problems. As a result, the flexibility of banks' balance sheets has suffered and it has made good banking sense to move towards increased short-term operations in order to maintain liquidity levels. Competition among the banks for short-term lending has become so fierce that the role of banks in the financing process is changing. Out of the increased competition has come the revolving underwriting facility (RUF), whereby banks guarantee access to the short-term money market rather than earn interest on the actual cash lent to borrowers. Another innovation in the Eurosecurities market is the note issuance facility (NIF) – medium-term loans (five to seven years) for high-quality corporations or high credit-rated governments financed by selling short-term negotiable paper (three to six months). The loans are underwritten by groups of banks, which agree to buy up any unsold notes at each maturity date. Other new borrowing methods include the sole placing agency revolving underwriting facility (SPARUF) and the tender panel (TP) whereby a group of banks bid competitively for notes and the underwriters take up any unsold notes at a fixed price. The banks' margin for gain on some of the new arrangements has been reduced to as little as 0.1 per cent (for acting as guarantor). The banks are also able to gain income, however, by selling the issue paper (known as Euronotes) to investors in the open market. The extent of the competition can be gauged if one considers that, in October 1984, Credit National (of France) asked Banque Nationale de Paris, Morgan Guaranty and Credit Suisse to arrange facilities for $500 million worth of Euronotes to be sold at $\frac{1}{4}$ per cent below LIBOR. The idea that prime borowers can access funds at lower rates than those charged between the banks themselves may at first seem nonsensical. A moment of reflection on the laws of supply and demand and on the concept of risk and return, which holds that the interest rate charged should reflect the riskiness of the borrower, should, however, throw some light on the matter. Why should guarantor banks be considered as the market's most favoured borrowers? With the evolution of the Euronote it will become increasingly difficult to distinguish between a Eurocredit and a Eurosecurity.

## The international bond market

The international bond market provides facilities for borrowing long-term capital outside the national borders of the issuer – either in one or several other countries. There are basically two types of international bonds: foreign bonds, which are not Euromarket securities, and Eurobonds which are. The differences between these two main forms of external bonds are as follows.

*Foreign bonds* This type of bond is underwritten and issued in one country while the issuer remains in another country. Usually, they are underwritten by a syndicate of domestic banks in the country of issue and then taken up by investors in the host country. The bond is normally denominated in the currency of the issuer's country but, in other respects, the placement procedure is similar to that for a domestic issue. Interest rates on foreign bonds tend to follow going rates of similar bonds in the host country but may be affected by regulations introduced to apply particularly to foreign bonds.

*Eurobonds* Issues of Eurobonds are denominated in one or more of the Eurocurrencies and arranged by international underwriting syndicates or investment banks. They can be sold in several countries simultaneously so that not only the underwriters but also the investors come from many countries. Important currencies for denominating Eurobonds include Eurodollars, Euro-Canadian dollars, Euromarks, Eurofrancs, Euroyen, European Units of Account (EUAs) and European Currency Units (ECUs).

**The foreign bond market**

During the 1960s most international bonds were foreign bonds, and most of these were issued in the US bond market because of the lower interest rates prevailing there at the time. Other important foreign bond markets at that time were West Germany and Japan and, to a lesser extent, Holland, Canada, France and Hong Kong. International organisations, state enterprises and governments have traditionally accounted for most of the foreign bond market, because these types of institutions are most able to circumvent regulations limiting access to domestic markets. Even today less than one-third of the foreign bond market is accounted for by private organisations, because of restrictions that limit access to domestic markets by foreign borrowers. With most foreign bonds being placed in the USA, the effect of the weakening dollar and US controls on foreign investments that followed the 1960s was to run down the number of foreign bond issues and increase the popularity of the Euromarkets. As a consequence the Eurobond market became much larger than the foreign bond market. The relative sizes of today's foreign and Eurobond markets can be gauged with reference to Table 6.1, which shows Euro- and traditional foreign issues of bonds from 1981 to 1984. In 1981 Eurobonds accounted for approximately three-fifths of the total annual value of externally issued bonds. By 1984 the value of Eurobond issues was over twice that of foreign bond issues. Despite this change in issuers' preferences, the US (Yankee), Swiss, West German and Japanese (Samurai) bond markets remain useful sources of long-term finance for certain classes of user.

The US or Yankee bond market is one of the largest foreign bond markets because of the importance of the US dollar in the international markets. An efficient underwriting system also accounts for some of the market's popularity. Most US bond issues are sold by US firms to foreign investors, a large proportion of the bonds being underwritten by investment banks, merchant banks and commercial banks based outside the US.

Switzerland has become another popular bond market by offering relatively low costs of borrowing, wide placing powers, and a relatively stable currency for denominating the issues. Measured

**Table 6.1 Eurobond traditional foreign issues of bonds (breakdown by currency).**

| | 1981 | | 1982 | | 1983 | | 1984 | |
|---|---|---|---|---|---|---|---|---|
| | $m | % | $m | % | $m | % | $m | % |
| EUROBONDS | 31294 | 100 | 50329 | 100 | 50123 | 100 | 81717 | 100 |
| US dollar | 25761 | 82.3 | 42228 | 83.9 | 39230 | 78.3 | 65334 | 80.0 |
| German mark | 1396 | 4.5 | 3253 | 6.5 | 4042 | 8.1 | 4324 | 5.3 |
| British pound | 535 | 1.7 | 846 | 1.7 | 2153 | 4.3 | 3964 | 4.9 |
| ECU | 153 | 0.4 | 823 | 1.6 | 2191 | 4.4 | 2938 | 3.6 |
| Canadian dollar | 688 | 2.2 | 1200 | 2.4 | 1067 | 2.1 | 2147 | 2.6 |
| Japanese yen | 410 | 1.3 | 598 | 1.2 | 233 | 0.5 | 1190 | 1.5 |
| Other | 2352 | 7.5 | 1381 | 2.7 | 1207 | 2.4 | 1820 | 2.2 |
| FOREIGN BONDS | 20514 | 100 | 25199 | 100 | 27050 | 100 | 27800 | 100 |
| US dollar | 6856 | 33.4 | 6025 | 23.9 | 4735 | 17.5 | 4294 | 15.4 |
| Swiss franc | 8118 | 39.6 | 11325 | 44.9 | 13500 | 49.9 | 13120 | 47.2 |
| Japanese yen | 2723 | 13.3 | 3317 | 13.2 | 3851 | 14.2 | 4872 | 17.5 |
| German mark | 1196 | 5.8 | 2109 | 8.4 | 2618 | 9.7 | 2419 | 8.7 |
| Dutch guilder | 439 | 2.1 | 854 | 3.4 | 933 | 3.5 | 860 | 3.1 |
| British pound | 911 | 4.4 | 1129 | 4.5 | 859 | 3.2 | 1649 | 5.9 |
| Other | 273 | 1.3 | 440 | 1.7 | 544 | 2.0 | 586 | 2.1 |
| TOTAL | 51808 | | 75528 | | 77173 | | 109517 | |

Source: OECD Financial Statistics Monthly

in terms of new issues, the Swiss market is now, in fact, larger than the US market. Innovation has been high in the Swiss market, which offers a wide variety of convertible, warrant, and variable interest rate issues. There are also dual currency bonds, denominated in Swiss francs but repayable in US dollars for investors interested in higher yields in return for some vulnerability to exchange rate changes. Japanese borrowers and US-based corporations have found the Swiss bond markets a particularly useful link with Europe. The relative importance of the foreign bond market in Switzerland can be gauged if one considers that foreign Swiss franc bond issues have exceeded domestic issues since 1981 and now stand in excess of Swiss franc 10 billion. Recently, popularity for Swiss franc denominated bonds has motivated the authorities to raise the ceiling on foreign public bond issues from Swiss franc 100 million per year to Swiss franc 200 million.

A further important bond market (which is likely to become more important in the future following deregulation moves) is the Japanese or Samurai bond market. Samurai bonds are bonds issued in Japan by non-Japanese issuers. In 1984 Samurai bond issues of yen 870 billion represented around 17 per cent of the world's foreign bond market but recent changes in Japanese regulations are likely to cause this figure to increase. For example, until 1984 only AAA and AA borrowers were allowed to issue Samurai bonds and limits on issues were yen 15 billion ($65 million) for sovereign borrowers and yen 20 billion ($87 million) for international agencies of which Japan is a member (such as the World Bank). The limits have now been raised to yen 20 billion ($87 million) and yen 30 billion ($130 million) respectively. Also, up to July 1984, only 70 corporations were eligible to issue Samurai bonds. Since single-A bonds were allowed, the number of issuers has doubled.

The West German Deutsche-mark market comes fourth in terms of volume of new issues behind the US, Swiss and Japanese bond markets. Around 10 per cent of new bond issues in West Germany tend to be international bonds. Recently, however, the rising dollar rates (against the Deutsche-mark) of 1983–5 have driven down prices of Deutsche-mark bonds and some difficulty has been experienced in placing some new issues.

The future of the foreign bond markets is uncertain due to the increasing popularity of the Euromarkets and uncertainty over whether countries participating in the system will continue to be able to combine operations of the markets with national objectives. Compatibility of domestic monetary objectives with the activities of the foreign bond market accounted for the rise of the Swiss, West German and Japanese bond markets. With the change towards variable exchange rates over which domestic governments are finding it increasingly difficult to exercise control, however, it is possible that monetary policy objectives and operations of the foreign bond markets will conflict. It is likely, therefore, that foreign bond markets will continue to diminish in size in comparison with the growing Eurobond market.

### The Eurobond market

Most international bonds issued since 1970 have been Eurobonds. The regulations imposed on international capital flows in the USA during the 1970s and 1980s accounted for a large part of the market's growth but other factors – such as domestic inflation, shortages of capacity, needs for diversification and other local factors – have accounted for the sustained interest in offshore markets. The market's origins as an alternative to the US markets are still apparent because the largest portion of Eurobonds still tend to be denominated in Eurodollars. European and Japanese currencies are, however, becoming increasingly popular for denominating Eurobonds.

Issuers of offshore bonds include governments, corporations, banks and international organisations. They tend to be leading institutions in their domestic economies that have had previous dealings with the syndicated Eurocurrency credit market. Investors in Eurobonds include private individuals, insurance companies, pension funds, banks, corporations and investment trusts.

In the early days, only high class (AAA) bonds were available in the market, but now lower class bonds are also underwritten. The two sources of potential risk that affect the quality rating on Eurobonds are the quality of the issuer and the quality of the currency (or currencies) in which the bond is denominated. With a wider range of bond types available in the Euromarkets, the number of bonds issued has increased enormously. Some reasons why investors and borrowers may prefer Eurobonds to other forms of long-term debt instruments are as follows.

- Compared with domestic bonds, Eurobonds offer better prospects for capital gains and are hence popular with growth-oriented pension funds and insurance funds.
- Investors can choose from available types of Eurobonds according to their attitudes towards exchange risk. If they think they can profit by it, investors may choose to bear exchange risk by buying Eurobonds denominated in a single currency. If, on the other hand, investors wish to reduce exchange risk, they can purchase multi-currency or 'cocktail' Eurobonds, which go some way towards diversifying exchange risk across several currencies.
- Eurobonds are generally exempt from withholding taxes and legal restrictions, and documentation is minimal.
- Many large borrowers prefer fixed-rate Eurobonds to variable-rate syndicated loans from a group of banks. Eurobonds are also better suited than syndicated loans for longer-term borrowing.
- Innovation has been high in the Euromarkets. An extremely wide range of types of financial instrument are now available to fulfil the needs of many different types of borrower and investor.
- A system of bearer bonds is operated in the Euromarket, which offers anonymity – a highly prized commodity for some investors. Whoever holds a Eurobond owns it. Registers of ownership are not kept so the identities of private clients can be kept secret.
- Eurobonds are simple, yet versatile instruments for borrowers and investors alike.

Eurobonds are issued in many currencies although the preference is for currencies that are relatively stable, tradable and fully convertible. The only constraint with regard to currency of denomination is that some countries (for example, West Germany) may choose to control the amount of new issues when Eurobonds are placed in the local market.

A well organised secondary market for Eurobonds has become established in centres such as New York, London, Luxembourg and Switzerland. The markets provide no trading floors as such for Eurobonds but operate along similar lines to foreign exchange markets with dealers engaging mainly in over-the-counter transactions. The London market has remained popular ever since its important early role in the history of Eurobonds. The Swiss market is important because it provides a useful business channel between Europe and the rest of the world. High standards of professionalism are encouraged in the Euromarket by the Association of International Bond Dealers (AIBD) formed in 1968 and which now consists of around 500 members. AIBD's most important function is to provide market-makers with rules and guidelines. Professionalism is an extremely important requirement for Eurobond transactions in the absence of any rules and regulations imposed by government laws. The volume of business to which AIBD's rules apply is currently estimated at around $50 billion.

*Eurobond issue procedure*

The bulk of Eurobond issues are underwritten by a group of less than 50 European and US syndicates. The issuing procedure is largely based on the traditional US underwriting system – that is, a tripartite arrangement between an underwriting group, managers and a selling group. The main stages in the Eurobond issue procedure are as follows.

1 Before the issuing procedure can commence, issuers must ensure compliance with any existing domestic restrictions or regulations that apply to the bond. Issuers may, for example, find it necessary to seek permission from government or central bank authorities, which may be concerned with maintaining the value of the country's currency in the international markets. Once formalities at the pre-issue stage are cleared with the financial authorities, the bond becomes eligible for the unregulated Euromarket.
2 The issuer approaches a Eurobond underwriting syndicate, which takes charge of the issue in return for an underwriting

fee. Negotiations between the syndicate and the issuer are the responsibility of the lead underwriter (or lead manager). Specific matters to be arranged at this stage include the coupon rate to be paid on the bond, the issue price and maturity date, and underwriting fees and services. An agreement specifying contractual relationships between the issuer and the intermediaries involved in the issue process can then be drawn up.

3 The lead underwriter arranges matters between a) the issue managers, b) the underwriting syndicate, and c) the group of selling agents. In conjunction with the selling agents the lead manager will then prepare a prospectus containing the following information:

- Financial and historical details of the issuer.
- Information on the guarantor and management of the issue.
- A description of the issue in terms of its amount, currency (or currencies), coupon rate, maturity, certificate sizes, and details of any protective covenants or other legal matters.
- Details of the underwriting procedure including the names and number of underwriters, how the risk is spread between underwriters, and the price paid to the issuer.

4 An agreement is drawn up between the issue's managers (usually banks) specifying details such as the extent of each manager's participation in the issue, managers' rights for resale, any joint-funding arrangements and provisions for default on the part of any individual underwriter. The managers then become the underwriters' principals and are committed jointly and severally to take up the issue in the event of a partial placement.

5 The selling agents then become responsible for distributing the issue in return for a commission. The selling group is usually large and geographically widespread in order to reach the many corners of the Euromarket. Other duties of the selling agents include arrangements for keeping the issue price stable for a short period after the issue is taken up by investors and keeping in line with any legal or regulatory developments. The advertisement finally published to attract the interest of potential investors is often referred to as the 'tombstone'.

The main differences between the Eurobond issuing procedure and that for a domestic bond are, firstly, the cost of issue (Eurobond issuing costs are around $\frac{1}{2}$ per cent higher than a domestic issue because of the number of parties involved) and, secondly, the fact that the Eurobond issue does not involve any firm commitment on the part of the underwriters to take up precommited amounts of the issue (they operate on a best-efforts basis). The additional costs for the issue (which are becoming smaller in the competitive environment of the 1980s) generally appear worthwhile to issuers who, against them, can set the attractive prospect of becoming accessible to investors all over the world. The loose arrangement between the underwriters (compared with, say, the UK domestic underwriting system whereby underwriters agree to buy up specified percentages of any unsold portion of an issue) need not be problematic provided that the lead underwriter can ensure adequate interest by a large enough number of co-underwriters. In some cases the risk of partial placement may actually be taken up by the issuer via a purchase-fund arrangement, whereby the issuer agrees to take up any bonds that fail to reach the issuing price during a specified period of time. Other alternatives for dealing with a partial placement include raising the coupon payments on the bond to make it more attractive to investors, selling off any unplaced bonds at a bargain price, or simply cancelling the issue.

*Recent developments in the Eurobond market*

Change is a permanent feature of financial markets and the Eurobond market is no exception to this general rule. Currently there are some influences at work that would suggest a future enlargement of the market and others that would suggest a future contraction. The emergence of the ECU and European bond markets fall into the former category whilst recent tax changes in the USA fall into the latter. Details of these main recent influences on the Eurobond market are as follows.

*Emergence of an ECU bond market* ECU denominated bonds have become prominent in the international bond markets as a convenient means of reducing exchange risk through the concept of a cocktail currency. The first ECU denominated bond was issued by an Italian communications firm in 1981 and, since then, the market has expanded rapidly. There were five issues in 1981, 19 in 1982, and 45 in 1983 amounting to over ECU 4 billion in only three years. Most of these issues were listed on the Luxembourg stock exchange for maturities between five and fifteen years at interest rates between 10 and 14 per cent. Currently, ECU denominated bonds account for almost 5 per cent of the total Eurobond market, a figure which, although on the increase, appears rather insignificant in relation to the extremely high percentage of Eurobonds denominated in US dollars (around 80 per cent). The significance of the ECU denominated bond extends outside the realms of Euromarkets, however, to wider matters. The ECU denominated bond is, in fact, just one small step towards a much greater use of ECUs in private capital transactions, since ECU money markets and capital markets work hand in hand towards increasing the demand for ECUs. Approval by EEC central bankers for promoting the use of the ECU as an official reserve asset has also had the psychological effect of boosting the ECU's share of private capital market transactions.

*The rise of the Euroyen bond market* Euroyen bonds are one of the latest developments in Japan's freeing markets. Before 1 April 1984, Euroyen bonds could not be issued by private corporations (Japanese or otherwise). Only selected governments and international agencies were permitted to issue Euroyen bonds before this date. Following the relaxation of rules in April 1984, however, around 140 Japanese corporations became liable to issue Euroyen bonds. A further deregulation move in June 1984 permitted all Japanese residents (rather than just selected residents) to borrow yen denominated funds in foreign markets. Yet another change in the rules occurred in December 1984, since when non-Japanese countries, local government and private corporations have been able to issue Euroyen bonds. Further deregulation moves are still under discussion in Japan, including the possibility of removing all restrictions on non-Japanese borrowing via Euroyen bonds. Yields on Euroyen bonds have now fallen below those on Samurai bond issues. The stage is set for the Euroyen bond to become an increasingly dominant instrument in the Eurobond market.

*Removal of the US withholding tax* The introduction of the Interest Equalisation Tax by the US authorities in 1964 had an enormous impact on the growth prospects of the Eurobond market. In July 1984 another US tax change occurred – the removal (in steps) of the 30 per cent withholding tax deducted at source on income paid to foreigners which, for ten years, had discouraged European investors from the US bond markets and encouraged the use of Eurobonds. The important question to be answered, therefore, is 'Will the removal of the withholding tax lead to a reduction in the size of the Eurobond market?' A large proportion of the Eurobonds have always been denominated in US dollars but now the tax removal will encourage more US companies to borrow domestically rather than in the international bond market. As this book goes to press the implications of the US tax change have not yet emerged. Meanwhile, investment bankers in Europe are hoping that the international bond markets will continue to provide a home for US dollars outside the US and also that the US investors' interest in bonds denominated in other currencies will continue. Rumours that the US authorities are considering operating a system of bearer bonds in the US market add to European bankers' fears of losing business to the USA.

## International bond instruments

To the investor the basic international bond offers the opportunity to receive a series of coupon payments and the repayment of a principal amount at the bond's maturity date. Alternatively, since there is a flourishing secondary market, holders may sell their bonds in the open market with the possibility of a capital gain. From this basic format many different arrangements can be devised and set into contracts to the advantage of borrowers and investors alike, according to their requirements. The fluid characteristics of financial instruments devised in the Eurocurrency market extends into the Eurobond market, where maturities, currencies, coupon rates and repayment terms can be built into a myriad of different financial arrangements. Some of the most common variations on the straight international bond are now described. Although not all possible variations are listed, the list should be long enough to illustrate just how flexible an international bond instrument can be.

### *Floating Rate Notes (FRNs)*

The FRN was an early variation on the basic Eurobond first issued by an Italian utility (ENEL) in 1970. FRNs are debt instruments on which interest rates are set, usually semi-annually, at a margin (around $\frac{1}{8}$ to $\frac{1}{4}$ per cent) above either LIBOR (the London interbank offered rate) or SIBOR (the Singapore interbank offered rate). FRNs are popular substitute instruments for fixed rate arrangements such as syndicated loans so they are commonly issued by banks. Besides the basic FRN, recent developments include FRNs with warrants and FRNs with convertibles. Because of their adaptability, the number of FRNs has increased at a rate of around 20 per cent per year since their inception in 1970. International banks are the major issuing houses of FRNs with Credit Suisse, First Boston, Morgan Guaranty, Merill Lynch,

Salomon Brothers and County Bank accounting for over 40 per cent of FRN issues. Currently, FRNs account for around one-third of the total Eurobond market, with new issues in 1984 reaching around US$ 25 billion.

*Multiple currency Eurobonds*

Eurobonds may be denominated in cocktails of currencies. Common multi-currency bonds issued in recent years include those denominated in European Units of Account (EUAs), European Currency Units (ECUs), Special Drawing Rights (SDRs), and European Composite Units (Eurcos). In these cases, the cocktail of currencies is specified according to internationally agreed proportions but alternative arrangements whereby any group of currencies may be used to denominate the bond are possible. Multiple currency Eurobonds are popular because they reduce currency risk below the level that would prevail if the bond was denominated in a single currency. Depreciation of one currency can be offset against appreciations in others over the maturity of the bond. The methods used to mix the currencies are either to maintain fixed exchange rates between the chosen currencies or to maintain fixed quantities of the chosen currencies. Payments to bondholders may, according to contractual arrangements, be paid in one or several currencies.

*Zero coupon/original discount bonds*

Zero coupon bonds (or original discount bonds or 'Euro-zeros') are one of the more recent innovations in the Eurobond market, the first Euro-zero being issued by the Pepsico Capital Corporation in 1981. They carry no coupons and investors' incentive for buying them is purely due to the deep discount on the face value of the bond, which allows them to reap capital gains at the maturity date. The Euro-zero is therefore a useful investment for an investor following a buy-and-hold strategy who wishes to avoid the frequent reinvestment of interest payments. Another attraction of the Euro-zero to certain classes of investor is that, as the bond approaches maturity, its appreciation value is not taxed until it is actually liquidated – and then only at the going capital gains tax rate. Some investors, depending on their national tax systems, may be able to escape tax altogether (for example, the Japanese before the Ministry of Finance in Tokyo closed the market to Japanese investors in March 1982).

*Eurobonds with warrants*

Investors in Eurobonds with warrants are provided, along with the fixed rate bonds, with a detachable warrant allowing them to purchase further fixed rate bonds at a specified rate at or before a specified future date. Issuers gain from this arrangement because they are able to reduce the cost of the issue by between 1 and 3 per cent in terms of capital value (between 0.2 and 0.5 per cent per annum in terms of yield). The investor holding the warrant may either hold onto it until it expires or sell it in a derivative market. The value of the warrant, whoever owns it, is determined by interest rate movements. If interest rates rise sharply the value of the warrant becomes zero (nobody wants the privilege of being able to buy bonds at a cost higher than the one prevailing in the market). If, on the other hand, interest rates fall the warrant ensures the holder of participation in the capital appreciation of the underlying bond.

*Convertible Eurobonds*

Convertible Eurobonds comprise an ordinary Eurobond plus an option to convert at some date into common stock or some other specified tradable instrument from the corporate issuer's capital structure. Hence, the convertible bond (like the bond with warrants) carries a yield that is slightly less than that on a non-convertible bond. Types of convertible Eurobond include equity convertibles, FRN convertibles and currency convertibles. Currency convertibles offer the right to convert into common stock at exchange rates prevailing at the time of the bond offering. A dual option convertible bond was issued in 1980, which allowed investors to choose between a conversion into either common stock of the issuer or non-convertible fixed interest bonds. Possible disadvantages to the investor (compared with a bond with warrants) are that convertible bonds must be redeemed if the conversion feature is exercised, and that conversions can be forced by having the bond called at the issuer's bequest

*Droplock bonds*

A 'droplock' is the name given to an FRN that is convertible to a fixed rate bond with a specified maturity either at the option of the holder or whenever the market interest rate (LIBOR or SIBOR) falls to a pre-specified level. Both the investor and the issuer are then 'locked in' to the new fixed rate until the bond matures.

Issuers gain on the arrangement if, after the lock drops, rates tend to increase. Investors stand to gain if, after the lock drops, rates continue to fall. The high interest rates of the mid-1970s accounted largely for the introduction of the droplock bond.

*Parallel bonds*

A parallel bond is a variation on a straight international bond whereby a large multinational company floats bonds simultaneously in several different countries. A recent example (March 1984) is provided by Texaco, which launched a $1 billion convertible issue via four separate underwriting syndicates in West Germany, Switzerland, Asia and the rest of the world outside the US. This was the largest fixed rate Eurobond issue to that date but, in general, parallel bond issues are infrequent, probably because of the complicated administrative procedure involved.

The above list of variations on the basic bond format should not be regarded as exhaustive. Innovation runs high in Euromarkets and virtually anything is possible. A recent hybrid, for example, was launched in February 1985 by Eléctricité de France – a $300 million floating rate Eurodollar bond with warrants to buy a fixed rate currency unit denominated bond. More novel features can be expected for the future design of Eurobonds.

## Swaps

It has been previously mentioned how the distinction between Eurorates and domestic rates is disappearing with moves towards deregulation in many countries, and also how the distinction between a Eurocredit and a Eurosecurity is becoming blurred through the evolution of the Euronote and increased competition between banks. A further innovative idea should also be mentioned in the trend towards integration of capital markets, not because it offers a new type of instrument in the international markets but because of its importance as a method of using the markets. The innovation in question is the 'swap' and it threatens to have a significant influence on world markets. Swaps allow arbitrage between markets, between instruments, and between borrowers without having to wait for the markets themselves to cast down the barriers. There are as many different swap arrangements as there are varieties of debt financing and, with the volatile exchange rates and interest rates of the 1980s, demand for them is high. The basic kinds of swap are the interest rate swap and the currency swap (as illustrated in Figure 6.1).

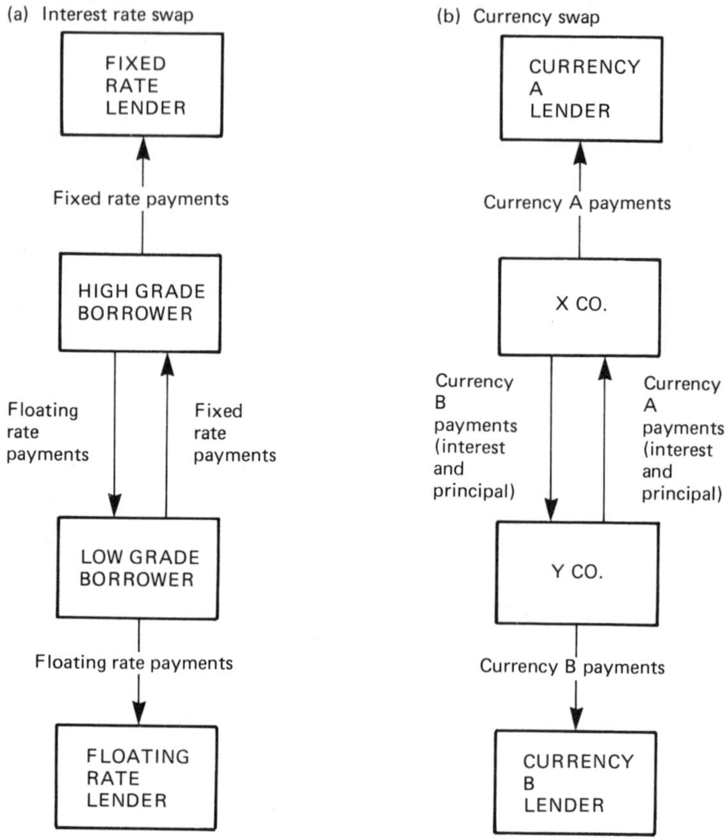


**Figure 6.1 The swap principle.**

*The interest rate swap*

With an interest rate swap, two unrelated borrowers borrow identical amounts with identical maturities from different lenders and then exchange the interest repayment cash flows via an intermediary. To understand how it works, consider the following example.

A high grade corporation can borrow fixed rate funds at 14 per cent or floating rate funds at 12 per cent. A more risky corporation is able to borrow fixed rate funds at 17 per cent and floating rate funds at 13 per cent. The high grade corporation therefore borrows fixed rate funds at 14 per cent and the lower grade corporation borrows floating rate funds at 13 per cent. The low grade corporation agrees to absorb 3 per cent of the high grade corporation's interest costs. After the exchange, the high grade corporation is better off because it has managed to borrow floating rate funds at 11 per cent (14 per cent minus 3 per cent). The low grade corporation is also better off because it has managed to borrow fixed rate funds at 16 per cent (13 per cent plus 3 per cent).

*The currency swap*

The currency swap operates in a similar fashion to the interest rate swap but each party becomes responsible for the other's currency payments. Consider the following example.

The going rate for foreign exchange transactions is £1 = $1.5. X Co. borrows £1 million. Y Co. in another country, borrows $1½ million. Y Co. agrees to supply funds to X Co. to pay interest on its pound sterling borrowings. When the underlying debts mature, at the termination of the swap agreement, X Co. and Y Co. exchange the nominal principal amount in each underlying currency.

The currency swap principle can therefore be used by borrowers to obtain currencies from which they are otherwise prevented because of excessive costs or foreign exchange risk. One or both parties involved may benefit from the arrangement.

*The swap market*

Many large banks are prepared to provide intermediary services in the swap market, which is expanding at rapid pace (over $70 billion worth of swaps at the end of 1984). Most of the banks and investment bankers engaged in swap business are situated in London and New York. For interest rate swaps Morgan Guaranty, Bankers Trust, Citicorp, Salomon Brothers and First Boston have already established a reputation. Leading arrangers of currency swaps include Salomon Brothers, Paribas and Morgan Guaranty. The volume of business is enough to render the matching of counterparties on a one-to-one basis unnecessary by the intermediaries. There is even support from some intermediaries for the idea that swaps, like options, should become tradable commodities. The main opponents to this idea are the commercial banks, which prefer to view swaps as being linked to credit decisions and hence, although assignable by negotiation, not tradable. As we have seen in other areas of the market, the case for making such distinctions is becoming increasingly difficult.

It would seem that swaps are popular with intermediaries and users alike as an aid to managing assets and liabilities. The overall effect of increased swapping activity is to bring domestic and international capital markets, short-term and long-term markets, and fixed rate and floating rate markets closer together as if the financial markets were one single melting pot of interest-bearing instruments. Although the swap principle is simple, there is room for deviations from the basic swap – such as swap options, zero-coupon swaps – and even swaps with government treasuries. The revolution has started and the implications for the Euromarkets have yet to be ascertained.

## Summary

The Euromarkets are becoming increasingly important sources of short- and long-term finance for governments and industry. Within the market the Eurodollar accounts for by far the largest proportion of all transactions but the currencies of other countries – for example, Europe and, increasingly, Japan – are becoming more frequently used. The variety of borrowing instruments in the market is extremely wide, ranging from short-term floating rate instruments to long-term fixed rate instruments. Innovation has been high in the market, the only constraint having been that, for any borrower wishing to raise funds, there must be investors willing to invest. Flexibility in contractual arrangements for reconciling the needs of lenders and borrowers has resulted in the adoption of many different instruments in the market (such as RUFs and NIFs). Latest developments in the Euromarkets include the emerging popularity of the ECU for denominating bond issues, an increased volume of Euroyen transactions as a result of the liberalising Japanese markets, and a potential threat to the Euromarket in the form of the US decision to withdraw withholding tax. A further development that could, through arbitrage possibilities, chip away at existing divisions between markets and instruments is the swap principle. At present there is some disagreement over whether the swap should be, firstly, legal and, secondly, a prudent business activity for those engaged in arranging swap agreements. The swap market is, however, flourishing even in its infancy and is backed by powerful multinational banks. Given the current trend towards flexibility and increased innovation in international financial markets, it is likely that the swap will stay and bring about further integration of not only divisions within the Euromarkets but also divisions between domestic and international financial markets.

## Further reading

### *The Euromarkets*


Altschul, J.S., 'A Taxing Problem for the Euroyen', *Euromoney* (UK), May 1984, pp 34–6.

Bamber, D., 'Annual Financing Report', *Euromoney (Supplement)* (UK), April 1984, pp 1–76.

Bance, N. and Bamber, D., 'Who's Doing What in the Euromarkets', *Euromoney* (UK), October 1983, pp 148–82.

Burgess, Roger, 'The Competition Intensifies as the Eurobond Market Expands', *Euromoney* (UK), February 1985, pp 117–28.

Campbell, K., 'Euromarkets: The Age of the Hybrid', *The Banker* (UK), vol 134, no 703, September 1984, pp 41–5.

Curtin, D., 'Now It's Grown Up, It's Fierce', *Euromoney* (UK), June 1984, pp 64–72.

Grant, C., 'The Liquefaction of the Euromarkets', *Euromoney* (UK), October 1983, pp 132–42.

Nora, S.M., 'Effects of US Tax Changes on Eurobonds', *International Financial Law Review*, (UK), vol 3, no 5, May 1984, pp 20–2.

Ollard, William, 'The Birth Pangs of the Euroyen Bond Market', *Euromoney* (UK), March 1985, pp 35–47.

O'Neill, J., 'The ECU as a Financial Instrument for Risk Diversification', *Business Economist* (UK), vol 15, no 2, summer 1984, pp 28–39.

Pakenham, K., 'Experiments in the International Bond Markets', *Amex Bank Review Special Papers* (UK), no 4, July 1982, pp 1–9.

Ramsden, N.F.E., 'The International Market for Floating Rate Instruments', *Bank of England Quarterly Bulletin*, vol 24, no 3, September 1984, pp 337–45.

Stoakes, Christopher, 'Here Come Euromortgages', *Euromoney* (UK), March 1985, pp 83–6.

'The ECU', *EEC European Documentation*, no 6, 1984, pp 1–51.

Yassukovich, S., 'Euro–Equities are Here to Stay', *Euromoney* (UK), June 1984, pp 64–72.

Youard, R.G.A., 'Everything You Need to Know about Syndicated Loans', *Euromoney* (UK), January 1984, pp 69–71.

*Swaps*

House, D.M., 'Documenting and Implementing a Loan Swap', *International Financial Law Review* (UK), vol 3, no 10, October 1984, pp 29–32.

Shirreff, D., 'Swaps – The Way into Any Market', *Euromoney* (UK), November 1983, pp 66–75.

Shirreff, D., 'Swaps, Managing the Future', *Euromoney* (UK), October 1984, pp 201–5.

Walmsley, J.K., 'Understanding Interest Rate Swaps', *Bankers Magazine* (USA), vol 164, no 4, July/August 1984, pp 44–7.

# 7 World stockmarkets

There are three basic types of stockmarket in the world: private organisations (such as the UK and the US), banking organisations (such as the West German market) where banks are the sole intermediaries, and state controlled markets (such as those of Latin America and France). All three types of systems are influenced at least to some degree by international pressure for increased cross-border portfolio investment. There is evidence of movement, particularly within Europe, towards bringing stockmarket standards, laws and accounting conventions more into line and towards improving lines of communication between markets. Deregulation is also occurring except in the most protected economies. The purchase of foreign quoted securities by domestic residents tends, along with direct foreign investments, to be one of the most frequently liberalised financial transactions. Issue of securities by foreign borrowers, on the other hand, tends to be less willingly liberalised but is becoming increasingly common. As a result the volume of international transactions in listed securities is growing. Within Europe, the last countries to remove major restrictions are Scandinavia, Spain, Portugal and Greece. Most of the world's industrial countries would appear to have accepted that mutual benefits accrue from international links between capital markets. Some new equity issues, particularly those of well-known multinationals, can now be issued and traded simultaneously in different markets across the world to provide a global shareholder base. Smaller companies may also, in many cases, seek access to foreign stock exchanges and make share issues into foreign markets.

This chapter reports on some of the major stockmarkets in the world with particular reference to facilities for and attitudes towards foreign investment. To provide a highly detailed description of every stock exchange in the world would, unfortunately, prove a mammoth task so the following pages provide primarily, an overview. The chapter relies heavily on facts and statistics from market descriptions to be found in books such as Paul Stonham's *Major Stockmarkets of Europe* and A.M. George and I.H. Giddy's *International Financial Handbook*, but every attempt has also been made to keep up-to-date with events reported in financial newspapers such as the London *Financial Times*. Recent reports by major central banks also prove useful sources. The result, hopefully, is a set of country 'cameos', which readers will find an interesting and useful overview of current trends and attitudes towards internationalisation from the major (and some of the minor) financial centres in the world.

## European stockmarkets (in general)

The European Economic Community (EEC), by the Treaty of Rome, is geared towards the creation of a unified European capital market. Progress towards this objective moves steadily but unevenly through the EEC political system, which does not have direct regulatory power over individual member states. The process cannot be rushed because of the different EEC countries' attitudes towards central regulation and the free market concept. For example, the UK and the Netherlands are traditionally self-regulating, open markets whilst those of France and Italy are relatively closed markets with complex regulatory and institutional frameworks. The overall aim of the EEC has therefore been towards the establishment of minimum standards for European stock exchanges. The EEC's *Code of Conduct Relating to Transactions in Transferable Securities* (1977) provides suggested rules of conduct for disclosure requirements by listed companies, for brokers and dealers, company directors, and controlling shareholders. Deregulationary moves and increased facilities for cross-border financial flows are also encouraged by the EEC authorities. Although progress is hardly occurring at breakneck speed, there is very little chance that moves towards internationalisation of European stockmarkets will be reversed.

*United Kingdom*

London and its financial institutions have a long history of service to international clients. Facilities for international investors in London include a large number of banks, an important stock exchange and a substantial market for foreign currencies. In addition, particularly since the abandonment of exchange controls in 1979, London intermediaries have been able to provide useful expertise and research for residents considering investing abroad or non-residents wishing to invest in the UK. Some larger brokers have even found it profitable to set up offices overseas to tempt foreign domestic investors to use the London market.

The size, sophistication, high trading standards, and professional organisation and supervision of the London stock exchange have given rise to its present status as one of the most important exchanges in Europe. The number of securities currently listed on the London stock exchange (around 3,500) represents half the total number of securities traded within the EEC, and around one-third of them are foreign listed securities. Large multinationals, in particular, find the UK exchange a suitable market for their shares. For example, GEC, IBM, Dutch Petroleum and Schlumberger alone account for 30 per cent of the market. Indeed, the sheer weight of overseas shares listed on the UK market can have a significant influence on the market's price index.

Withholding tax on foreign securities is 30 per cent basic but various arrangements with overseas countries allow investors to receive payments from holding UK stocks either tax free or partially tax free. For example, under double taxation agreements, foreign investors from many EEC countries and the US receive tax-free interest payments. Australian, Japanese, South African, Canadian and Malaysian investors pay a partial tax (between 10 and 15 per cent). These tax reduction arrangements reflect the underlying philosophy of the UK financial market which, since 1979, has been towards opening up the market to international influences.

Restrictions on the stock exchange are still being lifted by the Conservative government and there has been a rush by British and foreign (mainly US) banks to take shares in the new stock exchange system, devised largely during Norman Tebbit's term at the Department of Trade and Industry. The White Paper of February 1985 (*Financial Services in the United Kingdom*) outlines the basis of a new-style financial community for the UK which, increasingly, will be governed by a US-style system rather than the self-regulatory agencies of the present system. Other main changes for the new system are a move from fixed to negotiable broker's commissions and, for the first time since 1909, dual capacity (broker-dealers) is to be allowed on the floor of the stockmarket. Stock exchange revisions will also take into account EEC directives on matters such as listing requirements (standards of which are already high in the UK) as part of the general movement towards homogeneous minimum standards for EEC stock exchanges. The reforms are considered essential for promoting London as an international financial centre, for improving links with EEC countries and for taking full advantage of the market's geographical position, which allows it to catch the time zone between the closing of the Far East markets and the opening of the markets in North America. Other examples of removal of UK barriers to foreign transactions include agreements on the reductions of stamp duty (from 2 to 1 per cent) on securities transaction costs and the granting of licences to foreign-owned securities houses and banks. The government has also remained flexible in developing a financial framework for the foreign exchange, financial futures and traded options markets, which provide foreign and domestic investors alike with hedging and speculative opportunities. By the end of 1986 (sometimes referred to as the 'Big Bang'), by which time many of the proposals put forward in the 1985 White Paper will probably have been implemented, the UK will be one of the most internationalised financial markets in the world.

### *West Germany*

Foreign stocks were first introduced to the West German market in the 1950s. Frankfurt is West Germany's largest stock exchange (bourse), with seven others at Berlin, Hamburg, Hanover, Dusseldorf, Munich, Bremen and Stuttgart. Besides being the largest, the Frankfurt stock exchange also deals with approximately 70 per cent of foreign equities (around 200 stocks) and 80 per cent of foreign bonds. Dusseldorf, the second largest stock exchange, also provides facilities for foreign trading. Besides the stock exchanges, there is also an unofficial market for foreign shares. In fact, a West German company going public now has a choice of three types of market: the official trading market, the over-the-counter market, or the unregulated free market. Conditions for foreign investors in West German markets are generally the same as for domestic investors. The usual way for trading foreign shares is through the use of fiduciary certificates or through foreign security clearing associations, whereby the original share certificates remain in the home country of the issuer. Only a small percentage of foreign share certificates are actually physically deliverable in West Germany. For foreign holders of West German issues, the withholding tax to be paid is 25 per cent unless covered by inter-country tax agreements. Fees on West German stock exchanges tend to be higher than in most countries, but market users gain the benefit of the exchanges' efficient dealing and clearing systems, which are kept up-to-date with the latest technological developments. Plans are presently well under way to link West German electronic stock exchange systems with neighbouring countries (France and Belgium) and, already, the substantial telex over-the-counter market permits arbitrage with foreign stockmarkets with different trading hours.

Within West Germany, banks are an extremely important source of corporate finance and are responsible for a large proportion of security issues. They also manage unit trusts and generally play a direct role in financing investment – more so than in other EEC countries. Recently, however, West German businessmen have increasingly made use of the stockmarket. New launchings on the German bourse were three in 1982 (raising DM 319 million), and 21 in 1984 (raising DM 1.72 billion). More funds were raised on the bourse during 1982–4 than in the previous 20 years and there is no sign of an end to this trend.

Besides its stockmarkets, the importance of the Deutsche-mark as a trading and Eurocurrency, and efforts by West German banks to extend their international links, has increased the role of West Germany in international financial markets. Up to 1968–9 West Germany was traditionally a net capital importer but, since then, the West Germans have demonstrated a firm interest in overseas securities.

### *France*

France is one of the less attractive financial centres for foreign investors. Most foreign stocks issued in France are listed on the Paris stock exchange, which is relatively small and deals mainly in fixed interest securities. Foreign issuers of stocks on the Paris stockmarkets must comply with domestic authorisation requirements but, in addition, the requirements of the French Secretary of the Treasury. The additional requirements are: that the company must be listed on a stock exchange of its country or origin; that the intention that French residents can hold shares should be made explicit; and that all public documents and accounts distributed at shareholders' meetings should be translated into French.

Limited trading, complex administrative procedures and discriminatory taxes substantially reduce the attractiveness of the French financial markets to foreign borrowers and investors but there is a possibility that a change may occur in the future. Potential development and reform of the Paris stock exchange, in particular, has attracted a good deal of attention. For example, the Perouse Commission, which reported in 1980, investigated the markets and made several recommendations towards internationalisation. Main recommendations of the Perouse Commission included simplification of means of holding securities, increased efficiency of market clearing systems, facilities for securing increased anonymity of investors and, generally, more efforts towards attracting foreign investors. Suggestions for attracting foreign investors included an extension of market trading hours, simplified continuous quotation systems, more information for investors, lower taxes, and freedom for market-makers to act like their US counterparts. More recently, in March 1985, the French Government announced new measures to modernise and deregulate the Paris financial markets with a view to increasing competition and exposure to competing London and New York markets. The new measures include provisions for a financial futures market, more liberal rules on bond and share commissions, and the encouragement of intermediary activities. These ideas and the need to integrate French markets with those of other EEC countries may lead to increased attractiveness of the French financial markets to foreigners in the future.

### *Belgium*

Although the Belgian domestic market is open to foreign investment, like France, Belgium has one of the least internationalised markets in Europe. The domestic markets at Brussels, Antwerp, Ghent and Liège deal mainly in fixed interest public debt instruments and the capacity of the secondary market is hampered by government control of financial institutions. All issues of stock must have the permission of the Banking Commission, which regulates the market. Foreign issuers, in addition, must have permission from the Belgian Minister of Finance. Such permission is seldom granted to non-EEC residents. Foreign investors in

Belgian markets must pay withholding taxes deducted at source by Belgian issuers, who also have additional documentation to cope with if their stocks are taken up by foreigners. Although there are no foreign exchange restrictions on sales and purchases of foreign securities in Belgium, investors are forced to use the more volatile of two parallel currency markets (the other one being controlled by the central bank). Despite the administrative and other inconveniences, there remains interest by foreigners in Belgian securities and there are foreign issues of, in particular, UK, US and South African shares circulating in the Belgian market.

*Netherlands*

Amsterdam, the only official stock exchange in the Netherlands following the closure of stock exchanges at Rotterdam and Hague, dates back to the seventeenth century. It is not as large as the London stock exchange, listing only between 2,000 and 2,500 securities, although, in structure, there are many similarities. Historically, international interest has accounted for much of Amsterdam's development as a financial centre. For example, securities of the Dutch East India Company were traded on the exchange in the eighteenth century and funds raised through Amsterdam helped finance the Russian railways in the early nineteenth century. Today, foreign borrowers and investors are still welcome on the Amsterdam exchange, where Dutch multinationals account for a high proportion of issues. Government regulation of the exchange is minimal as also are capital controls but standards of operation and supervision are high from self-imposed regulations.

A recent development in Amsterdam is the setting up of the European Options Exchange (EOE) in 1978, which runs along similar lines to the Chicago Board Options Exchange. In 1985 the EOE extended its operations from dealing in securities options to include gold options. The hope is that the volume of EOE business will increase to become an international market capable of competing with New York and London futures markets.

*Switzerland*

Switzerland is open to foreign investments both into and out of the country. Swiss residents are free to invest in foreign securities – even if the securities are not listed on a Swiss stock exchange. Foreign residents in Switzerland have the same purchase and sale rights as natives. Foreign issuers face rules similar to those for domestic issuers with the additional requirements that permission must first be obtained from the Swiss National Bank (a refusal of which binds all Swiss stock exchanges) and that the nominal value of listed shares must exceed 1 million Swiss francs. Foreign investors must pay 35 per cent withholding tax on income from Swiss capital markets unless double-taxation agreements are available for tax avoidance or reduction. The main exchanges for international business are at Zurich, Basle and Geneva, with around 60 per cent of shares traded on the Zurich exchange being of foreign origin. Recently (1982–3) Swiss capital markets have been running at record levels attracting massive foreign investment from, in particular, the USA, Canada, Netherlands and West Germany.

### *Italy*

There are ten Italian stock exchanges at Milan, Rome, Florence, Venice, Naples, Trieste, Bologna, Palmero, Turin and Genoa, but the amount of trading that they handle is small. For example, Milan, which accounts for the largest proportion (around four-fifths) of equity trading, lists shares of just over 200 companies, some of which are never traded. Italian stock exchanges are under the control of the Treasury Minister via the Stock Exchange Commission and are also regulated by local authorities such as the Stock Exchange Delegation and the local Chamber of Trade. Most long-term finance in Italy is raised through state-controlled institutions and interest in internationalising the stockmarkets is low. Nevertheless, there is a foreign currency market, a spot market for equities and bonds, and a forward market for equities which, one day, may forge further links with world markets. Currently, however, overseas investors are prevented from investing in lire and Italians are unable to export lire for equity investment. Taxes on interest and dividends are deducted at source (32.4 per cent on ordinary shares and preference shares, 15 per cent on savings shares, and 12.5 per cent on bonds in 1984) unless double-tax agreements are in force. Foreign stocks are more or less cut off from the Milan exchange by a stringent 50 per cent non-interest bearing deposit rule.

The Italian stockmarket is notorious for its low standards of disclosure. Present regulations for domestic or foreign issuers do not require any specific disclosure at time of issue, nor is there a requirement to publish a prospectus to inform the general public. Some suggestions were put forward for improving the Milan stock exchange in a report of the Senate Commission for Finance (1977) but, even so, there remains a great deal of room for improvement.

Perhaps increased efficiency of the Italian markets will one day develop in line with increased exposure to world stockmarkets. Meanwhile, foreign investors on the Italian stockmarket must rely largely on investors' services provided by the larger Italian banks, which deal with many of the necessary formalities.

### *Luxembourg*

Liberal financial legislation (the over-the-counter Eurobond market is completely unregulated), an absence of foreign exchange controls, and no withholding taxes on foreign investors' income make Luxembourg the ideal location for an international financial marketplace. Hence, Luxembourg's market has become a major centre for Eurobonds. There are some foreign shares listed on the exchange but these are dwarfed by the volume of Eurobond trading. Both primary and secondary markets are dominated by banks and the establishment of foreign brokers and other forms of financial intermediaries is highly restricted. Standards of disclosure by issuing firms are maintained by the Commissaire du Contrôle des Banks – rather than by any form of securities commission – and this further reflects the dominating influence of the banks in this important centre for Euromarket activity.

## The US and Canadian markets

### *The USA*

The US offers investors and borrowers a wider range of financial services than any other single country in the world. The New York stock exchange has, for a long time, been the largest stock exchange not only in the USA but also in the world and lists around 2,000 ordinary and preference shares. Other important US stock exchanges are the American Stock Exchange (New York), the Midwest Stock Exchange (Chicago), Pacific Stock Exchange (Los Angeles), Boston Stock Exchange, Cincinnati Stock Exchange and the Philadelphia Stock Exchange. These stock exchanges are all willing to list foreign stock providing they meet prevailing listing requirements. The usual arrangement for foreign shares traded in a US market is to have the foreign shares deposited with a trust company (either in the USA or abroad) and have depository receipts called ADRs (American Depository Receipts) issued against them. The foreign shares can then be listed on the US exchange while the trust company looks after matters such as collection and distribution of dividends for a commission. The US markets are highly efficient with well developed information systems (stockmarket reports, newspaper, journals, electronic links and so on) that reach most corners of the globe. Investors' interests are safeguarded by the Stock Exchange Commission (SEC), the Securities Investors Protection Corporation (SIPC) and a series of legislative provisions. Along with investor protection measures, reasonable commissions, competitive earnings and a lack of restrictive legislation have attracted enormous volumes of foreign business to the US markets. The only major restriction on foreign interest in the US markets was the Interest Equalisation Tax (IET) placed on foreign issues between 1963 and 1974.

US investors wishing to buy foreign securities can do so through US stock exchanges, through the US 'over-the-counter' (OTC) market, or by purchasing them directly from a foreign market. The US markets therefore provide an important route for foreign portfolio investment both into and out of the USA.

Besides having well developed primary and secondary markets, the USA has led the world in developing tertiary or derived markets such as the Philadelphia Options Market and the Chicago International Money Market, which deal in stock options and financial futures. Many innovations in market technology – such as the NASDAQ electronic system for providing latest market prices in the OTC market – have also originated in the US. There are even plans afoot to link the NASDAQ system to foreign markets in order to extend the opportunity of making deals in less than five seconds to foreigners.

The influence of US stockmarket systems, market innovations and market technology on the systems developed and implemented in other corners of the globe cannot be understated. It would appear that the eyes of the world are focused on any new financial market idea or system originating in the USA to monitor the new development's success or failure. Other, smaller countries can then learn from US experiences in order to make judgements on whether similar systems would fulfil their own needs. In return, communication and willingness to do business remains high between the USA and other countries in the free world.

### *Canada*

Canada has well developed financial markets with stock exchanges in Toronto, Vancouver, Montreal and Winnipeg – Toronto being the largest. Disclosure and listing standards are high with standards controlled and regulated by the Investment Dealers Association (IDA) – a non-profit professional organisation consisting of around 80 investment firms – and the Securities Commission. There is evidence of a positive attitude towards internationalisation, particularly in the money markets. Canada and its currency have played an increasingly large role in international finance over the last 40 years owing, mainly, to a worldwide network of Canadian branches of banks and other financial institutions. Nowadays Canada and its institutions are often viewed as an important financial bridge between Europe (particularly the UK) and the USA. For Canadian borrowers there is evidence of a trend towards increased use of the domestic capital market, where a well-developed market for floating rate instruments allows borrowers to obtain funds domestically at low rates. The doors remain open, however, for access to the Euromarkets, if required. Foreign investors in Canada are faced with a withholding tax of around 25 per cent but, with Canada's tax treaties with other countries numbering over 30 (amongst them, the US and UK), there are many arrangements for avoiding double taxation of investment earnings. With a stable political economy and a highly active financial press for providing domestic and foreign investors with information, Canada remains a popular market for foreign users.

## The Asian-Pacific region (in general)

Markets in Asia and the Pacific region are becoming increasingly important in the international financial system. Australia, Hong Kong, Singapore and Malaysia all have stock exchanges that are actively seeking further integration with and importance in world markets. Japan, too, although traditionally a highly protected marketplace is now slowly opening up its doors to foreign interests. Even small moves towards opening the Japanese market are of great significance because of its enormous size (over 75 per cent of total capitalisation in the Asian–Pacific region and 80 per cent of turnover). For progress towards global stockmarket activity, the markets of the Asia–Pacific area provide the time-zone link between the markets of North America and Europe.

### *Australia*

Foreign capital, particularly in the form of direct investment, has played an important role in Australia's development. In the 1980s, private capital flows continue to flow into Australia, particularly from the USA, UK and Japan. The main restriction on investment in

Australia is that it should not run contrary to the public interest and hence permission must first be sought from the Foreign Investment Review Board (FIRB). Special permission is required if a foreigner's intention is to purchase more than 15 per cent of an Australian company's shares (or more than 40 per cent if several foreign interests are involved). Otherwise, except for normal stock exchange regulations, there are no exchange controls to restrict the purchase of shares. Both capital and income can be freely repatriated. Withholding taxes are 30 per cent basic but, for countries with tax agreements with Australia, this may be reduced to 15 per cent. Stock exchanges are at Sydney (established 1830), Melbourne, Perth, Brisbane, Adelaide and Hobart and Australians can buy and sell securities freely through the banks. Overall policy for the stock exchanges is provided by the Australian Associated Stock Exchanges (AASE), which is firmly committed to the idea of further unification. Regulation of the securities industry has been undertaken by the National Companies and Securities Commission (NCSC) since July 1981.

The present government is encouraging Australia's development as a significant and stable financial centre and has recently allowed an influx of foreign banks, including banks from US, Japan, Canada, Singapore, UK and other European countries. Australian banks, in particular Australia's largest bank (Westpac Banking Corporation), are keen to extend their international activities from their already extensive network in the Asian–Pacific region. Deregulation of the banking system and the decision to float the Australian dollar from December 1983 has led to innovations such as the Sydney Futures Exchange (SFE), which is now open to foreign participants. The SFE offers financial futures contracts in bills of exchange, US dollars, precious metals, Commonwealth bonds and stock exchange indices. There are also plans for a Eurodollars futures contract. The futures exchange, along with the rest of the Australian financial system, is responding quickly to deregulatory moves and increased exposure to world capital markets.

### *Hong Kong*

Hong Kong is a Chinese territory under British administration until 1997. It is ideally situated for financial and trade links throughout the Asian–Pacific region and maintains many links with Japan, Korea, Taiwan, Thailand, Philippines and China. Stock exchange activity in Hong Kong goes back as far as 1866 and now there are four stock exchanges (Hong Kong, Far Eastern,

Kam Ngan and Kowloon) listing around 200 companies and supported by well developed financial institutions. To date Hong Kong has remained attractive as a financial centre for foreigners owing to the *laissez-faire* attitude of the government, which allows complete freedom of funds into and out of the colony, imposes no exchange controls, and operates a simple, low tax system. The securities market is regulated by the Securities Commission, which was set up in 1974, and disclosure requirements drawn up by the Hong Kong authorities in 1977. Further disclosure regulations are being considered to meet the requirements of the International Accounting Standards Committee. There is also acknowledgement of the need to simplify securities administration by bringing the four stock exchanges under a central body.

The future of Hong Kong has for a long time remained uncertain in regard to the changeover from British to Chinese rule in 1997. Anxieties have to some extent been reduced, however, by the Sino-British negotiations of 1984 and confidence in the markets remains high. In fact, in January 1985, the Hang Seng Index rose 14 per cent, which made Hong Kong the best performing stock exchange in the world for that month. Political uncertainty has by no means dampened enthusiasm for new developments in the markets and this is reflected in the establishment of the Hong Kong futures exchange at the end of 1984. The futures market has opened its financial trading with a stock market contract based on the Hang Seng Index to allow speculators to take an interest in a large number of shares rather than in individual securities. There are also plans for a US dollar/yen contract. Perhaps one day we will see China, a centrally planned economy, using Hong Kong's futures markets for trading commodities.

### *Singapore*

Singapore maintains a free market in securities and foreign exchange. Foreigners can invest freely in Singapore and Singaporeans are free to invest abroad. The stock exchange of Singapore and the Securities Research Institute of Singapore have actively sought foreign business to improve the standing of the city-state as a popular international financial centre. Since 1980 Singapore has become a member of the International Federation of Stock Exchanges and now there are around 300 companies listed on the exchange. There are close links with Malaysia (which accounts for around two-thirds of companies listed on the stockmarket) and, indeed, some competition too. Singapore has, however, emerged as more successful than Malaya with regard to the encouragement of foreign capital.

A recent development in Singapore markets is the establishment of the Singapore International Monetary Exchange (SIMEX), which began trading in July 1984. With its convenient position on the globe, SIMEX is able to trade with Sydney and Hong Kong in the morning and with Europe in the afternoon. In 1974, market capitalisation of the Singapore exchange stood at around $8 billion. Ten years later, in 1984, market capitalisation exceeded $100 billion – more than twice that of Hong Kong. Continued development along these lines would ensure the future importance of the Singapore exchange as both a domestic and an international marketplace.

### *Japan*

Japan is the second largest economy in the world measured either in terms of gross national product or by volume of foreign trade. For many years, however, Japan's international importance in world financial markets has been small owing to the isolationist attitude of the Japanese Ministry of Finance (MoF). In the past, the MoF has restricted access of foreigners to Japanese capital markets and imposed rigid regulations on internal interest rates. The 1980s have, however, witnessed a changeover from Japan's financial markets being relatively highly regulated to their becoming relatively liberalised.

To monitor the process of change in Japanese attitudes towards open markets it is useful to look back to the period following the Second World War. At this time, and for the next two decades, Japan was in the process of developing its financial system as an important ingredient of post-war reconstruction and needs for protection were high. The MoF discouraged excessive competition between institutions and encouraged moves towards stability and protection of the interests of depositors and investors. With such an emphasis on financial stability, bank failures during this period were virtually unknown. Against this solid foundation for the financial system, however, it is necessary also to take into account the associated low interest rates that kept economic growth slow and reinforced the need to keep Japanese markets isolated from the rest of the world.

By the 1960s the rewards of controlled protectionism were beginning to pay off for Japan and the economy began to show signs of strength and growth. Some small moves towards liberalisation were taken. For example, foreign investment in Japan became possible through the use of depository receipts representing a number of Japanese securities and held by a foreign bank located in Japan. Any dividends or interest payable on the securities would, under the system, be translated into foreign currencies and delivered by the bank to the foreign investors. Issuance of depository receipts was controlled by the authorities, however, and limited to selected US and UK investors. Even into the 1970s, regulations on Japanese markets kept them almost completely cut off from the rest of the world. There were also extremely stringent listing requirements for foreign companies wishing to raise capital in Japanese markets. These listing requirements included minimum assets, minimum profits, minimum dividends, agreed amounts of shares available to Japanese investors, and the requirement that the shares should also be listed in the home country of the issuer or on a continuously traded over-the-counter market. Up to 1976 there were very few foreign shares traded on the Tokyo stock exchange. Those that were traded were limited to issues by foreign unit trusts, foreign mutual funds and large international corporations such as General Telephone and Electronics (GTE), International Utilities, and Pan Am. By the late 1970s, however, the volume of capital raised by foreign investment in Japan and Japanese investment abroad had increased substantially and the possibility of further deregulation appeared more likely than continued isolationalism. Indeed, in 1980 new foreign exchange laws were introduced and, by 1981, portfolio investment into Japan had expanded so that foreign ownership of shares traded on the Tokyo stock exchange had reached around 20 per cent. Led by the insurance companies and institutional investors, Japanese investment overseas also expanded. With the maturing Japanese economy, the pressures mounted between 1980 and 1984 for further deregulation, when a lack of domestic investment opportunities caused a swing in the personal investment sector away from bonds to higher yielding assets. In the three years up to 1984 Japanese savings amassed to create a pool of yen 600 trillion (million million) ($2.5 trillion) – more than twice Japan's gross domestic product. The closed economy no longer provided sufficient outlets for such sums and, in May 1984, after a visit from the US President, the present Japanese liberalisation package began to unfold. The new reforms would include further international usage of the yen, expansion of the Euroyen market and freer access by foreign entities to Japanese foreign exchange, money, bond and equity markets. Futures market activity in Japan has already begun with the introduction of a yen-bond futures contract on the Tokyo Stock Exchange in October 1985. The liberalisation process will gradually enhance the use of the yen as an international currency and increase access to yen financing. Although the MoF has yet to implement all of its envisaged reforms, it has clearly announced its intention for progressive but controlled deregulation. If the rule of thumb that weak economies impose regulations whereas strong countries open up their markets holds true, there can be little doubt about the continued liberalisation of Japanese markets. Even with the world recession of the mid-1980s, the Japanese economy continues to expand and attitudes remain keen for maintenance of free trade and development of the world economy.

### Summary

Private, bank-controlled and state-controlled stockmarkets alike are experiencing pressure in the 1980s for increased links with domestic markets in other countries. Within Europe the EEC countries have agreed on the long-term objective of creating a unified capital market but progress in this direction must wait upon the decisions of individual governments of member countries. Leading the movement towards unity and deregulation are countries that include the UK, Netherlands and Switzerland. Other European countries show progress towards an internationalised EEC capital market in various ways: through double-taxation agreements; through the acceptance of international stock exchange listing requirements and accounting standards; through the establishment of new, internationally-oriented markets; and through other links with stockmarkets both within and outside Europe.

In the US there is no sign of slackening off of activity geared towards providing more and more alternative means for participating in stockmarket activities. The influence of the US stockmarket system extends to Europe and other areas of the world not only with respect to market innovations but also in terms of electronic links for the transfer of information and securities. Canada, too, has extended its influence in the international markets via its network of financial institutions.

The third major area for stockmarket activity is the Asia–Pacific region. Here competition runs high with Australia, Hong Kong, Singapore and Malaysia all actively seeking development towards becoming significant international financial centres. Japan, following a long period of isolationism, is the latest country to begin lowering barriers to international money and capital transactions. The full impact of deregulation of the Japanese markets on the international markets has yet to be assessed – but it is bound to be significant.

The next logical step, now that the stockmarkets in major centres across the world have accepted the need for integration with other stockmarkets to at least some degree, is further progress towards round-the-clock global trading, seven days a week. This vision has already been mooted by stockmarket authorities in various countries, certainly in the US, and progress in this general direction is already taking place in the forms of links between individual groups of foreign-oriented stockmarkets. Some of the existing facilities for accessing foreign markets are described in more detail in chapters 8, 9 and 10.

**Further reading on moves towards internationalisation of financial centres in the 1980s**


Adam, N., 'How the Swiss Markets are Opening up', *Euromoney* (UK), August 1984, pp 20–30.

Azzam, H.T., 'Bahrain: A Regional Financial Centre', *Arab Bankers' Association Arab Banker* (UK), vol 4, no 5, September/October 1984, pp12–14.

Commission of the European Communities, *Code of Conduct Relating to Transactions in Transferable Securities*, Brussels, July 1977.

Commissione Finanze a Tesoro del Senato, *Indagine Conoscitiva sul Funzionamento delle Borse Valori in Italia*, Rome 1977.

Fingleton, E., 'Going Global Means Coming Home', *Euromoney* (UK), May 1984, pp 63–8.

Jao, Y.C., 'Hong Kong's Future as a Financial Centre', *Three Banks Review* (UK), no 145, March 1985, pp 35–53.

Johnson, P.B., 'Legislation for the International Futures Market', *International Financial Law Review* (UK), February 1984, pp 24–7.

Laakso, Jyrki, 'The Internationalisation of Finnish Banking', *Bank of Finland Monthly Bulletin*, vol 58, no 10, October 1984, pp 26–31.

Maenpaa, M.K., 'The Finnish Equities Market in the Process of Internationalisation', *Economic Review* (Finland), no 2, 1984, pp 3–10.

Ollard, W. and Lim, Q.P., 'The City Prepares to Take on the World', *Euromoney* (UK), February 1984, pp 28–36.

Osborn, N., 'The Rise of the International Equity', *Euromoney* (UK), May 1984, pp 63–8.

Osborn, N., 'Risk-Taking comes to Tokyo', *Euromoney* (UK), March 1985, pp 49–58.
Prindle, A., 'Japan Steps out Gingerly', *Banking World* (UK), vol 3, no 4, April 1985, pp 26–8.
Rybczynski, T.M., 'The UK Financial System in Transition', *National Westminster Bank Quarterly Review* (UK), November 1984, pp 1–12.
Sang-Myeon, L., 'The Internationalisation of Korea's Financial Markets', *Korea Exchange Bank Monthly Review*, vol 19, no 3, March 1985, pp 1–13.
Tay, A., 'The Great Call of China', *Euromoney* (UK), March 1985, pp 179–83.
'UK Financial Markets: International Integration and Change', *Morgan Grenfell & Co Economic Review* (UK), November 1984, pp 1–12.
Wheway, R., 'Cross-Frontier Housing Finance', *Journal of Chartered Building Societies Institute* (UK), vol 38, no 165, September 1984, pp 141–3.

## Appendix: Sources of information on world stockmarkets

*USA and Canada*

CANADA

*Newspapers*
*The Globe and Mail*

*Other regular publications*
*Business Life*
*Canadian Banker and ICB Review*
*Canadian Business*
*Executive*
*Investors Digest of Canada*
*The Canadian Business Review*
*The Financial Post*
*The Financial Times*

*General information*
Bank of Canada
Bank of Canada *Review*
*Canadian Almanac and Directory*

USA

*Newspapers*
*Wall Street Journal*
*Journal of Commerce*

*Newsletters*
*Babson's Reports*
*Kipilinger Washington Letter*
*Personal Finance Letter*

*Statistical services*
Moody's Investor Service
Standard and Poor's Corporation
The Value Line Investment Survey

*Other regular publications*
*ABA Banking Journal*
*Bank and Quotation Record*
*Barron's Commercial and Financial Chronicle*
*Financial World*
Federal Bank of Chicago *Economic Perspectives*
Federal Bank of Kansas City *Economic Review*
Federal Bank of Minneapolis *Quarterly Review*
Federal Bank of New York *Quarterly Review*
Federal Reserve Bank of St Louis *Review*
*Financial Analysts Journal*
*Forbes*
*Fortune*
*Magazine of Wall Street*
*Money Magazine*
*The Exchange*
*The Money Manager*
Annual reports:
  New York stock exchange
  American stock exchange
  National Association of Security Dealers

*Europe*

BELGIUM

*Kredietbank Weekly Bulletin*
*Revue de la Banque*

DENMARK

Copenhagen Handelsbank *Quarterly Review*
Danmarks Nationalbank *Monetary Review*

FINLAND

*Economic Review*
Union Bank of Finland *UNITAS Economic Review*

FRANCE

*Newspapers*
*Ag Hefi: Agence Économique et Financière*
*La Côte Deffossés*
*Le Nouvel Journal*
*Les Echos*

*Other regular publications*
*Banque*
*Bulletin des Opérations Financières*
*Inventir*
*La Vie Française*
*L'Expansion*
*Le Journal des Finances*
*Le Nouvel Economiste*
Annual report:
Commission des Opérations de la Bourse

IRELAND

*Business and Finance*
Central Bank of Ireland *Quarterly Bulletin*
*Irish Banking Review*
*Journal of Institute of Bankers in Ireland*

NETHERLANDS

*ABN Economic Review*
Bank Mees and Hope *Review of Financial Markets in the Netherlands*
De Nederlandsche Bank nv *Quarterly Bulletin*

NORWAY

Den Norske Creditbank *Monthly Survey*
Norges Bank *Economic Bulletin*
Norwegian Bankers' Association *Financial Review*

SWEDEN

Svenska Handelsbanken *Current Business in Sweden*

SWITZERLAND

*Credit Suisse Bulletin*
Swiss Bank Corporation *Economic and Financial Prospects*
Swiss Bank Corporation *Manual of Selected Swiss Shares*
*Statistical Yearbook of Switzerland*
*Swiss Credit Bank Bulletin*
Swiss National Bank *Annual Report*
Swiss National Bank *Monthly Bulletin*
*Switzerland in Figures* (Union Bank of Switzerland)
Zurich Stock Exchange *Annual Report*

UK

*Newspapers*
*Financial Times*

*Other regular publications*
*Banking World*
Bank of England *Quarterly Bulletin*
de Zoete and Bevan *Exchange Rate Monitor*
*Investment Analyst*
Lloyds Bank *Economic Bulletin*
Midland Bank *Review*
National Westminster Bank *Quarterly Review*
*Phillips and Drew Market Review*
*The Banker*
*The Stock Exchange Fact Book*

WEST GERMANY

Commerzbank *Business Notes*
Deutsche Bank *Bulletin*
Deutsche Bundersbank *Annual Report*
Deutsche Bundersbank *Monthly Bulletin*
West LB Girozentrale *Quarterly Economic Report*
Annual report:
  Frankfurt and Dusseldorf stock exchanges

*Asia–Pacific region*

AUSTRALIA

*Australian Banker*
*Australian Stock Exchange Journal*
National Australia Bank *Monthly Summary*

HONG KONG

*Far Eastern Exchange Year Book*
*Hong Kong Exchange Monthly Gazette*
*Hong Kong Exchange Year Book*
Kam Ngan Stock Exchange *Monthly Bulletin*

JAPAN

*Asian Wall Street Journal*
Daiwa Bank *Monthly Survey*
Sanwa Bank Sanwa *Economic Letter*

SINGAPORE AND MALAYSIA

*Asiabanking*
*Frazer's Circular*
*Securities Industry Review*
*The Kuala Lumpur Stock Exchange Gazette*

# 8 The foreign exchange markets

The foreign exchange markets provide two basic services without which international transactions related to trade, travel or the raising or lending of funds could not occur. The first service is the provision of facilities for changing money denominated in one currency into money denominated in another. Their second function is to provide facilities for reducing or hedging foreign exchange risk. This second function of the market has become particularly important since the 1970s since when exchange rates have been fairly volatile. Exchange market facilities have increased in size and range in line with increasing volatility of exchange rates. The foreign exchange markets of today are at a much higher state of development than they were 25 years ago and, unless there is a move back towards fixed exchange rate régimes, they will no doubt continue to expand in response to the risk-reduction needs of traders and investors. Providing that facilities for the reduction of exchange risk are available at reasonably low cost, there will be little grass roots demand for a return to fixed exchange rates.

Since there is such a strong relationship between the type of exchange rate régime and the demand for foreign exchange services, the first section of this chapter looks at the implications for foreign exchange markets from the various types of exchange rate régimes that have existed to date. The chapter continues with a look at the structure of the foreign exchange markets and the services that they provide. This is followed by an examination of the types of currency that are traded in the markets. One of these currencies, the European Currency Unit (ECU), is singled out for more detailed attention because of its extraordinary rise to fame and its implications for the future of international financial markets. Finally, some of the most recently established foreign exchange markets and the services they provide are described to illustrate how innovations occur in response to changes in the wider institutional and economic environment.

## Floating versus fixed exchange rates

Does it matter if exchange rates are fixed or floating? There would seem to be advantages and disadvantages of both systems. In this section the key issues at stake for traders, investors or borrowers when exchange rates are fixed, pegged or volatile are presented – along with the reason why foreign exchange markets have become so important since the 1970s.

### *Fixed exchange rates*

The main arguments in favour of a system of fixed or stable exchange rates are, firstly, that the real value of international cash flows can be known in advance of their occurrence; and, secondly, that interest rates in the long run tend (at least in theory) to be similar in all countries. The second of these points can be illustrated as follows.

Consider two countries, A and B. Country A is running a balance of payments deficit, suffers from rapid inflation and has high interest rates. Country B is in an opposite position with a balance of payments surplus, low inflation and low interest rates. On the assumptions of fixed exchange rates and zero restrictions on capital flows, the following changes should take place. Funds would flow from country B to country A in order to benefit from the higher interest rates. The increased supply of funds in country A would then tend to increase the availability of domestic credit and, through the interaction of supply and demand, reduce interest rates. Meanwhile, in country B, the reduction in the supply of funds would reduce the availability of credit and lead to higher interest rates. The lower interest rates in country A would lead to economic expansion and lower inflation (expectations of which partly determine interest rates), eventually clearing the balance of payments deficit. The flow of funds between countries A and B would continue until interest rates are the same in both countries and equilibrium is reached.

The illustration is rather simplistic and only for illustrative purposes. Departures from the real world include the assumption that inter-country cash flows are unrestricted, that lower interest rates automatically lead to economic expansion, and that the governments of countries A and B are content to sit back and ignore other developments in their economies whilst the progression towards interest rate parity occurs. In practice it is quite likely that the government in country B would consider slowing down or blocking the outflow of funds to or the inflow of cheap funds from country A. One way that the flows of funds between countries A and B could be moderated is via changes in currency values, but within the fixed exchange rate scenario of the illustration this possibility cannot be considered.

*Pegged exchange rates*

A pegged exchange rate system is the half-way house between completely fixed exchange rates and completely floating exchange rates – such as the situation that prevailed for a short period after the departure from the gold standard in 1971 (see Figure 5.2, page 72). Countries were, at that time, allowed to devalue or revalue their currencies to new pegged positions when appropriate. Under this situation, for countries A and B from the illustration, this would mean that interest rates could change to reflect the increased (decreased) value of the foreign currency in the event of a revaluation (devaluation). Currency flows between countries A and B would occur until a new equilibrium was reached whereby differences in interest rates would reflect expected future changes in exchange rates.

At first sight it might appear that the option to revalue or devalue provides governments with a useful tool for relieving pressure on their currencies in order to pursue domestic policies. In practice, the process can prove (and has proved) problematic. For example, suppose that a country decided to devalue its currency in order to increase the competitiveness of its exports and, hopefully, cure a balance of payments deficit. There is no certainty that the desired effect would occur and there could be further, unforeseen needs for further currency devaluations. A country deciding to revalue its currency, on the other hand, might be the cause of anxiety for exporters trying to remain competitive in the international market and also from the labour force because of the fear of increased unemployment. The inherited wisdom appears to be that short-run interventions in currency markets aimed at curing short-run problems are workable but that revaluations and devaluations that last for any length of time are the cause of problems for the future. The fact that most industrial countries now allow their currencies to fluctuate lends support to this view.

*Floating exchange rates*

The main advantage of freely floating exchange risks is that it allows governments to pursue domestic objectives with more freedom than if currency values are fixed. The domestic economy is insulated to some extent from the impact of foreign disturbances because currency values change according to the forces of supply and demand. A common argument against freely floating exchange rates is that it deters international trade and investment because of exchange rate risk caused by volatile currency values. Another view is that variable exchange rates leads to a misallocation of resources because traders and investors require a premium for bearing exchange risk. The evidence, however, is that such fears are largely unfounded. International trade and investment have not been reduced since the move to floating exchange rates in the 1970s – in fact, it has expanded rapidly. As for the suggestion that investors require a risk premium for overseas investments, this line of argument does not adequately take into account the role played by foreign exchange markets. At a small cost foreign exchange exposure can be hedged in the currency markets which, in effect, allows investors to become risk neutral, so that the volume of international funds flows need not be adversely affected This state of affairs could not prevail, of course, if currency markets were not available or had not reached their present level of development.

The debate over whether exchange rates should be fixed, pegged or volatile continues – mainly in academic circles. Most governments have already chosen floating or pegged exchange rates for their currencies and the result has been an increased need for services provided by the foreign exchange markets which include a wealth of innovations.

## The nature of foreign exchange markets

Within the foreign exchange market, which like any other market responds to forces of supply and demand, prices of individual currencies are expressed in terms of other currencies. Since the markets allow for the exchange of currency not only at present rates but also at rates that are likely to occur in the future, for any particular currency there are likely to be several different types of market. Firstly, providing the currency is a convertible currency, there is a spot market where currencies for immediate delivery can be bought and sold. Secondly, most currencies also have a forward market in which currencies for delivery at some future date (usually, one, three or six months hence) are traded. In forward markets, prices to be paid for a currency on a specified future date can be arranged now, the money not changing hands until the delivery date. Thirdly, for the world's most popular currencies, there are futures markets, which are rather like forward markets except that any gains or losses made by traders must be settled on a daily basis. The futures markets are arranged in such a way that traders are required to maintain margin accounts from which funds are added or subtracted depending on their misfortune or luck respectively. Finally, also for the world's most popular currencies, there are options markets dealing in instruments (not the actual currencies) that confer the right (but not the obligation) to buy or sell currencies at specified prices before or on a specified date. With spot, forward, futures and options markets available, the foreign exchange markets would seem complex enough already, but there are also markets that deal in hybrid instruments such as options on futures and other possibilities for which a real demand exists. Innovation and development of facilities for dealing in hybrid instruments proceeds at rapid pace in the foreign exchange markets.

### *The forward market for foreign exchange*

The forward market for foreign exchange is simply a market for foreign currencies that are to be delivered in the future. The operations can be compared with the forward market for commodities, which allows purchases or sales of commodities at a future date. Unlike for commodities, however, forward markets for currencies allow purchases and sales on any forward date. Forward markets are available for all the major industrial currencies for up to several years into the future but most transactions lie in the time-span between overnight and one year. From the beginning of the 1970s, besides facilities for regular currencies, there has also been active use of forward markets for Eurocurrencies. There is, however, some room for improvement in this market because some currencies (those of smaller and less developed currencies) are not actively traded.

Existence of the forward markets allows market users to speculate on interest rate movements and to cover or hedge against the risk that exchange rates will vary during a particular period, besides providing access to a useful source of liquidity. The cost of forward cover depends on the time value of money as evidenced by the relationship between the forward rate and the future spot rate. In practice the costs of using the forward market are directly affected by interest rates which, also representing the time value of money, influence the difference between spot and forward currency prices. If you like, money has a time value that can be seen either in interest rates or as the difference between spot and foward prices for currencies. If the currency in question is a Eurocurrency, the difference between the time values of money evidenced in interest rates on the one hand and in the difference between spot and forward rates on the other hand is likely to be small or non-existent. This is because of the unregulated nature of Eurocurrencies. If the currency is not a Eurocurrency, then there may be restrictions such as taxes or exchange controls which, as imperfections in the market, will cause more of a difference.

*The futures markets for foreign exchange*

Futures markets, like forward markets, have existed for commodities since the early days of shipping. Now there are futures markets for currencies too, their role being the provision of risk-reducing facilities for offsetting (partially or wholly) transactions with futures contracts in order to hedge risk. The difference between futures transactions and forward transactions is that forwards are agreements between two parties whilst futures are contracts traded on organised exchanges. Futures contracts are for specified sizes and settlement dates and are resalable in the market on any date up to the expiry of the contract.

*Currency options markets*

Currency options markets deal in bundles of contracts, which offer holders the right to buy or sell currencies at pre-specified prices up to or before the date when the contracts expire. The value of an option contract to the holder is determined by the difference between the price specified in the contract (the striking price) and the actual currency price prevailing in the foreign exchange market (the spot price). For example, the option to buy a particular currency would be valuable if the price specified in the contract was less than the actual currency price prevailing in the spot market. If spot prices were lower than the price specified in the contract the option to buy would be worthless. Options contracts are available in many different currencies for a range of maturity dates and striking prices. The concept of an option contract is not new, having been applied for many years to physical goods, financial instruments and securities. Popularity of the currency option is increasing fast, however, owing to the universality of the underlying asset – money. Some of the many types of currency options contracts available and examples of their use are described in chapter 9.

*The interbank market*

Vast numbers of buyers and sellers of currencies comprise the foreign exchange market yet there is no central marketplace and, except in some European centres, it is not possible to 'see' the market. Instead, the many billions of dollars worth of currency traded each day is arranged and controlled via telephone and telex links. Participants in the market rarely meet each other and are unlikely ever to see the currencies in which they deal as they are moved telegraphically across the world.

The channels through which funds in the foreign exchange market flow are given in Figure 8.1. The diagram shows that people wishing to exchange currencies are linked to one another via a financial mechanism that removes the need for them ever to meet face to face. At the heart of the system is the interbank market.

Most participants in the foreign exchange market find it convenient to conduct their business via the large commercial banks, which comprise the interbank market. Even large corporations (but not all of them) find that the interbank market provides a reasonably priced service that is not worth bypassing with other arrangements for direct access to the market. The role of the banks is to act as 'market-makers' and stand ready to buy and sell foreign currencies. Most of the interbank business is conducted by a small number of banks (about 20) that have a worldwide network of branches, but there is room for other participants. One way to view the market is as a series of layers.

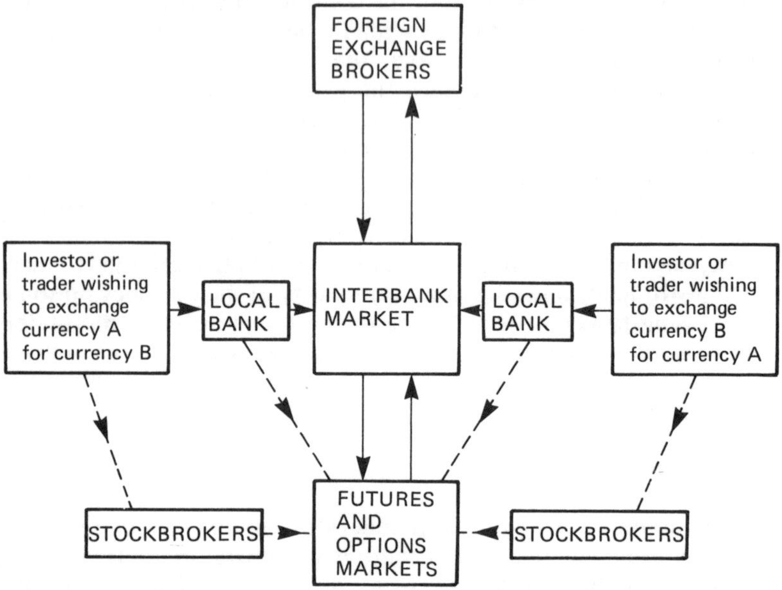


**Figure 8.1 Financial flows in the foreign exchange market.**

- The top layer of the interbank market comprises a few giant banks that assume leadership in the market and tend to dominate the system through direct links with each other and their complex network of branches.
- The next layer is composed of a much larger number of participants, most of which are large international banks. Activities of the international banks are limited to dealing in smaller amounts than the giant banks and through brokers rather than via direct links.
- Finally, the third layer of the interbank market is made up of many smaller banking institutions that tend to specialise in one or a few currencies in their own financial centres. They too rely on brokers' services but may also deal direct with other institutions of similar size.

The foreign exchange brokers in the interbank market provide the important function of bringing buyers and sellers of currency together in an efficient manner. Without this service a bank with business to transact would have to contact every other bank dealing in the same currency to ask prices before knowing where the best deal could be found. By using the broker system the bank is immediately informed where the best markets are because of the brokers' wide-ranging and speedy information and communications systems. The size and nature of broking organisations vary according to geographic location and clients' needs. Their activities ensure the smooth functioning of the market and that currency values at any moment in time are virtually the same all over the world.

Until recently the interbank market was the only channel through which foreign exchange transactions could take place. Since the 1970s, however, a number of new developments have occurred. For example, some multinational corporations have extended their activities in the market to become market-makers alongside the banks. Other developments include the options and futures markets, which link via stockbrokers to anyone (rather than just banks) who wants to take an interest in currency markets.

*Central banks' activities in the foreign exchange markets*

Besides the interbank activities of the commercial banks, central banks operating on behalf of their governments also, from time to time, play an active role in foreign exchange markets. Their role, according to their country's régime of fixed, pegged or floating exchange rates, is to attempt to keep exchange rates and fluctuations in prices for particular currencies within acceptable limits. One way a central bank can influence currency prices in the desired direction is via market operations (buying and selling currencies) aimed at influencing supply and demand. Thus, operating through its central bank, a government can maintain a certain amount of control over its currency's value. Besides their regulatory role, many central banks also operate as their government's principal banker for international and domestic payments and may handle foreign exchange transactions for public sector enterprises such as the post office or railways. Finally, central banks may also exchange currencies with international organisations such as the IMF.

## Types of currency in foreign exchange markets

The world's currencies can be classified in several different ways. Firstly, and most obviously, they can be categorised according to the geographical locations of the domestic economies to which they belong. Looking at the situation this way there are almost as many currencies as there are different governments. There are, in fact, more governments than there are currencies because some small countries prefer to use the currency of a neighbouring, more financially advanced country.

A second way to classify currencies is according to their degree of convertibility. In the interbank market currencies are either fully convertible, semi-convertible or non-convertible. Fully convertible currencies are the ones that are most actively traded locally and worldwide, the main convertible currency areas being the US and Canada, Asia and Western Europe. Semi-convertible currencies, for example those of Third World countries, can only be bought and sold by dealing with a local bank. Restrictions are likely to be in force that make the currency available only for authorised commercial activities. Finally, non-convertible currencies are currencies that are restricted by their monetary authorities (for example, in Eastern Europe). Rates of exchange for non-convertible currencies are artificially pegged and this often leads to the development of unofficial black markets for those currencies.

A third way to categorise currencies is according to whether they are straight currencies or composite currencies. For an example of a straight currency, look in your wallet. You will not yet find a composite currency in your wallet because it can be found only in the international capital markets. Examples of composite currencies include the EUA (European Unit of Account), the ECU (European Currency Unit) and the SDR (Special Drawing Right). At present these composite, or 'cocktail', currencies are used to denominate Eurobonds and other financial instruments but it is possible that, one day, a 'cocktail' currency will find its way into people's pockets. Of the current composite currencies the one most likely to take on this wider usage is the ECU.

### The (incredible) ECU

Believe it or not, in France, during the fourteenth century there was a coin known as an 'écu'. This is perhaps a symbolic coincidence for what may happen with the modern ECU. The ECU became the fledgling reserve currency of the European Community in a step towards a more integrated monetary system in the EEC in 1979, when eight EEC members joined the new exchange rate system. Participating countries of the present system contribute 20 per cent of their gold and dollar reserves in a three month swap and receive ECUs in return. FECOM (European Monetary Cooperation Fund) manages the fund but is not a central bank as such and does not intervene in currency markets. Each participating country has the central rate for its national currency set in relation to other members' currencies and to the ECU. Allowable fluctuation limits around the central rate are then agreed (currently 2.25 per cent above or below the central rate, except for the Italian lira, which may fluctuate 6 per cent) and national intervention is only required if fluctuations exceed the agreed limits.

The weight of each currency for calculating the ECU is determined by the economic strength of participating countries and facilities are available for changing the weights or for adding to or subtracting from the number of countries participating in the scheme. If the ECU currency basket is changed at any time, however, the value of the ECU against other currencies does not change. Table 8.1 shows how the ECU currency basket was calculated under the old system (13 March 1979) and under the new system (from 17 September 1984).

**Table 8.1**
**Calculation of the ECU currency basket**

| | National Currency Units | | Percentage Weights | |
|---|---|---|---|---|
| | 13 March 1979 | 17 Sept 1984 | 13 March 1979 | 17 Sept 1984 |
| Belgian franc | 3.66 | 3.71 | 9.3 | 8.2 |
| Danish krone | 0.217 | 0.219 | 3.1 | 2.7 |
| French franc | 1.15 | 1.31 | 19.8 | 19.0 |
| Deutsche-mark | 0.828 | 0.719 | 33.0 | 32.0 |
| Irish punt | 0.00759 | 0.00871 | 1.1 | 1.2 |
| Italian lira | 109.00 | 140.00 | 9.5 | 10.2 |
| Lux. franc | 0.14 | 0.14 | 0.4 | 0.3 |
| Neth. guilder | 0.286 | 0.256 | 10.5 | 10.1 |
| Pound sterling | 0.0885 | 0.0878 | 13.3 | 15.0 |
| Greek drachma | — | 1.15 | — | 1.3 |
| | | | 100 | 100 |

Source: EEC Council Regulations

On 28 September 1984, 1 ECU was worth:

| | |
|---|---|
| DM | 2.23435 |
| £ | 0.592711 |
| F.fr | 6.85877 |
| Lira | 1387.72 |

| | |
|---|---|
| FL | 2.51939 |
| B.fr | 45.3114 |
| L.fr | 45.3114 |
| D.kr | 8.08762 |
| Drach | 92.1597 |
| Ir.£ | 0.720910 |
| US$ | 0.738933 |

The ECU fulfils several functions within the European Monetary System (EMS) framework but recently EEC governments and operators in the international market have taken steps to extend the role of the ECU. Thus, within the official circuit the ECU provides a means of settlement of debts by central banks in their exchange market operations. Outside the official circuit, however, private markets have grown up where transactions are not affected by EMS rules. If you like, outside the EMS, some people treat the ECU as a normal currency. For example, the ECU has been used for private bank deposits since 1980. Over one hundred Eurobonds denominated in ECUs have been issued since 1981. Multinationals with subsidiaries in Western Europe use the ECU for accounting between subsidiaries. An ECU interbank market has emerged because of the increasing use of the ECU for financial and commercial transactions. Borrowers of ECUs now range from the USA and Canada, throughout Europe, to Asia and Australia. Financial instruments denominated in ECUs include floating rate notes (FRNs), revolving underwriting facilities (RUFs), Treasury Certificates, debentures, leasing contracts, invoices – and there are moves afoot to have ECU denominated travellers' cheques.

The fundamental attraction of the ECU is its stability – appreciations of strong member currencies can be offset against depreciation in others to provide an automatic hedging mechanism. Unbundling the currency basket at any time presents no particular problem with modern computer technology. On the other hand, there is often no need to dissect the ECU into its component parts. Traders in the new ECU interbank market have already decided that unbundling is not worth the bother and treat the ECU as a single currency. By the end of 1984 the ECU was being used for international bank lending more than the British pound or the French franc.

The future of the ECU would appear to be secure. How long will it be before governments and banks allow nationals and foreign residents to use it freely for all normal currency transactions?

**The new markets**

The interbank market was, until the 1970s, as mentioned, the only channel through which to conduct foreign exchange transactions.

Since that time, however, major innovations have taken place in the form of markets where brokers can deal face to face rather than over the interbank telephone and telex system. The first of the new markets was the International Money Market (1972), which opened in Chicago to provide a market that, unlike the interbank market, could deal in futures contracts for foreign exchange during specified trading hours. The IMM was followed by similar markets in London (LIFFE) and Singapore (SIMEX) and there are also plans for new futures markets in Hong Kong and Japan. Another new market offering foreign exchange services to a wider range of users than banks alone is the Philadelphia Stock Exchange (PSE) for currency options. As with the futures markets, currency options markets have now opened in other parts of the world.

The arrival of the new futures and options markets has greatly extended the facilities available to financial managers to reduce (or increase, if desired) exposure to exchange rate movements and interest rate changes. Most recently some new markets also provide facilities for taking a financial interest in changes in stockmarket volatility through stockmarket index options. The new markets link up around the world to provide facilities for exchanging financial instruments representing a large number of currencies, interest rates and entire stockmarkets.

Main features of the existing currency futures and options markets are now described.

### *The International Money Market (IMM), Chicago*

The IMM in Chicago, when it started business in May 1972, was the first market to provide facilities for forward and futures transactions for parties other than banks. Operations of the market run along similar lines to those of the interbank market with buyers and sellers transacting most of the business over the telephone or telex. It is an open auction market where authorised dealers can buy and sell contracts in foreign currencies (sterling, Deutschemarks, Mexican pesos, Japanese yen, Canadian dollars, Swiss francs and so on) with four fixed delivery dates each year. Some dealers act on behalf of clients and others have their own accounts for which they try to make profits. Standard contract sizes are £25,000, Canadian $50,000, DM 125,000 and yen 12,500,000 – which may appear rather large until you consider that buyers of contracts can operate on a 'margin'. That is to say, rather than hand over funds to cover the whole contract, buyers need only initially pay a deposit of less than 5 per cent of the contract's value as security against trading losses. The margin is then added to or subtracted from as prices move against or for the buyer. A safety valve is provided in the system in that the extent to which contract prices can fluctuate each day is limited, so large losses can be avoided. In its first year of operation trading on the IMM was less than 200,000 contracts but in 1984 the number was nearer 10 million contracts, which is evidence of a much faster growth rate than that of the interbank market.

*The London International Financial Futures Exchange (LIFFE)*

LIFFE opened in 1982 in London to provide a similar service to the IMM in Chicago. Indeed, experts from the Chicago exchange advised on the setting up of the new London market. LIFFE handles futures traded in Eurodollars, sterling, Deutsche-marks, Swiss francs, yen, and, most recently, a Financial Times Stock Exchange (FTSE) index contract which allows market users to hedge or speculate on the basis of future stockmarket trends. The FTSE index contract is now affectionately known as 'footsie' – to be played by one and all. Like the IMM, numbers of transactions at LIFFE were slow at the outset but now stand at over 3½ million per year. On its busiest day so far (30 October 1985) 34,591 contracts changed hands.

*The Philadelphia Stock Exchange (PSE) for currency options*

Another non-interbank market is the PSE options market for foreign exchange. The options are for spot currencies (Deutsche-mark, sterling, yen, Swiss francs and Canadian dollars) and are traded in bundles of similar size to those of IMM and LIFFE futures contracts. Owners of options are not locked into their contracts (as with forwards and futures) and, even if market trends move against them, stand to lose not more than around 5 per cent of the contract's value. The market has international links (over half the contracts traded in the market originate in Europe) and has proved popular on both sides of the Atlantic. Corporations, in particular, find the market useful for hedging foreign currency earnings, for hedging import or export costs, and for hedging bids for projects in foreign currencies (bidders know that, if a tender is accepted, the option protects against adverse currency movement before the project's completion date). As with the IMM and LIFFE, acceptance and use of the currency options market has been rapid.

*The Singapore International Monetary Exchange (SIMEX)*

SIMEX opened on 7 September 1984 to link with the Chicago money market and LIFFE in London. Futures traders can open positions in one market (say, LIFFE) and close them in another (say, SIMEX). Thus the opening of SIMEX heralded the arrival of round-the-clock, global trading in futures. Corporations, banks and other financial institutions in the Gulf-to-Tokyo time zone now have access to their own exchange and need no longer depend on those in the USA and UK. SIMEX has only recently started business so, at present, the range of contracts is currently limited to four (a three-month Eurodollar interest rate contract, a US dollar–yen contract, a US dollar–Deutsche-mark contract, and a gold futures contract). The possibility of a stock exchange futures contract based on the Tokyo stock exchange index is, however, under consideration. The volume of transactions on SIMEX is expected to reach between 3,000 and 5,000 transactions per day.

*The future development of currency options and futures markets*

Of the new markets that have grown up to deal in currency options and futures, the Chicago market is leading the field in terms of the volume of transactions handled. Worldwide, however, the use of currency futures and options markets is increasing at a remarkable pace as more uses for the new types of instrument are found. Countries like Hong Kong, Japan and Brazil are considering introducing or improving market facilities for trading in options and/or futures. Banks and pension funds find the markets particularly useful for controlling their portfolios. Some institutions have taken the initiative to offer customers packages that involve use of the options and futures markets. For example, a financial institution might offer clients fixed rate loans with the lender hedging in the futures market. Such packages are likely to become increasingly common because infrequent users of options and futures, especially if they are coming to the market for the first time, may find the methods of trading difficult or time-consuming to master. With customised packages, smaller and infrequent users can benefit from the knowledge of the staff working for larger institutions who have learned the skills necessary for successful trading. Some of the more straightforward uses of currency options and futures are described in the next chapter but the examples provided there barely scratch the surface of the many different methods of using the new instruments. For the professionals, some markets run regular courses to maintain up-to-date knowledge of the latest instruments and how they can be used. Education of market users is an important aspect of marketing the new markets in order to ensure their successful future.

## Summary

The demand for foreign exchange market facilities is largely dependent on the prevailing exchange rate systems. When exchange rates are fixed, demand for exchange market services is at a minimum. Floating exchange rates, however, give rise to problems of exchange risk for international traders and investors, who must then depend on foreign exchange market services to reduce the riskiness of their international funds flows. Facilities within the foreign exchange market for reducing foreign exchange risk include futures markets, forward markets, and options markets for the world's most commonly traded currencies. The interbank market has traditionally provided foreign exchange facilities (including facilities for hedging exchange risk) but there is now a trend towards provision of services by non-bank institutions. Recent examples of non-bank foreign exchange services by non-bank institutions include those provided by the IMM (Chicago), LIFFE (London) and SIMEX (Singapore). Further development of new currency markets can be expected in other areas of the world.

Besides changes in the structure of the foreign exchange market and the types of facilities available to traders, there are also changes in the nature of the currencies in which the markets deal. At one time only straight currencies could be traded. Nowadays, composite international currencies, such as the ECU, can also be exchanged. The markets' willingness to deal in new currency inventions could, potentially, lead to a much wider use of an international currency for everyday purchases and payments.

## Further Reading

*Foreign exchange markets in various countries*

Cabiallaveta, M., 'Structural Changes in the Foreign Exchange Markets', *Union Bank of Switzerland Business Facts and Figures*, June 1984, pp 3–5

Chrystal, K.A., 'A Guide to Foreign Exchange Markets', *Federal Reserve Bank of St. Louis Review* (USA), vol 66, no 3, March 1984, pp 5–18.

Cicchetti, C., 'The Beauty of the Boston Option', *Euromoney* (UK), February 1985, p 45.
Goodman, L.S., 'New Options Markets', *Federal Reserve Bank of New York Quarterly Review*, Autumn 1983, pp 35–47.
Jaycobs, R., Ramond, C. and Bilson, J., 'The Forex Services', *Euromoney* (UK), January 1984, pp 148–59.
Ollard, W., 'Egypt: Laying the Basis for a Free Market', *Euromoney* (UK), February 1985, pp 107–15.
Peagan, N., 'The New York Futures Exchange', *Euromoney Supplement* (UK), January 1984, pp 1–37.
Powers, J.G., 'Chicago Faces the Next Challenge', *The Banker* (UK), vol 134, no 699, May 1984, pp 109–19.
Spence, A., 'London's Burgeoning Crop of New Futures Markets', *The Banker* (UK), vol 134, no 702, August 1984.
'The Foreign Exchange Market in Belgium', *Kredietbank Weekly Bulletin* (Belgium), March 1984, pp 1–5.
Tourret, R., 'A Future with SIMEX', *Asiabanking* (Hong Kong), no 48, March 1984, pp 50–3.

*Options and futures*

'Financial futures', *Euromoney* (UK), October 1984, pp 318–50.
Fitzgerald, M.D., 'Traded Options: A Successful Innovation', *The Banker* (UK), vol 134, no 699, pp 103–7.
Geske, R. and Roll, R., 'On Valuing American Call Options with the Black Scholes European Formula', *Journal of Finance* (USA) vol 39, no 2, June 1984, pp 445–55.
Goldstein, H.N., 'Foreign Currency Futures: Some Further Aspects', *Federal Reserve Bank of Chicago Economic Perspectives* (USA), vol 8, no 6, November–December 1983, pp 3–13.
Raj, S., 'Financial Futures', *State Bank of India Monthly Review*, vol 22, no 12, December 1983, pp 536–9.
Spence, A., 'Financial Futures', *Banking World* (USA), vol 2, no 10, October 1984, pp 41–5.
Sutton, W. and Shourbaji, M.T., 'Treasury Bond Options', *Arab Bankers' Association Arab Banker* (UK), vol 4, no 6, November–December 1984, pp 22–3.
Yamey, B.S., 'The Economic Performance of Futures Trading', *Three Banks Review* (UK), no 141, March 1984, pp 33–43.

# 9 Techniques for the international financial manager

The domestic, overseas, Euro- and foreign exchange markets provide many opportunities for risk taking (in the quest for profit) and risk reduction (in the quest for financial stability). Objectives of financial managers, whether engaged in domestic or international operations, are often described in terms of the joint needs for wealth maximisation and risk minimisation. The difference between the tasks undertaken by domestic and international managers in fulfilling these objectives is that, unlike his domestic counterpart, the international financial manager must deal in more than one currency and in more than one country. Since financial markets differ between countries, managers must be aware not only of the different financial and economic environments in which they operate, but also of the techniques required to operate in them safely and profitably. Of particular importance for international operations are techniques for forecasting the financial environment, for managing foreign-denominated assets and liabilities, for managing exchange rate, interest rate and political risks, and for performance evaluation and control in an international setting. Successfully applied, the techniques enable managers to identify and respond to opportunities and imperfections in world markets to the benefit of the organisations that they serve.

Complete coverage of the wide range of techniques available to modern international financial managers is impossible given the size and scope of this book and there is a need for selectivity. The information contained here therefore covers only selected areas that a) are not normally dealt with in traditional text books on domestic financial management, and b) relate to developments examined elsewhere in this book. More specifically, the techniques selected for attention are as follows:

- *International diversification* The potential advantages and pitfalls from portfolio investment in foreign countries.
- *The cost of capital for the international firm* The mathematical basis for techniques aimed at measuring capital costs as a prerequisite step towards their minimisation.
- *Multi-currency capital budgeting* How domestic capital budgeting techniques must be adapted to take into account variations in currency values that are likely to occur during the lifetime of overseas projects.
- *Political risk* Why managers should be aware of political developments in foreign countries in which they do business.
- *Managing exchange risk* The art of dealing successfully with variations in currency values which affect a wide range of business activities. (Forecasting and basic theories for understanding exchange rates are also included in this section.)
- *Trading techniques* Hedging, arbitrage and speculating for profit or risk reduction, including examples of trading techniques using the new markets.

## International diversification

The last 30 years have seen an increase in diversification at several levels in the world economy. Large firms have discovered advantages of 'putting their eggs in several baskets' and have diversified direct investments geographically and across industries to become today's multinational corporations. Smaller investors and the professional investment and pension fund managers who look after their interests have also become aware of the potential benefits of international diversification. At the heart of the concept of international diversification is the notion that economic conditions and shareholders' returns in different (domestic and foreign) markets are less than perfectly correlated. If this is indeed the case, it is possible to reduce portfolio risk by selecting individual securities in such a way that their risky characteristics offset each other. Sometimes information on inter-country correlation coefficients is not available but, even in these situations, a simple naïve diversification strategy (a large number of investments in as many countries as possible) could forseeably also achieve a reduction of portfolio risk. A second attraction of international diversification is the possibility of finding assets in foreign markets that offer a higher return (after tax and transaction costs) than assets in the domestic market with a comparable amount of risk. The potential gains to be achieved by cross-border security selection along these lines are largely determined by the degree of integration of the domestic and foreign markets. If the markets are fully integrated and money and capital are allowed to flow freely between them, then the investors in both countries face similar sets of risk and return opportunities. If, on the other hand, the markets are segmented, risk-return opportunities facing investors in each country are likely to be different. A quick look back at Figure 3.1(c) (page 26) should serve to illustrate the potential gains to be made from cross-border investing if markets are segmented.

*Gains from international diversification*

The question of potential benefits from international diversification has been the subject of many journal articles including those by Grubel (1968), Lessard (1973), Levy and Sarnat (1970), Solnick (1974) and Agmon (1972). The overall conclusions from the studies is that Markowitz diversification techniques can be most usefully employed by investors in smaller, less developed countries. Investors in more advanced countries such as those in Western Europe and North America are less likely to benefit from Markowitz diversification but are still likely to gain risk reduction benefits from employing a naïve diversification strategy. For investors looking for securities in foreign markets that offer higher returns than those in the domestic market for similar risk levels (on the assumption of segmented markets), the evidence is that such opportunities regularly occur. One method that international managers might use to identify desirable foreign investments involves the following steps:

*Step 1* Collect information on:

(i) the Beta (systematic risk coefficient) of the foreign security in its own capital market (Bfi).
(ii) the expected return on the foreign market's market portfolio or market index (ERmf).

(iii) the riskless rate of return (or the three-month Treasury bill rate) in the foreign market (Rff).
(iv) the Beta of the foreign security in relation to the market portfolio (or index) of the domestic capital market (Bfi*).

*Step 2* Find the expected return (ERfi) on the foreign stock using the following equation based on the capital asset pricing model (CAPM) developed by Sharpe (1964), Mossin (1966) and Lintner (1965 and 1969).

$$ERfi = Rff + Bfi\,(ERmf - Rff)$$

*Step 3* Subtract from ERfi any taxes and transactions costs that would have to be offset against gross returns from the foreign investment to find the net return to the investor (ERfi*).

*Step 4* Use the CAPM equation again to find the expected return (ERi) that the foreign security (with systematic risk Bfi*) would be associated with in the domestic market, thus

$$ERi = Rf + Bfi^{*}\,(ERm - Rf)$$

where Rf is the risk-free rate in the domestic market and ERm is the expected rate of return on the domestic market portfolio (or index)

*Step 5* Compare ERfi* with ERi.
If ERfi* is higher than ERi, then the return on the foreign stock is higher than for a domestic security with the same systematic risk level. The foreign stock would therefore appear attractive and a potential purchase.

The method described assumes that the markets in both the domestic and foreign markets are efficient and also that the CAPM is a valid aid to security selection decisions. Both of these assumptions are reasonably justifiable in the more developed markets. The remaining drawback of the method is that it is rather cumbersome and requires estimation procedures for most of the key variables. With modern computers and information technology, however, this, too, should not present too much of a problem.

Refinements to the model could be introduced to encapture further aspects of international investment activities. For example, measures of exchange risk (for variable currencies) and political risk (for the risk that overseas earnings may not be able to be repatriated) could also be incorporated into the model. Another approach would be to use not two CAPM equations (one for the domestic market and another for the foreign market) but a single international asset pricing model (IAPM) such as that put forward by Solnick (1974). The IAPM is a more complex version of CAPM and attempts to model equilibrium risk and return levels in an international setting. At its current level of development, the IAPM is rather difficult to use because it requires many adjustments for different countries' interest rates and exchange rates. Also, the IAPM requires estimation of a suitable index to represent an optimum portfolio selected from international markets. Currently the only world index available is the Capital International World index based on the performance of 18 leading stock exchanges. The search for more sophisticated indices and measures of political and exchange risk continues.

*Evidence from the pension fund industry*

Despite potential shortcomings of the theoretical models for international diversification and asset selection, there is no doubt that professional portfolio managers of mutual funds, unit trusts and pension funds are becoming attuned to the idea of investing and diversifying abroad. Increasingly, changes in the laws, professional skills and attitudes are leading to increased geographical spreads of the investments chosen for managed portfolios. In the USA, for example, the Employee Retirement Act (ERISA) 1974 was passed to encourage trustees of pension funds to diversify their portfolios as far as possible. Spurred on by financial theorists who drew attention to the potential of international diversification for increasing returns and decreasing risk, US pension plans looked favourably at overseas markets and are now estimated as having over $15 billion invested in foreign equities – a large proportion of which are Japanese growth stocks. Management of ERISA overseas funds is becoming an increasingly specialist job in the USA with around 80 per cent of the overseas business being handled by around 20 per cent of the managers.

In the UK, Japanese and US securities are popular additions to pension funds portfolios, especially since the removal of UK exchange controls in 1979. Around 15 per cent of UK pension funds are now invested in overseas equities. Japanese investors, too, reacted quickly to the removal of regulations in 1980, which permitted up to 10 per cent of pension trust portfolios to be invested in foreign securities. In other countries, the proportions of pension funds invested overseas are (according to estimates published in the financial press) Italy 7 per cent, Switzerland 35 per cent, Netherlands 41 per cent, Belgium 24 per cent and West Germany

12 per cent. Unfortunately, the exact extent of international portfolio diversification is difficult to estimate with precision because overseas investment figures are often aggregated to include direct foreign investment or portfolio investment in the domestic market. If the financial newspapers are anything to go by, however, the trend is definitely towards more overseas portfolio investment.

With investors from more and more countries (even Japan) becoming more willing to invest outside their national borders, the face of international investment management is changing. In response to increasingly fierce competition, the trend is towards more marketing of international funds to international clients. New types of specialist intermediaries are beginning to emerge on the financial scene who can advise clients on the choice of specialist managers for international investments. Managers with previous experience of managing an internationally-diversified portfolio and with knowledge of techniques for managing exchange risk are increasingly in demand.

*Remaining restrictions on international diversification*

It is not yet possible for all investors in all countries to diversify internationally. Limitation on international diversification include direct controls on capital movements and indirect controls such as taxation of earnings from foreign investments and currency restrictions. Non-governmental restrictions of a practical nature also remain, such as limited resources on the part of individual investors who are unable to invest on such a large scale. Where investment institutions such as unit trusts and investment trusts are accessible to small investors, however, the practical limitations are minimised leaving government policies and ideologies as the most important restriction on international diversification.

The decision to allow or disallow international investment is closely tied in with governments' views of the free market system – and whether it is economically beneficial for the free market system to operate in their own country. Conceptually, a world free market system in which there would be no restrictions on international diversification would have the following characteristics:

- Complete knowledge by all market participants.
- Free access to assets over national borders.
- An absence of monopolies worldwide.
- Free movement of assets across national borders.

The concept of a world free market, needless to say, is far from being reached in the real world. The market systems of countries such as the USA, most European countries and, increasingly, countries in the Asian–Pacific region do approach the free market concept, however, and, as long as links between them remain open, provide the beginnings of a world free market. The factors that would bring about increased movement towards a free world market are political factors (moves towards liberalism) and economic factors (the stronger the economy the stronger the incentive to lower international barriers). Meanwhile, even with a world market that falls short of the free market concept, there are many opportunities for successful overseas diversification, either where restrictions are minimal or where the extra costs of restrictions are outweighed by the additional returns or lower risk characteristics of overseas securities.

## The cost of capital for international firms

Managers of international firms, like their domestic counterparts, are involved in the process of seeking out projects and investments that are worth more than they cost in their search for earnings. That is to say, money raised at a cost should be invested so that it generates returns in excess of that cost. The cost of a firm's capital is therefore important both as a concept and as a yardstick for gauging the desirability of investment alternatives. The main reasons why a manager must know the firm's cost of capital are: firstly, to be able to compare it with the cost of capital of other firms engaged in similar activities (if, by comparison, the firm's cost of capital appears excessive, it may be possible to reduce capital costs by changing the firm's capital structure); and, secondly, knowledge of the firm's cost of capital provides a useful yardstick or discounting criteria for evaluating new projects.

Analysis of the firm's cost of capital is an inexact but necessary science. It is 'necessary' because it allows managers to know a desirable new investment when they see one, and 'inexact' because estimation procedures normally enter into the calculations. A common method for estimating the firm's cost of capital involves piecing together a jigsaw of the costs of the various elements of the capital structure (some of which are not known with certainty) according to their relative proportions. When added together according to their respective proportions the total cost of the subdivisions of the firm's capital structure combine to provide a weighted average cost of capital (WACC). An alternative method of estimating the firm's cost of capital is via the capital asset pricing model (CAPM) of Sharpe (1964), Mossin (1966) and Lintner

(1965, 1969). The first of these two general methods is, essentially, a 'bricks-and-sticks' approach focused directly on the firm's actual capital costs. The second, CAPM, approach involves looking at the firms securities (to see how risky they are) and then looking at the market to find the cost of capital normally associated with securities with that level of risk. The essential principles of each approach are as follows:

*Method 1 – The Weighted Average Cost of Capital (WACC)* The estimated costs of each element of the firm's capital structure are combined according to the following formula:

$$\text{WACC} = \sum_{i=1}^{n} \text{pi ci}$$

where n = the number of different sources of capital in the firm's capital structure (bonds, ordinary shares, preference shares, retained earnings, and so on).

pi = the proportion of the firm's total capital structure represented by each source of capital (expressed as a fraction).

ci = the after-tax cost of each component of the firm's capital structure.

Conventional procedures for estimating the cost of capital for each segment of the firm's capital structure, in a domestic setting, are as follows:

- *For long-term debt* Use the rates specified in the firm's debt agreements adjusted for tax.
- *For equity* Use the rate of return normally required by the firm's shareholders (this is where estimating WACC becomes 'inexact').
- *For retained earnings* Use the same rate of return as for the rate of return on equity. The same rate as for equity is used here because retained earnings are, ultimately, shareholders' funds whether they be paid out as dividends or reinvested in the business to produce future earnings.

For the manager of an international firm, where the capital structure comprises elements raised in different countries and, quite likely, in different currencies the calculation becomes more complicated. This is because payments on capital raised in more than one country will be subject to exchange rate risk. For dealing with the exchange rate risk two alternatives are available. Firstly, the cost of each element of the firm's capital structure could be estimated using a forecast of expected exchange rate movements. Secondly, rather than keep the exchange risk, a hedging procedure could be adopted and the cost of the hedge added to the cost of capital estimate. Thus, for a bond, the borrowing cost could be estimated as either

| | | |
|---|---|---|
| Amount borrowed (plus costs of issue) | *minus* | Discounted value of repayments (coupons and principal) including estimated exchange rate gains or losses |

OR

| | | | | |
|---|---|---|---|---|
| Amount borrowed (plus costs of issue) | *minus* | [ Discounted value of repayments (coupons and principal) | *plus* | Discounted value of costs of hedging exchange rate risk ] |

depending on which strategy was followed.

In practice there are difficulties estimating future exchange rate gains or losses but, providing that no major forecasting errors occur near the beginning of the series of cash flows, a reasonable estimate could still result. This is because any errors near the end of the cash flow would be discounted at lower rates than those near the beginning.

*Method 2 – Using CAPM* CAPM is a useful tool for estimating the cost (or shareholder's required rate of return) of equity capital in efficient markets. To use the CAPM method the firm must first find the Beta risk of its stock (B), which measures the extent to which the firm's shares are influenced by the overall riskiness of the market. Betas for stock exchange listed corporations can be found in publications such as the *London Business School Risk Measurement Service* (for UK listed firms). Smaller firms would have to find their own Beta by examining their past returns in conjunction with returns on the market (or market index). When the Beta is known, it can be entered into the CAPM equation and the expected return for shareholders (cost equity of capital for the firm) found, thus:

$$ERi = Rf + Bi\ (ERm - Rf)$$

| where | | | |
|---|---|---|---|
| | ERi | = | expected return on firm's equity |
| | Rf | = | the risk-free rate (possibly estimated as the going rate of return on a three-month Treasury bill) |
| | ERm | = | the expected return on the market (possibly estimated from a market index) |
| | Bi | = | the sensitivity of the firm's securities to market risk |

Having estimated the cost of equity capital using the CAPM method, the resulting figure can then be combined with the cost of debt capital using the WACC formula.

The drawbacks from using the CAPM method are that the cost of capital estimated is what the firm's equity capital *should* be under the assumption of CAPM – not what it actually is (the assumptions of CAPM have been criticised by, among others, Roll (1977)). A problem also arises if the firm's capital is raised in markets in several countries because several CAPM equations (one for each market) would have to be used.

Whichever method for estimating the cost of capital is employed, judgement will enter into the calculation. If the lack of an exact method is a cause of concern for financial managers, they might find solace in knowing that, even if an exact method was available, as soon as it was used and a figure for the firm's cost of capital arrived at, the figure would be out of date. This is because market costs and prices constantly change. A rough estimate of the cost of a firm's cost of capital is, however, better than none.

## Multi-currency capital budgeting

Capital budgeting involves deciding on which investment projects should be undertaken given the firm's resources and its cost of capital. There are various criteria for deciding which projects should be undertaken. Well-known capital budgeting criteria include the payback method (whereby the project that returns the initial outlay most quickly will be chosen), the internal rate of return method (IRR) (whereby the project that offers the highest rate of return will be chosen), and the net present value (NPV) method (whereby a project will be undertaken providing that the discounted value of its future cash flows exceeds the required initial outlay). Each of these methods requires a forecast of likely future positive and negative cash flows and, if these cash flows are denominated in more than one currency, will also require an estimate of future exchange rates. There are two methods available for reducing estimated future cash flows denominated in foreign currencies to net present value. The main steps involved in each method are as follows:

*Method 1 – Convert, then find NPV*

*Step 1* Estimate future cash flows in foreign currencies.

*Step 2* Convert to domestic currency at forecasted exchange rates.

*Step 3* Calculate present value of cash flows using the discount rate for the domestic currency.

*Method 2 – Find NPV, then convert*

*Step 1* Estimate future cash flows in foreign currencies.

*Step 2* Calculate present value using discount rates appropriate for the foreign currencies.

*Step 3* Convert to domestic currency using spot market rates.

Even working from the same set of forecasted future cash flows, it is possible that two managers, one following method 1 and the other following method 2, would arrive at different figures. The size of the difference would be determined by the degree of skill employed for estimating future exchange rates and, if forward market prices were used (for step 2 of method 1), by the degree of efficiency and lack of bias in the foreign exchange market.

## Political risk

Besides opening themselves up to exposure to exchange rate risks, investors and lenders in foreign markets face another – political – risk that can be defined as the risk to a prospective flow of funds from political acts of a sovereign government. Examples of political risks include nationalisation, expropriation, war, riots, corruption and occupation by a foreign power. Sometimes the political risk process is gradual (say, via the introduction of taxes on overseas capital) and sometimes the process is more speedy (say, via a few tanks and rockets). Another form of political risk, mainly undertaken by lenders, is the possibility that a foreign government may simply refuse to repay or service its debts.

Information on political risk appears mainly in the banking literature (as a consequence of the current debt crisis). This information can, however, also be usefully employed by other lenders and investors. According to the Euromoney country risk ratings (*Euromoney*, October 1984) countries with around zero political risk include the USA, Germany, Japan, UK, Switzerland,

Australia, Canada, Sweden and Finland. At the other end of the spectrum, countries with less than ten marks out of 100 for political stability include Venezuela, Nigeria, Bolivia, Haiti, Lesotho, Zambia, Chile, Senegal, Ghana, Dominican Republic, Sudan, El Salvador and Uganda. Methods of assessing political risk vary as do the rankings arrived at by different surveys, but such investigations provide managers with at least a rough guide.

Some managers would argue that political risk does not exist. That is to say, they consider that lending or investing abroad is no more risky than lending or investing at home, especially when international diversification allows the reduction of political risk by spreading it over several countries. Depending on their country of domicile, some of these managers may have a good point!

The lesson to be drawn from attitudes towards political risk for today's troubled areas is plain. A stable political environment encourages the foreign investment required for economic growth. Revolutionary changes and the possibility that assets will become 'frozen' only deter economic assistance from free market forces. Even if the political risk level is not high enough completely to cut off the supply of foreign funds, those that are forthcoming will require an additional premium to compensate for the higher risk – thus making overseas funds more expensive.

## Managing exchange risk

Exporters waiting to receive payments in foreign currencies, importers intending to pay foreign suppliers in foreign currency, investors in foreign assets, and corporations issuing bonds in foreign markets all face exposure to exchange risk. The risk arises from the possibility that changes in exchange rates will occur between the time when a financial arrangement is entered into and the time when the cash flows actually occur. On a foreign investment, for example, if it is necessary to change funds denominated in one currency into funds denominated in another, both parties to the agreement could lose (or gain) from unfavourable (or favourable) movements of exchange rates between the two currencies.

The two main steps involved in dealing with foreign exchange risk are, firstly, to predict the likely size of exchange rate movements and their effects on expected cash flows and, secondly, to make arrangements to reduce the exchange risk to acceptable levels. These two tasks are more easily said than done. Predicting exchange rate movements can be a complex and expensive process which, unless large currency fluctuations are likely, may not be worth the bother. To find the likely effect on cash flows, too, can be a complicated affair, particularly for a firm with a large volume of multi-currency transactions (although, with modern computerised information and management accounting systems, the task could be completed with some precision). As for reducing the exchange risk to an acceptable level, the job requires deciding what an 'acceptable level' is, and then selecting the required risk reducing activity from a variety of alternatives. The 'acceptable level', remembering that exchange risk can work for or against managers, is likely to depend on the forecast of future exchange rate movements. If currency values are going to change in their favour, then there is hardly any point in taking steps to protect themselves from the currency fluctuations when they occur. If the currency fluctuations are likely to be detrimental to their cash flows, then, of course, some risk reduction activity would be appropriate. The problem in practice is, of course, complicated by the fact that currency movements are not always easy to predict. Generally speaking, therefore, most firms try to minimise their risk of losses from exposure to exchange rates by either ensuring that assets and liabilities in different currencies are equal and close together with each other in time (this process is known as 'matching'), or by hedging the exchange risk in the foreign exchange or money markets. As an example of 'matching', consider a bank selling dollars foward to one customer buying dollars forward at the same time, thus reducing exchange rate risk to zero. Only someone who is very sure that future exchange rate movements will be favourable will let exposure to exchange risk remain uncovered.

With the latest developments in the currency markets there are now many alternatives at the disposal of managers for reducing exchange rate risk. They can choose between using spot, forward, Eurodeposit, futures or options markets and between a variety of strategies. For example, a manager requiring a foreign currency in three months' time could buy the currency in the forward market, buy the currency now in the spot market and put it into the Eurodeposit market for three months to gain interest, buy the foreign currency in the spot market to be rolled over at regular intervals within the three months' period, or take no action at all in the hope that the price of foreign currency will become more attractive during the three month interval. Depending on the course of action chosen and the progress of currency prices, the result will be either a cost or a profit.

Readers requiring further details of how exchange rate risk can be managed and hedged would find it useful to look at Brooke and Remmers (1977) or Rodriguez and Carter (1984).

*Forecasting*

Techniques for forecasting trends in the domestic and international financial environments are invaluable tools for the financial manager, especially if they produce good (accurate) forecasts. Forecasts may be drawn up for inflation, market prices, interest rates, exchange rates and other financial variables either by statisticians or financial analysts within the firm or by specialist agencies claiming expertise in particular fields. Even though forecasts, in practice, tend to be less than perfect predictions of the future (even when drawn up by an expert) they provide a useful planning tool in an essentially uncertain financial environment. They should be treated as sources of information (rather than crystal balls), the accuracy of which diminishes the farther they go into the future. Most managers would be pleased enough (and probably surprised) with a reasonably accurate forecast of key financial variables up to one year into the future.

Types of forecast fall into two main categories. Firstly, there are 'fundamental' forecasts, which use macroeconomic data and fundamental characteristics of the object of the forecast to predict long-term trends. Secondly, there are 'technical' forecasts, which use past and recent data to predict short-term market movements. Technical forecasts usually involve the use of charts for monitoring market movements over time and are particularly used by traders in the money and foreign exchange markets. Technical analysis, besides its cheapness and relative simplicity, is claimed to incorporate market psychology in its predictions but suffers from a lack of theoretical justification (why should the future continue along lines suggested by the past?). Fundamental forecasts usually involve statistical models, often computerised, and can be complex and expensive (and inaccurate because of the long time-scale under consideration). Both techniques, if widely used in the market, could be accused of becoming the basis of self-fulfilling properties (because of the buy and sell orders they instigate) – although market traders could well argue that this is precisely why forecasts are so useful.

*What determines exchange rates?*

As mentioned, future exchange rates are difficult to predict. A comparison of forward rates and previous spot prices will show this to be true (although *on average* forward prices tend to be fairly good predictors of future spot prices). Ultimately, currency prices, like the prices of any other commodity, are determined by supply and demand. Unfortunately, however, the supply and demand for a currency is difficult to predict because it depends on so many national and international factors – and on up-to-date data that are not always available. Even if up-to-date data were available, it would only provide a rough guide to tomorrow's prices and an even poorer guide to next month's prices. Difficulty in predicting future exchange rates is the main reason behind the growth of the many facilities in currency markets for hedging exchange rate risk.

Although currency prices are difficult to predict, there are some theories available to explain exchange rate movements, which may help estimation procedures. In an area of great uncertainty even a rough guide to the future is better than none. The two types of theory available for explaining exchange rates are 'equilibrium theories' and 'partial equilibrium theories'. Equilibrium theories establish general relationships between key variables and tend to hold up on average and in the long run. They are not particularly useful for explaining today's or tomorrow's prices but are useful for explaining prices in general over, say, a period of one year. Partial equilibrium theories are more useful for explaining and predicting short-term price movements (but can, unfortunately, be wrong). They are useful, however, to academics for explaining why at any moment in time actual prices are different to what the equilibrium models would predict – and useful for financial managers engaged in trying to outguess the market.

The equilibrium theories link together inflation rates, interest rates and exchange rates as follows:

*The law of one price (purchasing parity theory)* states that the price of goods in one country must equal the price of the same goods in another country translated at the current exchange rate.

*Fisher's theory of interest rates* states that nominal interest rates reflect real interest rates and the expected level of inflation. This means that differences in money rates between two countries can be brought about only by differences in inflation rates between the countries.

*The interest rate parity theory* states that differences in interest rates between two currencies must be equal to the difference between the spot and forward exchange rates for the two currencies.

*The expectations theory of forward rates* states that the difference between today's forward and spot rates is equal to the expected change in the spot rate.

The theories link together in the following way:

| Difference in interest rates between currencies | = | Expected difference in inflation rates | = | Expected change in spot rates | = | Difference between forward and spot rates |
|---|---|---|---|---|---|---|

Or, for currencies A and B:

$$\frac{1 + rA}{1 + rB} = \frac{E(1 + rA)}{E(1 + rB)} = \frac{E(S\ A/B)}{S\ A/B} = \frac{F\ A/B}{S\ A/B}$$

where rA = interest rate in country A
rB = interest rate in country B
E = 'expected'
S = 'spot'
F = 'forward'

It is important that managers understand the nature of the theories described above – and, in particular, their limitations. The simple model described for linking together inflation, interest and exchange rates is concerned with equilibrium, long-term relationships. That is to say, the model decribes the situation towards which variables gravitate – not the situation that exists at any particular moment in time. Take, for example, the interest rate parity theory, which links differences in interest rates to differences in spot and forward rates for any two currencies. There is evidence, particularly in offshore markets where many traders use the theory for quoting prices, that, in general, the theory holds up. At any moment in time, however, there may be a slight difference between what the model predicts and actual market prices. If any such difference did exist, market traders would immediately be alerted to the possibility of making riskless gains through arbitrage activities. Their actions, through the laws of supply and demand, would bring the relationship between exchange rates and interest rates back into equilibrium – until the next deviation, which would spark off the arbitrage process again. (For further information on the interest rate parity theory in the Euromarkets, *see* Agmon and Bronfield (1978) and/or Frenkel and Levich (1975).)

Another way to see the limitations of the model provided by the equilibrium theories is through the relationship between forward rates and actual spot rates on the forward date. The expectations theory of forward rates holds that if, today, the 30 day forward rate for any currency is X, then in 30 days' time the spot rate for the currency will be exactly X. Needless to say, this exact relationship does not hold up all of the time because managers and traders in the currency markets are not perfect forecasters. On the other hand, if one looks at average long-run relationships between spot rates and previous forward rates, it can be seen that, in general, the two draw very closely together (*see*, for example, Cornell (1977) and Frankel and Johnson (1978)).

At this point readers will no doubt be asking themselves 'What good are equilibrium theories if they do not help forecast future exchange rates with precision?' The best answer available is that knowledge of the equilibrium theories gives managers a guide as to how currency prices should react – eventually. They can be used to find out when a currency price is out of equilibrium, a state of affairs to which (in theory at least) it must return. That is, every time the equilibrium theories are wrong, market traders stand to make gains (or losses) either through arbitrage or through out-guessing the market. The theories hold up better in efficient markets than they do in inefficient markets. For managers this implies that in an efficient market it is probably wise to take market prices as up-to-date reflections of available information. In inefficient markets, on the other hand, discrepancies between the 'value' and 'price' of currencies are likely to exist and work for or against the interests of the firm. Hedging activities, too, are more justified and speculative activities more subject to variable results (profits or losses – depending on managers' forecasting abilities) in inefficient markets.

## Trading techniques

There are three basic types of trading activity in which managers may become involved – hedging, arbitrage and speculation. Hedging activities aim to reduce financial risk and are particularly appropriate for dealing with exchange rate fluctuations. Arbitrage activities are aimed at making riskless profits by buying and selling assets without holding onto them. Speculation involves entering into a risky situation in the hope of gain. Techniques and simple examples for each of these basic trading activities are now provided.

### *Hedging*

Hedgers are worried people. They are so concerned about their potential losses that they are willing to pay for their removal. The basics of hedging operations are as follows:

| | |
|---|---|
| Start situation | Mr X has entered into a financial arrangement and is worried that adverse financial conditions will occur to the detriment of his cash flows. |
| Required action | Mr X enters into another financial arrangement whereby, if the adverse financial conditions do occur, any losses from the first financial arrangement can be offset against gains from the second financial arrangement. In statistical terms, Mr X should try to ensure that the cash flows resulting from his first financial arrangement are perfectly negatively correlated with those resulting from his second arrangement. |
| Possible outcomes | 1 *The adverse financial conditions do occur* Mr X is not worried because losses on the first financial arrangement are offset against gains from the second arrangement.<br>2 *The adverse conditions do not occur* Mr X has not made any gains from hedging operations. He is content with the situation, however, because he has not made any losses on his original financial arrangement (except for transactions costs). |

Hedging is a general technique that can be used in a wide variety of financial situations. The examples that follow are geared specifically towards hedging to remove risks that arise through multi-currency operations.

*Hedging examples using the forward market*

*Hedging exchange rate risk* Suppose that Mr X, in the UK, is expecting an inflow of dollars in three months' time and is worried that, by that date, exchange rates will have moved so that the expected inflow of dollars will not buy as many pounds sterling as they will today. Mr X's alternatives are as follows:

- He can wait until three months' time and accept whatever exchange rate prevails on that day; OR
- He can buy sterling in the three month forward market at today's forward price.

If he adopts the second of these approaches, Mr X is hedging. The cost of his hedge will be determined on day 90 when the difference between today's forward price and the spot price in three months' time is known. Mr X's motive for entering into the hedge is that the certainty of knowing what his future cash flows will be in terms of pound sterling outweighs the possibility that future spot exchange rates could, in fact, work in his favour.

*Covering interest rate risk* Suppose Mr X lends £1 million for a year in the UK at an interest rate of $r_A$. At the end of the year Mr X's funds would have increased to £1 million × $(1 + r_A)$. An alternative plan for Mr X would be to buy another currency, say dollars, with his £1 million and lend out the funds in the USA at a rate of $r_B$. In this case, at the end of the year, Mr X's funds could be worth £1 million × S × $(1 + r_B)$ (where S = the spot rate in dollars per pound sterling). If Mr X is still not satisfied because of uncertainty about the future interest rate on dollars in the USA, he could sell the dollars forward into pounds sterling. In this case the accumulated amount at the end of the year would be 1 million × S/F $(1 + r_B)$ (where F = the forward rate for converting dollars into pounds sterling). Mr X would thereby no longer be subject to the fear that future spot rates would turn against him.

### *Hedging using the futures markets*

The use of financial futures provides a flexible alternative to using the forward markets for hedging risk. To see how hedging with futures can be performed, consider the following example.

A payment of £1 million is expected in the USA by Mr X who is concerned that sterling might depreciate against the dollar over the next three months (which would depreciate the dollar value of sterling receipts). Mr X could hedge by buying dollar futures. The transactions might proceed as follows:

| Cash market | Futures market |
|---|---|
| *Day 1* | |
| Mr X awaits receipt of £1million on day 91.<br>The spot exchange rate is $1 = £0.8333 (£1 million = $1,200,050) | Mr X buys dollar futures contracts at $50,000 per contract at an exchange rate of $1 = £0.8333 (Total value is $4,200,000 costing £999,960) |
| *Day 91* | |
| The £ has fallen to $1 = £0.9091<br>£1 million is now worth $1,099,989<br>Loss = $100,061 ($1,200,050 – $1,099,989) = £90,965 | Mr X sells futures contracts at $1 = £0.9091<br>This yields £1,090,920 (1,200,000 × 0.9091)<br>Gain = £90,960 |

The loss from the weakening pound sterling is almost completely offset. The offset is not perfect because the $1,200,050 in the cash market is offset against $1,200,000 in the futures market (because dollar futures contracts are denominated in $50,000 units, perfect matching is impossible).

The example assumes that exchange rates in the spot and futures markets have moved together. In practice, this would not occur very often – spot and future prices are more likely to change by different amounts and the hedge would not be as perfect as in the example. Differing rates of change between spot and futures markets would lead to additional gains or losses from hedging operations.

*Arbitrage opportunities in foreign exchange markets*

Arbitrage in currency markets involves making riskless profits by buying and selling currencies. Activities of arbitrageurs relate to market efficiency in the following way. Arbitrage activities make the market efficient (because, through supply and demand, they bring prices for currencies into line). On the other hand, in an efficient market, arbitrage opportunities do not exist (because, in an efficient market, currency prices are in line). That is, arbitrage opportunities in currency markets are rare but, when they do exist, the activities that they generate make the market efficient once more and the arbitrage opportunities disappear – until the next time.

Before the introduction of pocket calculators, arbitrage opportunities were more prevalent than they are now because it took traders longer to work out that currency prices were not in line. Nowadays, pocket calculators have been replaced by computers that continually scan world market prices and are programmed to identify arbitrage opportunities as soon as they occur. Once upon a time the man with the fastest pencil made the highest profits from arbitrage. He was replaced by the man with the quickest fingers for pressing calculator buttons. With modern computer technology, the man with the quickest fingers has been replaced by the man who can get to the telephone quickest to place his buy and sell orders. Perhaps the next step is for the computers to be programmed to make the required telephone calls – in which case arbitrage opportunities would become very rare indeed.

If managers are lucky enough to spot an arbitrage opportunity, the following types of transaction could be the vehicle for generating riskless profits.

*Triangular arbitrage* If one unit of currency A exchanges for one unit of currency B, and one unit of currency B exchanges for one unit of currency C, then one unit of currency C *should* exchange for one unit of currency A. If it does not, then there is an opportunity to make immediate profits via triangular arbitrage.

*Space arbitrage* Space arbitrage involves buying currency in one market and selling it immediately, at a profit, in another market. The markets involved may be separated geographically by a large distance (for example, arbitrage between London and New York markets) or between markets within closer proximity (for example, between the International Money Market and the interbank market in the same city).

*Interest arbitrage* Interest rates on different currencies may not be the same. For example, the interest rate on pounds sterling is likely to be different to the interest rate on US dollars. If such differences do exist it is sometimes possible to borrow in one currency and lend in another at a profit. Opportunities for interest arbitrage are rare, however, because the interest rate parity theory (which states that the nominal interest rates between two countries should be equal to the forward exchange rate discount or premium) tends to hold most of the time. That is to say, the interest rate on a unit of currency A will equal the interest rate on a unit of currency B covered in a forward market. If an opportunity for arbitrage should arise, it would not last for very long, because of the actions of the large international banks which can move vast amounts of funds rapidly around the world.

*Speculating in modern markets*

'Speculation' is not a dirty word. Speculators attempt to outguess the market and its participants with regard to future prices in order to try to make profits. The activities of speculators play an important part in maintaining the efficiency of foreign exchange markets (forwards, futures and options markets) and keep the markets liquid. Without speculators there would be less opportunities for hedgers to use the foreign exchange markets to reduce exchange risk. This makes sense if the reader considers that for everyone wanting to buy an asset there must be someone else willing to sell it. The exact amount of speculative activity in the foreign exchange market is difficult to gauge from information on the number of deals. That is to say, holding an asset that would secure a high return if exchange rates increased could benefit either a speculator or a hedger attempting to cover an exchange risk. Information on the number of deals would not cast light on the motives (speculative or hedging) for the transactions.

At one time the only speculators in foreign exchange markets were the banks and international institutions. Now, however, just about everyone has access to the market through facilities such as the IMM, LIFFE and SIMEX.

*Speculating with foreign exchange options*

Foreign exchange options contracts specify the right to buy or sell foreign exchange at a specified price (the striking price) either within a specific period (the American option) or a specified date (European option). Contracts that confer the right to sell are called 'puts' whilst contracts that offer the right to buy are known as 'calls'. Buyers of options pay a premium for the privilege. If market rates during the option period move to the advantage of the option holder, the option can be exercised at a profit. If, on the other hand, market rates move against the interests of the option holder, the premium paid at the outset will be lost. For example, suppose a three months' European call option on £10,000 cost \$400 (or \$0.04 per pound sterling) and the striking price is set at \$1.30 per pound sterling. The buyer of such an option would have the right to buy £10,000 at \$1.30 per pound sterling in three months' time and would have paid \$400 for the privilege. If the spot price at the end of the option period is \$1.25 per pound sterling, the option would be valueless because sterling could be bought more cheaply in the spot market. If, on the other hand, the spot price at the end of the option period is \$1.35 per pound sterling, the option would be valuable. It would be worth £10,000 $\times$ (1.35 $-$ 1.30) = £500. If spot currency prices changed to \$1.40 per pound sterling during the three months, the option would be worth £1,000 – and so on.

The relationship between the value of a call option and the spot price of the underlying currency is shown in Figure 9.1(a). The profit from buying the call is the difference between the striking price (A) and the spot exchange rate (B). The option comes into the money only if the spot exchange rate (B) is greater than the striking price (A).

The situation for a seller of a put is shown in Figure 9.1(b). The put seller's opportunities for gain and losses are a mirror reflection of those for a buyer of a call. Benefits only accrue if the spot exchange rate (B) is less than the striking price (A).

By buying both a call and a put simultaneously (this combin-

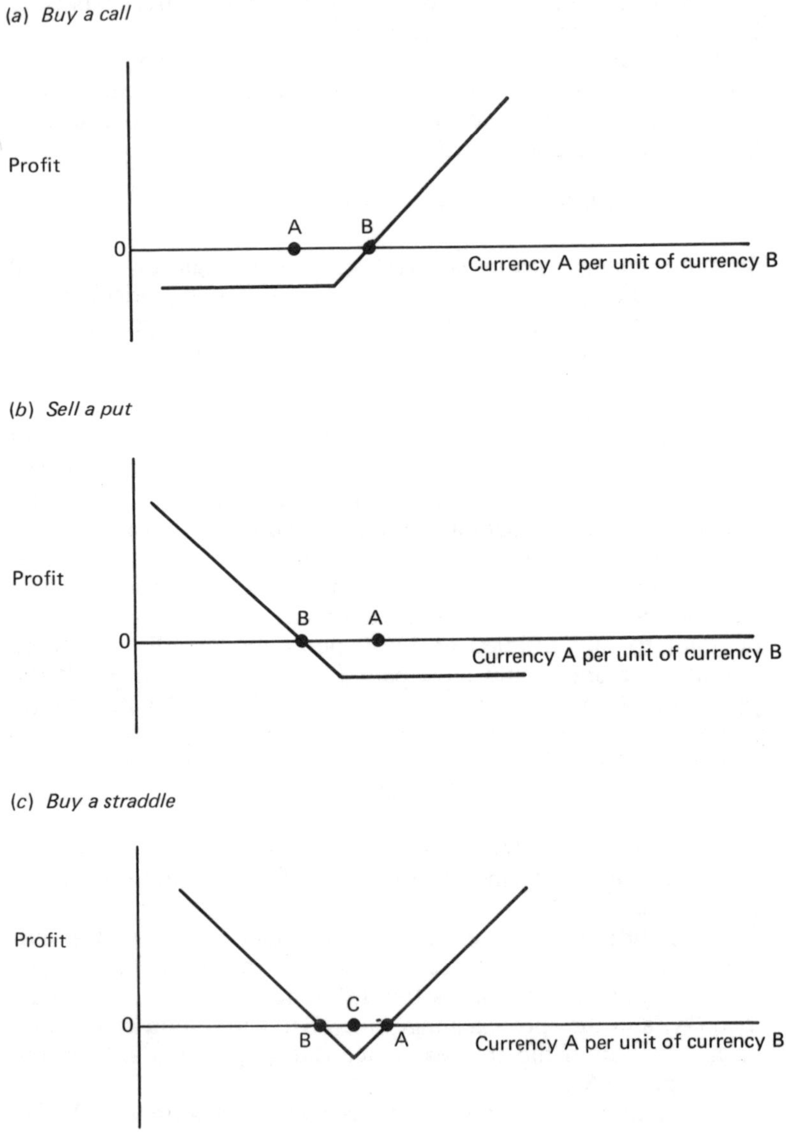


**Figure 9.1 The relationship between currency options values and spot prices.**

ion is known as a straddle), the option buyer stands to gain if exchange prices move either above A or below B, as shown in Figure 9.1(c). The straddle allows option buyers to take an interest in the amount of market variability.

Of course, more complicated ways of using the options markets are possible. New approaches for using currency options constantly spring from both inside and outside of the market and range from low risk, low possible returns strategies to high risk strategies with high possible returns. Futures options continue to be popular with hedgers and speculators because potential losses are limited to the amount paid out for the initial premium.

### *Speculating with stockmarket index options*

The US, UK, Hong Kong and Australian financial markets as well as those in some other countries have facilities for speculating on market movements, in addition to opportunities to speculate on price movements of individual currencies and securities. The new speculative facilities are known as index futures and index traded options. As with other types of option and futures contracts, the amount required as a deposit by the stockbroker is only a fraction of the amount that would have to be paid if the intention was to invest in all the shares represented by the underlying assets. Also, as with other types of options, the alternatives for index options include the buying and writing of calls and puts and the writing of straddles. Small investors have found the index options a simple outlet for playing hunches about forthcoming market movements.

## Summary

Financial techniques have changed and continue to change in response to the increased range of facilities in world stockmarkets. Today financing and investment across national borders is possible in most countries in the free world and there is a need for financial managers to keep up-to-date with new developments. Managers who can identify imperfections between financial markets and take appropriate actions stand to make extra profits. Financial managers who are unaware of international developments run the risk of cutting into their profits or operating at the mercy of international forces which increase the riskiness of their operations. In particular, modern financial managers should understand the potential gains and drawbacks of international diversification, raising capital in foreign markets, capital budgeting in more than one currency and how to deal with exchange and interest rate risk. The key to becoming a successful international financial manager would appear to be in understanding foreign exchange markets and using them to the advantage of the firm. At minimum, managers should know how to use the new markets to reduce risk to acceptable levels. At maximum, if managers can outguess the market with skill and judgement, the new markets offer many opportunities for boosting returns via speculative activities.

## References


Agmon, T., 'The Relations Among Equity Markets: A Study of Share Price Co-movements in the United States, United Kingdom, Germany and Japan', *Journal of Finance*, September 1972.

Agmon, T., and Bronfield, S., 'The International Mobility of Short-term Covered Arbitrage Capital', *Journal of Business Finance and Accounting*, 2, summer 1978, pp 269–78.

Brooke, M.Z. and Remmers, H.L., *The International Firm*, Pitman, 1977.

Cornell, B., 'Spot Rates, Forward Rates and Exchange Market Efficiency', *Journal of Financial Economics*, 5, 1977, pp 55–65.

Frankel, A. and Johnson, M.G. (eds) *The Economics of Exchange Rates: Selected Studies*, Addison-Wesley, 1978.

Frenkel, J.A. and Levich, R.M., 'Covered Interest Arbitrage: Unexpected Profits?', *Journal of Political Economy*, 83, April 1975, pp 325–38.

Grubel, H.G., 'Internationally Diversified Portfolios: Welfare Gain and Capital Flows', *American Financial Review*, vol 58, 1968, pp 1299–1314.

Lessard, D.R., 'International Portfolio Diversification: A Multivariate Analysis for a Group of Latin American Countries', *Journal of Finance*, vol 28, 1973, pp 619–33.

Levy, H. and Sarnat, M., 'International Diversification of Investment Portfolios', *American Economic Review*, vol 60, 1970, pp 668–75.

Lintner, J., 'The Valuation of Risk Assets and the Selection of Risky Investments in Stock Portfolios and Capital Budgets', *The Review of Economics and Statistics*, February 1965, pp 13–27.

Lintner, J., 'The Aggregation of Investors' Diverse Judgements and Preferences in Purely Competitive Security Markets', *Journal of Financial and Quantitative Analysis*, December 1969, pp 347–400.

Markowitz, H.M., 'Portfolio Selection', *The Journal of Finance*, 1952, pp 71–92.
Mossin, J., 'Equilibrium in a Capital Asset Market', *Econometrica*, October 1966, pp 768–83.
Rodriguez, R.M. and Carter E.E., *International Financial Management*, 3rd edn, Prentice Hall, 1984.
Roll, R., 'A Critique of the Asset Pricing Theory's Tests', *Journal of Financial Economics*, March 1977, pp 129–76.
Sharpe, W.F., 'Capital Asset Prices: A Theory of Market Equilibrium under Conditions of Risk', *Journal of Finance*, September 1964, pp 425–42.
Solnick, B.H., 'Why not Diversify Internationally Rather than Domestically?', *Financial Analysts Journal*, vol 30, 1974, pp 48–54.

**Further reading on techniques for financial managers**

Belongia, M.T. and Santoni, G.J., 'Hedging Interest Rate with Financial Futures: Some Basic Principles', *Federal Reserve Bank of St. Louis Review*, (USA), vol 66, no 8, October 1984, pp 15–25.
Brealey, R. and Myers, S., *Principles of Corporate Finance*, 2nd edn, McGraw Hill, 1984.
Brown, C.T. and Gardener, E.P.M., 'Financial Futures – New Tools to Tackle Old Problems?', *Accountancy* (UK), vol 94, no 1008, December 1983, pp 113–16.
Brunner, T., 'Currency Options in the Service of Exchange Rate Hedging', *Credit Suisse Bulletin*, vol 90, autumn 1984, pp 12–13.
Discepolo, A.J. and Burchett, S.B., 'The Long Hedge is Here to Stay', *Euromoney* (UK), March 1984, pp 195–6.
Fabozzi, F.J. and Zarb, F.G., *Handbook of Financial Markets: Securities, Options and Futures*, Dow Jones–Irwin, Illinois, 1981.
Frankel, A.B., 'Interest Rate Futures: An Innovation in Financial Techniques for the Management of Risks', *Bank for International Settlements Economic Papers*, no 12, September 1984, pp 1–24.
George A.M. and Giddy I.H. (eds), *International Finance Handbook*, (vols I and II), Wiley-Interscience, 1983.
Goodman, L.S., 'New Options Markets', *Federal Reserve Bank of New York Quarterly Review*, autumn 1983, pp 56–60.
Howard, C.T. and D'Antonio, L.J. 'A Risk-Return Measure of Hedging Effectiveness', *Journal of Financial and Quantitative Analysis* (USA), vol 19, no 1, March 1984, pp 101–12.

Pippenger, J.E., *Fundamentals of International Finance*, Prentice Hall International, 1984.
Powers, M. and Vogel D., *Inside the Financial Futures Market*, 2nd edn, John Wiley and Sons, 1984.
Rothestein, N.H. and Little, J.M., *Handbook of Financial Futures*, McGraw-Hill Book Co, 1984.

# 10 Informational and technological aspects

The amount, nature and speed of information available to marketeers and market users is an important aspect of and a driving force behind the internationalisation of stockmarkets. Much of the growth of international financing and investment has to do with technological change in the information processing and transmission industry. The more information is available, the more able is the market to arrive at fair prices so that current prices reflect current values of the securities for sale and purchase. Indeed, the external efficiency of markets is measured in terms of the ability of stock prices to reflect information. If all information on past price movements is reflected in stock prices, the market is said to be weak-form efficient. If stock prices reflect all publicly available information, then the market is semi-strong efficient. If stock prices reflect all information (which would render inside information on particular firms useless), the market is said to be strong-form efficient. Internal efficiency, too, is improved with up-to-date electronic links between markets and the people and institutions that use them. For markets to become efficient on an international scale it is important, therefore, that financial newspapers, computer links, and the host of other information services should be able to operate freely and wthout interference from influential pressure groups. The needs for worldwide up-to-date information extends not only to matters concerning individual securities but also to matters concerning whole markets. Time and effort spent by market authorities on informing market users across the globe of the existence, nature and progress of their respective markets has the effect of raising market efficiency worldwide. Instant communication across the globe is already bringing borrowers and lenders closer together.

As might have been expected, private interests are leading the informational and technological revolution in world stockmarkets. The scope for providing information services is increasing. For trading and clearing securities, banks and market organisations have shown great willingnesss to take up new automated facilities developed by private computer firms. Alternatively, impetus and expertise for installing the new systems has arisen from inside the markets themselves. As a result, dealing and settlement has become quicker and more reliable and the amount of uncertainty and ignorance has decreased. The future dissemination of information across the world will be determined largely by the climate for freedom of the press and by political factors. Given minimum needs for secrecy, maximum freedom of the press and continued technological development, a highly sophisticated, instantaneous, worldwide information system should arise naturally enough out of the free-market system.

## Market intelligence: the need to keep up-to-date

The desire for worldwide information and the desire to invest and finance across national borders feed off each other. Information on markets promotes their usage and the needs of internationally-oriented traders stimulates a real demand for more information. The amount of required information increases with the number of markets that are accessible to marketeers, borrowers and investors. Borrowers, for example, would ideally like to have real time information on nominal interest rates worldwide, exchange rates, flotation fees, transactions costs, taxes, channels for funds transmission and a host of other statistics for making more informed decisions. The better their knowledge, the cheaper it will be to secure the required capital. Investors, too, benefit from up-to-date information so that they can ensure the highest possible returns on their capital for any desired level of risk-taking.

Virtually every leading newspaper – such as the London *Financial Times* and the New York *Wall Street Journal* – provides a report

processing, and high-technology clearing systems has increased banking efficiency and brought about further integration of the world's financial markets. For large and giant banks the new technology means improved coordination of domestic and overseas branches, high-speed feedback on national and international developments, and speedier interaction with the markets. The old style telephones and telexes are being phased out and replaced with electronic equipment that links branches to central bank and central bank to the market.

Automated clearing systems have been in use since the 1970s. Clearing systems remove the need for banks to present cheques or make transfers directly to each other by providing facilities for settling accumulated lists of the transactions on a net basis through a central bank. An example of such a system is provided by CHIPS (Clearing House Interbank Payments System), which has been operated since 1970 by the New York Clearing House. CHIPS operates between 7.00 am and 4.30 pm with a final settlement at the Federal Reserve at 6.00 pm. A dozen full-member banks use the system for sending and receiving payments advices and for linking with a much larger number of associated-member banks. Most of the associate-members are overseas branches of US banks which can send and receive messages and payments via their own computer terminals. A similar system – CHAPS (Clearing House Automated Payments System) – operates in the UK.

SWIFT (Society for Worldwide Interbank Telecommunications) provides another example of a high-tech banking facility. Formed by banks in Western Europe and the USA in 1973, SWIFT is jointly owned and non-profitmaking and provides an interbank system for carrying information about financial transactions. The system has been upgraded over the years and is now available in Europe, the USA, Asia and Latin America. By 1984 SWIFT had over 1,000 member banks operating in over 40 countries of the world. The enlarged membership has led to economies of scale so that smaller countries – such as Taiwan, which joined SWIFT in 1984 – can afford to link into the system. It is estimated that start-up costs for SWIFT can now be recouped in only three years. One effect of widespread use of SWIFT is a movement towards standardised automation procedures in the processing departments of member banks. Flexibility of operations can still be achieved, however, via member banks' in-house processing systems. Some members have even introduced facilities for customers who can afford the necessary computer equipment to use the facility for their own cash management purposes. Money transfers are becoming faster and errors fewer as the system is updated.

Besides the banks' private systems, most banks, particularly those engaged in international operations, also have machines linking them to the older TELEX system. TELEX provides not one information network but a series of interconnected networks run by different companies across the world. Although the TELEX system follows no standard format, individual banks (or groups of banks) can arrange their own internal systems to suit their own purposes.

For lending operations, too, the amount of information and data services for banking is increasing. Computerised techniques (such as multiple discriminant analysis (MDA) and Z-scores) are available for assessing credit risks. For the larger banks, facilities such as those provided by the Institute of International Finance (IIF) are available to provide information on sovereign borrowers. The IIF provides member banks with information on up to 50 developing countries via online computer terminals and printed country reports.

The most visible signs of change, however, are in the field of retail banking where, in an attempt to lower costs, high speed electronic transfers are now being used for payments services. Automatic teller machines (ATMs) are becoming increasingly used to provide customers with a 24 hour, seven days per week sevice. Even in Japan the increasingly affluent society is putting pressure on the banking industry to give the automatic teller a much larger role. Latest developments include home banking facilities and point-of-sale terminals in supermarkets. To the banking customer these developments mean lower transaction costs and easier facilities for shifting funds between uses according to going rates of return. In the wake of the technological progress, behavioural changes in the way people manage money are beginning to occur and the populace as a whole is beginning to feel more aware of financial processes. On a larger scale, corporations with direct links to the banks now have facilities for managing cash flows and investing surpluses in short-term maturities with increased efficiency.

The overall effect of the new banking technology is that interest rates for borrowers and lenders come nearer and nearer to that which is appropriate according to current market conditions. Faster communications between customers, banks and financial centres ensure that, except where market imperfections exist, capital moves quickly to where it can earn the highest return, ironing out differences between rates of return for similar financial instruments and securities.

One potential threat to the banking system as we know it should perhaps be mentioned. It is possible that new electronic information technology could overthrow the current masters of the deposit-taking business because non-bank institutions armed with the new technology – in particular, ATMs – find it easy to increase their share of the business. The advent of ATMs means that it is no longer necessary for deposit-takers to have an expensive network of high-class properties situated in prime positions nationally and internationally. An electronic box on a street corner or near the check-out at a supermarket is all this is required. With such stiff competition one can be sure that the banking system will continue to adopt the new technology at pace.

## Information technology for the markets

In this section some of the most important market clearing and information systems are described in (approximately) historical order – from the 1950s to 1986. An exact chronology is difficult because some of the systems have non-high-tech origins and have become increasingly computerised over the years. None of the systems described have reached a static state of development. New information stores and programming subroutines are continually being devised to cope with the changing marketplace. The following list is selective covering some of the developments in the USA, UK, Tokyo, France, Luxembourg and Belgium. They are chosen either because they are already installed or because firm plans for their installation are currently under way. A much larger list of information systems would have resulted if they were selected from the multitude of suggestions for potential new systems put forward by specialist computer hardware and software firms, which are attempting to enter the market intelligence industry.

### *SICOVAM*

An example of an early stock exchange clearing system is provided by the French Société Interprofessionelle pour la Compensation des Valeurs Mobilères (SICOVAM) created in 1949. The system, which now operates both nationally and internationally is the most important clearing system in France and is subject to control by the Ministry of the Economy. Around 70 per cent of securities quoted on the Paris stock exchange are deposited with SICOVAM and facilities are also available for handling registered foreign securities. Functions carried out by SICOVAM include the opening of accounts for securities on behalf of member stockbrokers and banks, the receipt of deposits for French bearer securities, registration of foreign nominative securities, provision of links with foreign clearing systems, and arrangements for transfer of ownership. For foreign securities, SICOVAM now has links with Amsterdam, Belgium and Tokyo and it is possible that further international links will be forged in the future.

*NASDAQ*

The National Association of Securities Dealers' Automated Quotation System (NASDAQ), the US over-the-counter market, links around 6,000 dealers. Exact, instantaneous wholesale price quotations are provided nationwide from all the dealers who make the market for over-the-counter stocks. The system works so quickly and efficiently through electronic links that the need to make arrangements by telephone has been virtually eliminated. In fact, NASDAQ is, in terms of volume of transactions, the fastest growing stock exchange in the world.

The origins of NASDAQ go back to 1971 when computer screens were first used to convey price information. As a method for bringing together the previously unorganised arrangements for small stocks, which were unable to be listed on a main stock exchange, the system was an immediate success. By 1974 annual turnover was up to a billion shares, and by 1983 turnover was up to 16 billion shares. Today the system lists around 4,000 shares with a market value of around $200 billion.

In 1979 the National Market System (NMS) was developed to provide NASDAQ users with improved information on transactions. Information on the most actively traded NASDAQ shares includes best bid and offer quotes, last trade information, and the actual price in the market. Market-makers must honour the prices that appear on the screens. A second level of access to NASDAQ provides information on the market, rather than particular stocks. A third level of access, still under development, is known as the Computer Assisted Executive System (CAES) and aims to enable traders up to 3,000 miles away to buy and sell shares via computer terminals. The NASDAQ system is highly regarded in stockmarkets across the world and serves as a model for systems installed in other countries.

*INSTINET*

INSTINET provides a screen-based trading system for US stocks on either NASDAQ or other exchanges. The system carries bid and offer prices for around 3,500 US stocks and there are plans to extend the system abroad to the UK and West German stock exchanges (although it is competing for acceptance with SEAQ in the UK).

*Euroclear*

The Euroclear Clearance System plc handles the greater part of international bond trading activity. It is a cooperative owned by 120 shareholders, each of which is restricted to a maximum holding of 3 per cent of the shares. The number of participants in the system (mainly financial institutions but also several large corporations) is currently around 1,500. The present system grew out of a previous system installed in 1968 by the Morgan Guaranty Trust Company and is an important guardian of market efficiency. A network of depository banks ensures the safety of the 10,000–plus securities denominated in around 20 currencies handled by the system, which provides a link between Europe, USA, Far East, Middle East and Canada. The depository banks also provide services such as facilities for currency conversion and coupon payments. Operations are run from the Euroclear Operation Centre in Brussels in such a way that only around 5 per cent of the securities handled actually require physical transfer.

The older Euroclear system relied on telexes for communications but nowadays validation and upkeep of accounts is performed by an electrical communications system known as EUCLID. Participants in the system are provided with visual display units (VDUs), which, besides facilitating operations, offer an automatic security system because the information on the seller's VDU and the buyer's VDU must match exactly before a deal can go ahead.

A new facility has operated on the Euroclear system since June 1983. This allows automatic borrowing and lending in order to speed up operations and increase market efficiency. Bond borrowing can now operate smoothly from a pool of securities that are available for automatic lending to selected market participants.

Plans for the future for Euroclear include a system for clearing internationally traded equity securities and, possibly, an over-the-counter market.

*Cedel*

Cedel provides a similar service to Euroclear but is financed by Citibank and based in Luxembourg. Like Euroclear, Cedel facilitates and reduces the cost of international trading and makes the transfer of securities between buyer and seller a simple book-keeping operation.

*TALISMAN*

In 1979 the UK stock exchange introduced Transfer Accounting, Lodgement for Investors, Stock Management for Jobbers (TALISMAN) – a computerised settlement system for buying and selling company securities from a central pool. Before the introduction of TALISMAN, sellers would hold onto securities as long as possible before making a transaction. Now, however, securities can be predelivered from sellers via the jobbers to a nominee company (SEPON), which pools securities for delivery at a later date. The advantages of the system include cost savings, more dealings and speedier settlements (the system can handle up to 45,000 transactions per day). Already the major proportion of UK broking firms are linked into the TALISMAN system but there is still room for expansion and, as development costs are recouped, the service becomes less expensive and more affordable for smaller broking offices. Development of TALISMAN keeps pace with the times. For example, plans are now being made to adapt the system for the emergence of the broker-dealers in the UK market. A large reprogramming exercise is underway because the system no longer needs to recognise that brokers and jobbers have separate roles.

*EPIC and Topic*

EPIC is two computers that are at the heart of the UK stock exchange's market information systems. Essentially, the computers' main jobs are to share and disseminate information fed in by 25 price reporters monitoring over 3,000 securities. The central information bank can transfer information onto other computers such as Hotline, Valueline, Reuters, Datastream and Prestel's Citiservice, which pass on the data, at a price, to customers. EPIC also makes its computerised information available to the stock exchange's Topic Screen network, which currently includes around 2,500 Topic terminals.

*SEAQ*

Stock Exchange Automated Quotation System (SEAQ) is the system that currently is expected to replace the Topic system for the UK stock exchange. The new system will link office and floor traders receiving quotations and trade reports from those who are making the market. Individual direct computer links to SEAQ will be available, via terminals, for in-house computers owned by the market-makers. Different levels of access will be available to satisfy various user needs. The work will be shared between SEAQ and the older Topic system so that SEAQ provides a means for quotations and trade reports whilst Topic will continue to disseminate competing quotations to members. Future plans for SEAQ include a central limit order book, which could automatically execute orders when prices move far enough in the desired direction, and fully interactive terminal facilities.

*CORES*

The Computer-assisted Order Routing and Executive System (CORES) is a recent technical innovation on the Tokyo Stock Exchange. The system was partially implemented in 1983 (for 430 stocks) and a second stage of implementation (to cover a further 750 stocks) was implemented in May 1985. As a trade-matching system for stock exchange members, CORES has virtually replaced the need for face-to-face trading for a large segment of the market. The system also provides stock exchange members with information on stocks, turnover and market conditions. Despite its sophistication, CORES does not yet cover the 250 most actively traded stocks on the Tokyo exchange, nor does it allow access for non-member firms of the exchange. Plans to extend the CORES system are not included in the present liberalisation package system for the Japanese financial system.

*INTEX*

INTEX is a Bermuda-based, completely automated system for futures trading. The idea for INTEX originated in the USA in 1981 and, after years of development, there are now plans to extend the system worldwide. When (if) the extended system becomes operational, futures dealers across the world will be able to watch the market from visual display units, tap buy and sell instructions into their terminals, and execute their transactions within two or three seconds. After the transaction, parties to each end of the deal would receive confirmation of the deal on computer print-outs. Operations would be controlled by processors located in London, Bermuda and Hamilton via high-speed communication links. The intention is to start INTEX operations with dealing facilities for gold, US treasury bonds, freight and silver futures – trading in which currently reaches around 40 million contracts per year. Eventually, the designers and sponsors of INTEX hope that the system will become international, offering a much wider range of contracts 24 hours per day.

### Electronic information services for fund managers

Fund managers are late beneficiaries of the last 30 years of technological revolution. Up-to-the-second information on prices, at one time, ended behind the doors of the dealing rooms. Now, however, things are changing with more and more computer software firms experimenting with new products aimed at catching the fund managers' interest. Leaders in the electronic information industry include Reuters, Quotron, Datastream and Telerate but there is room for competition by smaller, specialist firms. Until now, the information sources available directly to fund managers have been geared mainly towards coverage of daily prices – and these were wiped from the screen at the end of the day. The systems now under development provide facilities for sharing and processing data in various analytical forms. Pie charts, graphical comparisons, Beta calculations, search facilities, trend analysis, bar charts, ratio analysis and other forms of data manipulation will soon be as available to the fund manager as to the experts whom they consult. International electrical information systems could also figure in the near future for fund managers, thus providing a useful aid to international financial activities.

### Personal finance computer links

Whilst the banks and markets improve their communications and information systems, small investors are not being left out. Several countries have already conducted successful home banking experiments which, one day, will link a large proportion of small savers to their banks and, possibly, to the markets themselves via their television screens. Large banks, such as the Chemical Bank in New York (which has around 15,000 subscribers), the Bank of America in California (10,000 subscribers) and the UK's Midland Bank (around 1,000 subscribers) are leading the experiments but other institutions, such as the UK's Nottingham Building Society, are also offering home banking services. Facilities offered by present systems include a visual display of the last, say, 120 bank statement entries, a check on standing orders, facilities for paying bills and limited facilities for swapping cash between current and interest-bearing accounts. The systems currently offered do not yet extend to the payment of cheques, payment of cash or transfer of funds for more than a limited range of investment opportunities. Home banking is, however, still in its infancy and may one day extend to link individual and small savers to world markets. Other examples of access to markets from the home include home dealing in stocks (for example, Hoare Govett's 'Stock-watch' – a file on Prestel's Citiservice).

### Secrecy laws – the final barrier?

It was mentioned earlier in the chapter that governments, rather than technologists, would be the main constraint on worldwide transmission of information in the future. Secrecy is an aspect of information dispersion that is soon likely to attract increased attention. Already governments are faced with problems caused by countries such as Switzerland, France and the UK, which have secrecy and blocking laws aimed at restricting certain classes of financial information. An example of information that may currently be blocked is provided by documents located in a particular country at the request of a foreign court. Secrecy laws may also apply to matters such as the disclosure of business records or the identity of bank customers. It is likely that the future could see increased blocking of information by governments, which may find such activities the last line of defence after being swept along with trends towards easing of restrictions on markets and financial institutions. As when considering the cases for free or restricted financial markets, it is difficult to weigh up the pros and cons of restrictions on information. On the one hand, secrecy laws can protect individuals, organisations and markets. On the other hand, they can encourage fraud and reduce the efficiency of world markets. The topic is too complex to be dealt with in further detail here. Discussion and a more comprehensive examination of the subject is likely to follow in the financial newspapers and journals in the near future. Meanwhile, the USA is currently waving the banner for complete freedom of information.

### Summary

Information and communications technology is bringing about major structural and functional changes in the financial markets.

The range of new market services is extending rapidly, led by a new information technology industry. Developments such as microchips and satellites mean that information is becoming available more cheaply, and more quickly (instantaneously). Software firms are finding more and more ways of serving the information needs of the many different kinds of operators in the markets. The banks are linked more closely now than ever before and the technology they have introduced has extended to the man in the street (or at home) via automatic teller machines and home banking services. In the markets, dealing and settlement have become quicker and more reliable. The race now on is to speed up the transactions side of the business so that it can keep up with the instantaneous reactions of the price and monitor screens. Instantaneous worldwide communication is already possible. Costs of the new technology are falling. The last stage in the story of worldwide information systems will be decided by governments, which must now ask themselves, 'Are we ready for complete freedom of information?'

**Further reading on market technology and financial information systems**


Barron, M.J., 'Microcomputers, Financial Statement Analysis and the Data Needs of Financial Analysts', *Accounting and Business Research* (UK), vol 14, no 56, autumn 1984, pp 291–309.

Collyns, C. and Horiguchi, Y., 'Financial Supermarkets in the United States', *Finance and Development* (United Nations), vol 21, no 1, March 1984, pp 18–22.

Donovan, J.F., 'The Impact on Industry of New Banking Technology', *Journal of the Institute of Bankers in Ireland*, vol 86, no 3, July 1984, pp 134–43.

Dordick, H.S., 'The Emerging World Information Industry', *Economic Impact* (USA), no 46, 1984, pp 66–73.

'Exploring Telecommunications Alternatives', *ABA Banking Journal* (USA), vol 77, no 2, February 1985, pp 52–5.

Kirchner, E.J., Hewlett, N. and Sobirey, F., 'Report on the Social Implications of Introducing New Technology in the Banking Sector', *Commission of the European Communities*, 1984.

Koch D.L., 'The Emerging Financial Services Industry: Challenges and Innovation', *Federal Reserve Bank of Atlanta Economic Review* (USA), vol 69, no 4, April 1984, pp 25–30.

Laidlaw, A., 'EFT and the Law', *Banking World* (UK), vol 3, no 3, March 1985, pp 39–40.

Lim, Q.P., 'Trading Stocks Across Frontiers', *Euromoney* (UK), May 1984, pp 110–12.
Loviton, C., '2004: Memories of the Future', *Transition Journal of Financial Service Strategy* (USA), vol 4, no 9, November 1984, pp 28–32.
'New Challenges: International Operations and Information Technology', *EEC Epargne Europe Bulletin*, no 521, April 1984, pp 1–2.
Siobhan, H., 'Deregulation: Plugging In for the "Big Bang"', *The Banker* (UK), vol 134, no 705, November 1984, pp 85–8.
'The One-World Capital Market', *Euromoney* (UK), October 1984.
Winder, R., 'The Final Days of the Trading Floor', *Euromoney* (UK), October 1984, pp 80–91.
Winder, R., 'Forget the Service: It's The Data We Want', *Euromoney* (UK), October 1984, pp 97–103.
Witt, H.J., 'Technology and Banking in the Years to Come', *World of Banking* (USA), vol 4, no 2, March/April 1985, pp 12–16.
Wooden, J.H., 'The Financial Services Business in Perspective', *Bankers Magazine* (USA), vol 167, no 2, March/April 1984, pp 28–31.
Wriston, W., 'The Information Standard', *Euromoney* (UK), October 1984, pp 92–5.

# 11 Summary, conclusions and potential future developments

This, the last chapter, is not the final chapter in the story for the internationalisation of money and capital markets. Many of the driving forces and contributory influences that have brought about the phenomena, and the effects felt by the many participants in the world's financial system, have already been documented. The remaining tasks are to provide a summary of what has happened to date and some pointers for the future. The summary re-covers the key changes that have occurred in the financial markets over the past 20 years. Providing a realistic outlook for the future is a little more problematic since none of it has yet happened. History is a less-than-perfect indicator of future events. The approach taken, therefore, is to look at developments that are currently up for discussion, under consideration or under way in the financial markets and in the financial institutions and point out where they are likely to lead if followed to their logical conclusions. Whilst not providing a clear-cut vision of the future, this will at least draw readers' attention to the key issues at stake so that they may formulate their own likely scenario.

**The internationalisation of money and capital markets: A review of the process to date**

The process of financial innovation, structural and functional modifications in the money and capital markets, deregulation, technical innovations, greater lending and borrowing and increasing competition in the 1970s and 1980s has led to a significant change in the financial marketplaces in the world. It is sometimes said that markets have no memory but it is unlikely that the same will be said of the history books of the future, which will look back on the events that have occurred in the financial markets during the past 20 years as an important chapter in the story of mankind. The main events and their implications for the markets, the banks and other financial institutions, the non-financial institutions, the financial managers, and the man in the street are as follows.

*Erosion of barriers between markets*

Demand for capital at the right price remains high in the 1980s among both developed and developing nations as the world seeks its way out of the deepest recession since the 1930s. Consequently, huge volumes of money, capital and securities continue to pass through the domestic and international financial marketplaces. Some are in a stronger position than others to influence events both at an international level through political persuasion or at a domestic level through controls (or lack of them) on cross-border trafficking of money and capital. In the present climate, deregulation abounds – both within banking systems and in the wider world financial system. Where deregulation is not occurring fast enough, the international banks, markets and corporations find further means and justification for profitable existence by setting up new markets outside the jurisdiction of governments. Within markets where, at one time, it was possible to clearly distinguish between domestic and foreign sections, and credit and capital sections, the barriers are being eroded in response to competition and free-market forces. The problem for market regulators has become either to gain control over the external markets, which are largely the cause of the changes, or to moderate domestic restrictions in order to bring the domestic markets more in line with their external counterparts.

*Increased exposure to international economic forces*

The effect of increased exposure to the external financial markets has been increased exposure to international economic forces and increased volatility of exchange rates in comparison to the years before the abandonment of exchange controls in the 1970s. The markets' answer to the problems of exchange rate and interest rate volatility has been a new range of financial instruments, techniques and facilities for trading in the essentially uncertain environment so that, at an acceptable price, immunisation against exchange rate and interest rate volatility can be purchased. Performance of the new facilities has been enough to avoid a reduction in the amount of overseas trading and investment.

*Movement towards freer markets*

Leading the movement towards freer marketplaces worldwide has been the USA, the dollar, the Eurodollar and the innovations occurring in US markets. Challengers for the lead role include Western Europe (because of its potential international influence when it has reconciled the internal problems of the many countries and varied political approaches that currently constitute the EEC) and Japan (because of the size of its markets if its progress towards financial liberation proceeds to the heart of its financial system). Latecomers, who may yet play a larger role in the movement towards freer markets, are the Less Developed Countries (LDCs).

*Harmonisation and improvement of professional standards*

Across the world, professional standards for dealing with financial matters are improving in line with methodological and technological advances. There is increasing recognition of the need to provide information and services that are equally acceptable to domestic and foreign clients. The accounting profession, for example, continues its quest for truer and fairer ways of providing investors and other interested parties with the financial information that they require, and it has set up channels for discussion on international accounting standards. Professionals in the markets continue to raise listing standards, find more effective ways to reduce insider trading, improve trading floor supervision, provide more effective information and clearing systems, and extend the range of securities traded. Information and security for the foreign investor is becoming more and more similar to that available for domestic investors.

*Wider access to markets*

The range of people who can take an interest in the world's financial markets has been extended. At one time wealth constraints meant that only those who could afford to buy and sell securities could take a chance on the market. Nowadays, with innovations such as stock options and index options, taking a financial interest in the market can cost as little as a bet on a horse. The extension of market facilities to more and more levels of society increases consciousness of financial affairs among the populace of many countries, reducing the distinction between 'them' and 'us'. The free market system is increasingly likely to be viewed as operating to the potential advantage of all, rather than of the few. Other repercussions for the man in the street from the internationalisation of stockmarkets include international cheque cards, home banking facilities, and a much wider range of financial services accessible in the high street branches of the financial institutions, from a machine at the back of the supermarket or on the street corner – or from an armchair in the home.

*Increased flexibility of intermediation techniques*

The financial markets' role is changing from that of providing a channel for different types of credits and securities to that of a melting pot in which any combination of risk, expected return and liquidity can be accommodated at the right price. Within the banking system, for example, domestic banking has been superseded by international banking which, in turn, has given rise to multinational banking. Increased competition between the banks, technological developments and liquidity problems resulting from the debt crisis have led to a further range of financial instruments which complement those developed in the stockmarkets. The distinction between a credit instument and a security, as a result, has become blurred with the evolution of revolving underwriting facilities (RUFs) and note-issuing facilities (NIFs) in the Euronote market.

Increasingly, intermediaries, in their role as financial tailors, are prepared to cut the cloth to measure rather than offer ready-made, off-the-peg financial instruments. Where markets and financial institutions have been slow to respond to changing financial needs, industry itself has become equipped for accessing the required funds, fixed or floating rate, at competitive prices. The swap principle allows floating rate debt to be exchanged for fixed interest obligations incurred by another borrower. The facility is now extending to second and third class credit risks. Commercial banks continue to provide floating rate debt in the full knowledge that it is likely to be 'swapped' – thus contributing further to the fluidity of the financial markets' melting pot.

*Changing roles for the international institutions*

Within international institutions such as the IMF and the World Bank discussions are now in progress aimed at curbing the effects of the debt crisis and reconciling individual countries' needs for protectionism or free markets. At the IMF, the system that has been flexible enough to cope with developments during the last 40 years is now under scrutiny for its continued suitability following the deregulatory explosion and market innovations of the 1980s. One of the relatively new innovations, the Special Drawing Right (SDR) is being actively promoted as the new international reserve asset for the international financial system because of its representativeness of global interests. At the World Bank attempts at guiding private capital for world development are under way to supplement its own lending activities. If these attempts succeed, the interests of governments, private corporations and individuals will become interlinked with the needs of the LDCs and the movement towards freer markets.

*The nature of money is changing*

The system of one country, one currency, no longer applies. With the advent of 'cocktail' currencies there are now more currencies than there are countries – and, for the international monetary system, the newly devised currencies are proving extremely popular. The dollar is still the main currency of international finance but its position may well one day be challenged by a 'cocktail' currency such as the European Currency Unit (ECU).

*Versatility and new techniques for financial managers*

Perhaps the most influential, yet least documented contributory force towards the internationalisation process has been not the changes in the markets and the financial system but the changes in the attitudes of financial managers. Their willingness and ability to look outside their domestic financial environments in search of profitable opportunities overseas has been one of the most important influences on market innovation and change. The basic role of financial managers to seek out maximum returns for minimum risk taking is a prerequisite for corporations, markets, banks and, indeed, the rest of the financial system. Nowadays, financial managers have a wider range of alternatives for fulfilling this role and satisfying their employers' or clients' needs. For financial managers engaged in overseas operations the onus has been on them to master a host of new techniques for identifying profitable opportunities and for dealing with the inconvenient effects of volatile interest rates and exchange rates. The new techniques include forecasting foreign exchange rates, internal control procedures for multi-currency operations, risk assessment and hedging techniques, and new techniques for capital budgeting and investment analysis in an international setting. Continued mobility of capital across national borders will remain dependent on the ability of financial managers successfully to use and improve the new techniques.

## The future?

'Where is it all leading?' is always an important and timely question since, just as the number of possible answers is infinite, so is the number of strategies available to mankind for dealing with the situation. With the internationalisation of money and capital markets, the need is to contemplate developments on a world scale and examine key issues likely to affect the affairs of many nations so that the future can be managed towards the benefit of all those concerned. Key issues falling into this category include the future for the Euromarkets (because of their size and wide geographical spread), the future for the developing countries (because, via the debt crisis and trade links, developments in those countries have implications for the rest of the world), and the future for the international monetary system. The outlooks for these vehicles of change, along with the general outlook for the mobility of money and capital around the world, are now examined.

### *The future for the Eurobond market*

'Will the Eurobond market die?' is a question presently on the lips of many European bankers. The question has come and gone several times before in the history of the market. This time it has arisen in response to the US repeal of withholding taxes. The fear is that, just as introduction of regulations helped create the market, the removal of the same regulations could help destroy it. Current concern over the US deregulatory move is, in some respects, therefore, just another shade of a recurrent phenomenum, although the size of the sums involved this time could have a more significant impact than on previous occasions. Optimistic Eurobankers take cheer in the memory that a previous, equally significant deregulatory move, the removal of the Interest Equalisation

Tax in 1974, was too late to halt the march of the Euromarkets. Why should the removal of the withholding tax in 1984 be any different? Besides, the Euromarket would lose to the dollar market only if similar interest rates were offered for similar risk levels and if the dollar market should continue to hold a competitive advantage. Further strength is lent to the future of the Euromarkets by the increasing popularity of bonds denominated in currencies other than dollars. The increasing demand for the ECU and other currency 'cocktails' for denominating bonds has already been documented. With strengthening links between EEC countries, the future may also see increasing use of European Eurocurrencies for denominating bonds. It would seem improbable therefore that the Eurobond market would completely disappear in the near future; there would still be room for a small Euromarket. There would also remain a need for a Eurobond secondary market for a decade or two – even if no new issues came onto the market.

Returning to the issue of deregulation and its effect on the Euromarket, it is here (if anywhere) that the seeds of destruction for the long-term future of the Euromarkets are sown. Whilst there is still a regulatory distinction between domestic and external segments of financial markets, there is room for a Euromarket. If the regulatory distinction is removed, then the demand for the Euromarket disappears. Another way of viewing such a development is that, if the domestic markets deregulate, they all become part of the Euromarket. Deregulation is, seen in this light, a threat to the Euromarkets but not a threat to the internationalisation of money and capital. If the deregulatory trend continues, there would be structural and geographical changes that might cause some concern for particular operators in financial markets – but the internationalisation process would just keep rolling along.

### *The future for the developing countries*

LDCs need to protect their economies and provide a sounder footing for growth. Only mature economies feel secure enough to open up their capital markets to the rest of the world. The implication is that, unless economic development can be assured, the internationalisation of stockmarkets will stop at the doors of the LDCs.

In order to improve the economic positions of the LDCs and increase the likelihood of open-door financial policies, there are two sources of help to which the LDCs can turn – self-help and international help – both aimed at economic growth. Despite political and social problems in many countries, motivation for self-help remains strong in the LDCs. With regard to international help, there is room for better understanding between industrial countries and the LDCs. Many LDCs may still cling to the idea that foreign investment is a form of exploitation and a threat to the domestic political system. The internationalisation of capital markets along with Coca-Cola, commercial radio and other aspects of modern civilisation do, without doubt, lead to cultural change – for better or worse – but there is not necessarily a threat to national sovereignty. Unless this fear can be removed, the LDCs are likely to continue to enforce restrictions that repel foreign investment and lengthen the process of economic recovery. Meanwhile, the only course of action for the industrial countries in Western Europe and the US is to encourage and wait, and, in the meantime, to support the developing countries in their growing pains if at all feasible.

One of the best ways to encourage investment, trade and aid to flow to the LDCs is through further channelling of funds by international financial intermediaries. Such organisations may be set up on the initiative of the LDCs (individually or jointly) or by the industrial countries to their mutual benefit. There is a case for more financial intermediaries for channelling funds towards the developing countries under a wide range of political ideologies. Socialists would argue from a moral viewpoint that aid, possibly in the form of cheaper-than-average funds, should be available for building up the economic infrastructure of under-developed countries in the name of equality. Capitalists, also arguing from a moral point of view, would support the need for more information about profitable opportunities in the LDCs in the name of the free market system. Either way there is a need for intermediaries. The system of finance currently furnished by the World Bank and its subsidiaries cuts across political ideologies offering, on the one hand, cheap loan facilities for the developing countries and, on the other hand, information and profitable opportunities for prospective investors. The internationalisation of stockmarkets could, foreseeably, provide a further incentive for the provision of such facilities. Ultimately the future of the LDCs will be determined by the degree of confidence felt by these countries towards Western capitalism or Eastern communism, because it is towards these two main political creeds that the developing countries can turn in their struggle for growth. In the name of world peace and the continued existence of the free market system, developed industrial countries cannot afford to lose developing countries and their productive resources to advocates of the centrally planned economy. This thought alone should provide political motivation at an international level to maintain mutually acceptable financial and trade links with the LDCs, along with the necessary intermediaries.

From the point of view of the industrial countries, a particularly significant factor influencing present attitudes is the debt crisis that has given bankers in the US and Western Europe great cause for concern. International dialogue arrived at drawing up new and realistic repayment schedules is much in evidence amongst banks, LDCs and international organisations. Proposals put forward to solve the problem are numerous – the Barclays scheme, the Lever scheme, the Morgan Grenfell scheme, the Zombanakis proposal, the Soros proposal, the Soloman proposal, the *Economist*'s proposal, the Rohatyn scheme, the Menen proposal, and the Weinert proposal (see *Amex Bank Review*, vol 2, no 5, June 1984 for further details) to name but a few. Despite the political risks, it is likely that the world's bankers will eventually find an acceptable course of action and that lending to and investment in LDCs will continue into the 1990s and probably also into the twenty-first century if industrialisation is not to be rushed. Reasons why capital is likely to continue to flow to the developing countries include the following.

1 Shortfalls of domestic savings in LDCs have led to a strong demand for external development capital. (This capital would be more easily attracted if restrictive legislation was eased.)
2 Most of the lenders presently caught up in the debt crisis (mainly the banks) have already opted for restructuring of loans and debt servicing arrangements as the way out of their predicament. The alternative would have been to incur enormous bad debts. Thus, in order to avoid the possibility of non-repayment of interest and/or capital, lenders must now offer even more capital in the hope of economic growth for the LDCs and eventual repayment for themselves. Shrewd lending policies backed up with directives are the order of the day and, hopefully, the result will be the economic growth required by the LDCs.
3 One of the main difficulties for the LDCs for paying off their debts has been falling prices for the raw materials they produce following the price boom of 1976 and 1977. This trend need not continue and the future could see higher prices from their trading activities leading to healthier current account balances and incentives for further lending to and investment in the LDCs. A successful end to the economic recession among the industrial countries leading to stronger demand for imported raw materials would have the desired effect on export prices for the LDCs.

4 Although many LDCs have suffered in the past from OPEC price rises, there is an opposite side to the coin. LDC deficits are balanced by surpluses for OPEC countries, which must now find investment opportunities for the funds they have amassed. At least some of this surplus is likely to be recycled into industrial activities in the LDCs.

5 The giant banks have traditionally been the lenders to LDCs but now there are moves afoot to encourage international lending and investment in the LDCs from both private and public entities. Spurred by the knowledge that, in the long run, only growth of LDC economies will assure repayment for existing debt, the banks and financial authorities of developed nations have seen fit to encourage the transfer of private capital to LDCs via the following types of arangements:

- Improvement of country-risk evaluation techniques.
- Pooling of information by lenders already caught up in the debt crisis.
- Contingency planning by lenders (individual and collective) for encouraging further lending.
- More information links between LDC borrowers themselves and between LDC borrowers and lenders.
- Discussion often leading to implementation of directives in conjunction with loan facilities and arrangements.
- Improved procedures and new plans for rescheduling existing debt.
- Continued assistance for capital-scarce countries to obtain foreign exchange by banks.

In a nutshell, the main reason and hope for continued export of capital to LDCs is that lenders and investors have learned that funds should not go unaccompanied by the financial expertise required to ensure their successful investment. Without this assistance, economic development would be almost impossible.

To end this section on an optimistic note, consider the case of Japan which, 40 years ago, was a developing country. The lesson to be learned from the Japanese example is that industrial progress and economic maturity can take a long time even if economic policies are successful but that, once economic prosperity is achieved, moves towards opening up the economy to international economic forces pose no real threat. Let us wish today's LDCs the same degree of success.

### *The future for money and the monetary system*

Concern amongst the governments of the world and the international financial organisations for the stability of international monetary arrangements is unremitting. It is now over 40 years since the Bretton Woods conference, however, and the problem of how currency values should be controlled internationally still has no universally agreed solution. Calls for change are frequent, being sometimes for a change in specific aspects of the current IMF system and sometimes for a complete overhaul of international monetary arrangements. The events of the 1980s heighten awareness to the ever-present potential need for reform in response to deregulation, technological advances in the markets, the continuing debt crisis, increased innovation in foreign exchange markets, increased sensitivity of funds to interest rate differentials, wider exchange rate fluctuations, decreasing control over monetary flows and increased interdependence of financial market conditions. Never before has so much happened at once, so it is hardly surprising that the current system is questioned for its wisdom. On the other hand, what can the IMF and international monetary authorities do? What could be more appropriate than the current system, which allows almost complete flexibility for individual monetary authorities to do what they feel is best? Floating, pegged or fixed exchange rates are all possible under the present system. What else is there? A possible answer to this question is the provision of a more unified system of international monetary arrangements. Unification is the only missing ingredient from the present system, which consists of a hotch potch of individual monetary policies. Whether or not a unified approach should or will be forthcoming is, of course, another question. After all, the gold standard was a unified, international standard but it buckled under the individual needs for flexibility of the various countries. Would not a unified international approach therefore be a backward step? Surely the large international capital movements of present times and the ease with which they take place would render such a solution impractical. Such a suggestion could only find acceptance if the stability of the international monetary system could be assured.

One radical but often mooted solution to the problem of maintaining adequate monetary control in an integrated world financial market is that of a common currency – possibly a 'cocktail' currency – backed by a joint internationally-owned strong central bank. Ten years ago such a suggestion was only for academic discussion but, following the events of the first half of the 1980s, the practical implementation of such a possibility is once more up for scrutiny. After all, the concept is not so far away from the present situation, which allows for the compatibility of different currencies and for special arrangements when the stability of a particular country's financial system is in jeopardy. Moves towards an international currency unit (for example, the ECU) are already occurring in the free markets. Why should a system involving a strong international bank and a mutually acceptable international currency pose any further threat to the freedom of trade arrangements, international capital movements, or government control than the present system?

Proposals for the strong central bank, single currency alternative have been put forward by Cooper (1984) along the following lines.

- The central bank would be governed by national representatives in proportion to the share of participating nations' GNP that they represent.
- Stability and liquidity of the international financial system would be ensured in a manner similar to that already performed by central banks catering for the needs of their particular economies. The difference between the present system and the envisaged future system is that the internationally-owned central bank would be in a much stronger position to be effective than the central banks of individual economies.
- The system would use a currency similar to that of the modern SDR or an alternative acceptable 'cocktail' currency.
- Economic well-being of member countries would be maintained by open-market operations.
- The international central bank would set minimum standards and operate as a lender of the last resort for the central banks of individual countries but would not impose detailed regulation on domestic banks.
- Representation of individual countries and the structure of the international central bank and the international monetary arrangements would be under constant review.

Cooper's claim is that such a system could not become a reality until the twenty-first century because, until then, world political problems would render it infeasible. An alternative view is that, with current world problems so tightly interlinked with developments in the financial markets which themselves are in a state of rapid change, there is a need for a new system along the suggested lines before the envisaged date. Cooper argues that the system would only become acceptable to all countries if they had already achieved satisfactory states of development and standards of living. Until then the LDCs would still feel the adverse effects of integrated, internationalised financial markets. Again, an alternative suggestion is that a strong international central bank with a sufficiently flexible policy could be the best solution to bringing the developing free world safely into the next century. Macroeconomic financial management has for a long time seemed idealistic, mainly because of the different interests of countries across the world, but perhaps a more formal structure for macroeconomic financial planning and control is not so far away. The difficulties encountered by individual governments in managing their own economic affairs in the rapidly changing international financial environment, although unfortunate, have a certain unifying effect. The successful futures of strong and weak are interlinked via, among other things, the internationalisation of money and capital markets. The dialogue has already begun.

*The future for capital mobility and the integration of capital markets*

It is an understatement to say that the universal, integrated, one-world capital market is not yet here – but will it ever arrive?

One way in which the situation could arise (in theory) is if all governments were able and willing to set real rates of interest and returns for risk taking to an international standard. Needless to say, this alternative has proved infeasible to date because of competitive attitudes between governments and the influence of the Euromarkets, which has rendered control over domestic interest rates extremely difficult. The other way it could arise (again, in theory) is if the international markets grew in influence so much that individual economies were forced to throw in the towel, deregulate completely, and become, in effect, an extension of the international market. Of course, theory and practice are seldom, if ever, in harmony and there is a grey area to be considered that ranges from 'more-or-less free world markets' to 'more-or-less protected world markets'. Nevertheless, with the increasing size and influence of the Euromarkets, the evidence suggests that some progress along the second of the described routes to an integrated world capital market is already under way.

In practice, the extent to which private capital is free to respond to investment opportunities abroad will continue to depend on the efficient development of exchanges and financial markets, on the imposition or reduction of official restrictions on foreign investment, and on the degree of security perceived by funds providers for their overseas business interests. Prediction of how governments will respond to the relevant matters is not simple in the absence of a strong and unequivocal argument for or against protectionism. Modern cost-benefit analysis has yet to develop a technique for assessing foreign policy with regard to international financial flows for something as large as an economy. The future trend lies with how the governments of the world evaluate the pros and cons of integrated markets, on attitudes to the new freedom at government level, and on how much individual governments feel able to resist external pressures such as the influence of the Euromarkets, rapid-developing market technology and the rate of development of new financial instruments. Attitudes towards the new developments differ and are difficult to rank in order of importance or influence. Perhaps the best way to illustrate attitudes is via the following quotation from Raymond Bertrand, a former director of financial affairs for the OECD, whose words probably apply almost as well today as they did when they were written in 1981. He writes (p 18):

> National attitudes . . . normally reflect the standpoint of the burcaucratic establishment . . . which can be qualified according to a scale of reference ranging from *dirigiste* to *liberal*.
>
> Some liberals are fundamentalists, opposed to non-market mechanisms, others are repelled more by the ineffectiveness of capital controls than by their wickedness, as it were.
>
> Among the dirigistes can be found doctrinaires who deny any useful economic function to private capital movements, fanatics of national autonomy in monetary policy and of independence, cynics who enjoy the power given to an administration by the right to say no (particularly to big business).
>
> Between liberals and dirigiste lies a majority of pragmatists, happy to enjoy the freedom granted by others, but not averse to pulling a string or two of their own *à l'occasion*.

Bertrand's words neatly describe the range of bureaucratic attitudes that must be reconciled within international organisations to secure each step towards progress. If bureaucratic attitudes have changed since 1981, it is likely to be in response to factors that include the unforeseen variety of financial instruments that arose through free market forces during later years and the increased popularity of the Euromarkets. As a result of these developments, it has been learned that restrictions on domestic markets only lend more weight to the international markets, and that the exchange rate fluctuations caused by uneven economic development are not such a bad thing because free market forces provide facilities for their effective removal through new types of financial instrument.

Another way of classifying attitudes of bureaucracies and governments is according to the state of economic development of the nations that they represent. Political and economic stability usually have priority over the free market system, which could always be adopted when a satisfactory level of development has been achieved. It was mentioned in chapter 4 that free international movements of capital give weak economies the opportunity for development – yet at the same time expose the economy to dangers from the world economy. Perhaps the future attitudes towards open markets and international capital mobility among the developing countries is therefore tied in closely with the future stability and safety of the world economy and the international organisations that have arisen for its protection. Here a unified approach to world problems is required arising either from strong leadership or from recognition of mutual weaknesses and common interests. Recent events such as the renewed rise in dollar interest rates, concern over unsettled conditions in the US banking system, and concern over repayment conditions for the world's heavily-indebted countries detract from the confidence felt in the international markets and have had the effect, temporarily at least, of slowing down the rate of international capital movements. For the international mobility of capital to be readily acceptable by all participants, the fear of such international disturbances must be eased – either by removal of the offending disturbances or via more effective international arrangements for spreading their adverse effects over time. Paradoxically, this would seem to require reconciliation of the free market concept of individual freedom to operate to the best advantage with the concept that such freedom will not be forthcoming unless it operates to the mutual freedom and advantage of all – at a national level at least.

## Summary

Widespread changes continue to occur in our financial markets at a faster pace than ever before. Effects of the changes are being felt at all levels of business and society and in a multitude of different types of organisation around the world. Distinctions between currencies, between markets and between financial instruments have been eroded leaving the financial system in a fluid state ready to respond to the needs of borrowers and lenders in an extremely flexible manner.

The future is likely to see structural changes in markets and organisations across the world, which may cause short-run problems for those caught up in the process of change. The overall movement towards further links between markets, further technical and financial innovation and further deregulation is, however, likely to continue. Individual markets and financial institutions may be phased out or take on less significant roles but the overall movement towards internationalisation will continue to sweep the world's markets.

Problems abound – particularly in the short run – the main one currently being that of turning the internationalisation process to the best advantage. Except for the largest economies, individual countries face great difficulty pursuing policies against the tide of international economic pressures and are forced into coalitions for joint discussion and joint action. This joining together is in itself a further step towards the internationalisation process. Leaders of industry, commerce and governments are being led more and more towards systematic discussion of international matters, particularly the pros and cons of controls on international trade and finance. Incentives for cooperation are strong because the positions of individual nations are weak in response to international economic forces.

## References

Bertrand, R., 'The Liberalisation of Capital Movements – An Insight', *The Three Banks Review*, no. 132, December 1981, pp 3-22.

Cooper R.N., 'A Monetary System for the Future', *Foreign Affairs*, vol. 63, no. 1, 1984, pp 116-84.

# Bibliography

## Books


Brealey, R. and Myers, S., *Principles of Corporate Finance*, 2nd edn, McGraw Hill, 1984.

Dunning, J.H. *Studies in International Investment*, George Allen and Unwin, 1970.

Freear, J., *The Management of Business Finance*, Pitman, 1980.

George, A.M. and Giddy, I.H. (eds), *International Finance Handbook*, Wiley-Interscience, 1983.

Johnston, R.B., *The Economics of the Euro-market: History, Theory and Practice*, Macmillan Press Ltd, 1983.

Kindleberger, C.P., *International Money*, George Allen and Unwin, 1981.

Kindleberger, C.P., *A Financial History of Western Europe*, George Allen and Unwin, 1984.

Kubarych, R.M., *Foreign Exchange Markets in the United States*, Federal Reserve Bank of New York, August 1978.

Lees, A. and Eng, M., *International Markets*, Praeger, 1975.

Levy, H. and Sarnat, M., *Portfolio and Investment Selection: Theory and Practice*, Prentice-Hall International, 1984.

Park, Yoon S. and Zwick, Jack, *International Banking in Theory and Practice*, Addison Wesley, 1985.
Pippenger, J.E., *Fundamentals of International Finance*, Prentice Hall, 1984.
Polakoff, M.E., Durkin, T.A. *et al, Financial Institutions and Markets*, 2nd edn, Houghton Mufflin Co, 1981.
Quinn, B.S., *The New Euromarkets*, Macmillan, 1975.
Rodriguez, R.M. and Carter, E.E., *International Financial Management* 3rd edn, Prentice-Hall Inc, Englewood Cliffs, 1984.
Sarpkaya, S., *The Money Market in Canada*, Houstons Standard Publications Ltd, Toronto, 1977.
Stonham, P., *Major Stockmarkets of Europe*, Gower, 1982.
Thomas, Brinley, 'The Historical Record of International Capital Movements to 1913' in Adler, J.H. (ed), *Capital Movements and Economic Development*, Macmillan, 1967.
Tygier, C., *Basic Handbook of Foreign Exchange: A Guide to Foreign Exchange Dealing*, Euromoney publications, 1983.
World Bank, *IDA in Retrospect*, Oxford University Press, 1982.

**Journals**

American Express International Banking Corporation, 'The LDC Debt Crisis: Proposals for a Solution', *Amex Bank Review* (UK), vol 11, no 5, June 1984.
American Express International Banking Corporation, 'LDC Debt. The Next Phase', *Amex Bank Review* (UK), vol 11, no 5, June 1984.
American Express International Banking Corporation, 'Europe's $500 billion Foreign Debt. How Serious a Problem?', *The Amex Bank Review* (UK), vol 11, no 7, September 1984.
Australian Stock Exchange, 'The Japanese Stockmarket', *Australian Stock Exchange Journal*, February 1982.
Banco di Roma, 'A Foreign Investor's Guide to the Italian Stock Exchange', *Banco di Roma*, September 1984.
Banca Nazionale Del Lavoro, *Italian Trends*, vol 25, nos 9 and 10, September–October 1984.
Banker The, 'Internationalising the Market', *The Banker*, May 1984, pp 85–6.
Banker , The, 'Ruffing out a Euro Commercial Paper Market?', *The Banker*, January 1985.
Banque Brussels Lambert, 'The European Monetary System and the ECU after the First Six Years', *Report from Brussels*, no 122, December 1984, pp 1–8.

Bertrand, R., 'The Liberalisation of Capital Movements – An Insight', *The Three Banks Review*, no 132, December 1981, pp 3–22.
Biger, Nahum, 'Capital Market Integration. Some Evidence from Foreign-Controlled Securities', *Journal of Economics and Business*, no 34, 1982, pp 207–13.
Bird,G., 'Reforming the Fund: the Future Role of the International Monetary Fund in the International Financial System', *The Three Banks Review*, no 140, December 1983, pp 3–21.
Black, S.W., 'Exchange Policies for Less Developed Countries in a World of Floating Rates', *Essays in International Finance*, no 119, Princeton University, 1976.
Blondeel, J., 'Ten Billion ECU', *Euromoney*, October 1984.
Bobb, Euric, 'The Role of International Banks in the Financing of Economic Development in the Late 1980s and Beyond', *Quarterly Economic Bulletin of the Central Bank of Trinidad and Tobago,* vol IX, no 1, March 1984, pp 62–72.
Brock, W.E., 'Trade and Debt: The Vital Linkage', *Foreign Affairs*, vol 62, no 5, 1984, pp 1037–57.
Brown B., 'The USA's Growing Dependence on Foreign Savings', *Phillips and Drew Market Review*, May 1984, pp 13–15.
Campbell, K., 'Euro-Clear: Bonding the Market', *The Banker*, July 1984.
Carew, E., 'Shake-up in Sydney', *Euromoney*, October 1984, pp 334–5.
Carli, G., 'Money Markets – Trends and Challenges', *Banco di Roma Review of Economic Conditions in Italy*, no 3, September–December 1984, pp 305–16.
Chazan, J. and Frame, W., 'The Swap Market', *Canadian Banker*, vol 91, no 5, October 1984, pp 30–2.
Chrystal, K.A., 'A Guide to Foreign Exchange Markets', *The Federal Reserve Bank of St. Louis Review*, vol 66, no 3, March 1984, pp 5–18.
Clausen, A.W., 'New Tasks Ahead for International Financial Institutions', *Credit Suisse Bulletin*, vol 90, autumn 1984.
Cooper, R.N., 'Towards an International Capital Market', paper presented to *The International Economic Association*, Algarve, August/September 1969.
Cooper, R.N., 'A Monetary System for the Future', *Foreign Affairs*, vol 63, no 1, 1984, pp 166–84.
de Lattre, A., 'A Status Report on the Institute of International Finance', *The World of Banking*, May–June 1984, pp 19–21.
Deutsche Bundesbank, 'The European Monetary System: Structure and Operations', *Monthly Report of the Deutsche Bundesbank*, vol 39, 1979, pp 11–18.

Dini, L. 'The Changing International Monetary System', *Banco Nazionale Quarterly Review*, December 1984, pp 423–31.
Done, K., 'Revolution in the Swedish Money Markets', *The Banker*, October 1984, pp 97–100.
Dordick, H.S., 'The Emerging World Information Industry', *Economic Impact*, no 46, 1984.
Drabenstoff, M. and O'Mara McDonley, A., 'Futures Markets: A Primer for Financial Institutions', *Economic Review,* Federal Reserve Bank of Kansas City, November 1984.
Dunning, J.H., 'Capital Movements in the Twentieth Century', *Lloyds Bank Review*, April 1964.
Ehrlich, Edna E., 'The International Diversification of US Pension Fund Portfolios', Federal Reserve Bank of New York, research paper, December 1981.
Ehrlich, Edna E., 'International Diversification of Institutional Portfolios: The Pension Funds', *Federal Reserve Bank of New York*, research paper, April 1982.
EIB, *European Investment Bank Information Sheet*, no 41, October 1984.
Fautz, W., 'Deregulating the Yen Financial Markets', *Economic and Financial Prospects* (Swiss Bank Corporation), no 4, August/September 1984, pp 1–4.
Flenda, C., 'The Internationalization of Banking and Its Economic Advantages', *Banco di Roma Review of Economic Conditions in Italy*, no 3, September/December 1984, pp 365–87.
Franzen, Thomas, 'Reflections on the External Position and Foreign Loans', *Sveriges Riksbank Quarterly Review*, no 2, 1984, pp 22–32.
Friedman, Irving S., 'The Key Role of Bank Lending', *Economic Impact*, no 46, 1984, pp 23–9.
Goodman, D. and Radford, P., 'The World Bank: Its Role in Financing Development', *Barclays Review*, vol LIX, no 3, August 1984, pp 55–61.
Goodstadt, L., 'Hong Kong's Uncertain Futures', *Euromoney*, October 1984.
Gordon, M., 'The Options Increase for Philadelphia', *Euromoney*, October 1984, pp 349–50.
Governor of the Bank of England, 'The Euro-Currency Market', *Bank of England Quarterly Bulletin*, vol 11, no 2, June 1971.
Governor of the Bank of England, 'The Role and Future of the International Financial Istitutions', *Bank of England Quarterly Bulletin*, vol 24, no 4, December 1984.
Grant, C., 'Hoping for a Stock Reaction', *Euromoney*, August 1984, pp 46–52.

Grinspun B., 'The IMF Essay. Support US Debtor Nations', *Euromoney*, October 1984, pp 22–4.

Hawkins, S., 'Yen Bonds – A New Era', *Phillips and Drew Market Review*, June 1984.

Helcowicz, G.P., 'Pension Fund Investment', paper presented at 7th annual UK Insurance Economists Meeting, Nottingham University, 3 April 1985.

Hooper, P. and Kohlhagen, S.W., 'The Effects of Exchange Rate Uncertainty on the Prices and Volume of International Trade', *Journal of International Economics*, vol 8, November 1978, pp 483–511.

International Monetary Fund, *Annual Report of the Executive Directors for the Fiscal Year Ended April 30 1977*, Washington DC, 1977.

International Monetary Fund, *Articles of Agreement of the International Monetary Fund*, Washington DC, 1978.

International Monetary Fund, *Annual Report*, 1983.

International Monetary Fund, *Exchange Arrangements and Exchange Restrictions Annual Report*, 1983.

Jeker, R.A., 'The Swiss Banks' Services for Foreign Clients', *Credit Suisse Bulletin*, vol 90, autumn 1984, pp 5–7.

Klopstock, F.H., 'The Euro-Dollar Market: Some Unresolved Issues', *Essays in International Finance*, no 65, Princeton University, March 1968.

Leigh S., 'International Equity Performance in 1983', *Phillips and Drew Market Review*, January 1984.

Lessard, Donald R., 'World, Country and Industry Relationships in Equity Returns', *Financial Analysts Journal*, January/February 1976, pp 32–8.

Lim, Q.P., 'Will the Eurodollar Market Die?', *Euromoney*, October 1984, pp 68–77.

Lloyd, W.P., Goldstein, S.J. and Rogow, R.B., 'International Diversification of Real Assets: An Update', *Journal of Business Finance and Accounting*, vol 8, no 1, 1981, pp 45–50.

Lomax, D.F., 'Prospects for the European Monetary System', *National Westminster Bank Quarterly Review*, May 1983, pp 33–50.

Lutolf, F., 'Should Switzerland join the Bretton Woods institutions?', *Economic and Financial Prospects* (Swiss Bank Corporation), no. 5, October/November 1984.

Makridakis, S.G. and Wheelwright, S.C., 'An Analysis of Interrelationships Among the Major World Stock Exchanges', *Journal of Business Finance and Accounting*, vol 1, no 2, 1974, pp 195–215.

Maldonado, R. and Saunders, A., 'International Portfolio Diversification and the Inter-temporal Stability of International Stock-market Relationships, 1957–78', *Solomon Brothers Center for the Study of Financial Institutions*, working paper no 197, January 1980.
Mayer, H.W., 'Some Theoretical Problems Relating to the Euro-Dollar Market', *Essays in International Finance*, Princeton University, no 79, February 1970.
Minikin, R., 'The Japanese Banking System', *Barclays Review*, vol LIX, no 3, August 1984, pp 58–69.
Morgan Guaranty Trust Co, 'Japanese Exchange-Control and the Yen', *World Financial Markets*, Morgan Guaranty Trust Co of New York, March 1981.
Morris, J., 'Financial Futures. Chicago's Options to Stay Ahead', *Euromoney*, October 1984, pp 318–26.
National Bank of Egypt, *Economic Bulletin*, vol 35, no 4, 1982, pp 382–5.
National Bureau of Economic Research (NBER), *Project on Foreign Trade Regimes and Economic Development*, Krueger, 1978.
Oba, T., 'The Yen must Play a More Important World Role', *Euromoney*, October 1984, pp 63–5.
OECD, 'International Financial Markets', *Financial Market Trends*, OECD, June 1984, pp 25–83.
OECD, 'The Impact of New Assets and Intermediation Techniques on the Functioning of Financial Markets', *Financial Market Trends*, OECD, June 1984, pp 12–24.
OECD, *Economic Outlook*, no 35, July 1984.
Ogai, H., 'Will Liberalisation Boost the Yen?', *The Banker*, July 1984, pp 33–9.
Okumura, H., 'Financial Liberalisation Gathers Pace', *The Banker*, January 1984.
Padraic, F., Adam, N. and Ollard, W., 'The Great Deregulation Explosion', *Euromoney*, October 1984, pp 55–61.
Pakenham, K., 'Experiments in the International Bond Markets 1970–1982', *Amex Bank Review Special Papers*, no 5, July 1982.
Parry, T.G., 'Arguments For and Against Foreign Investment in Australia', *The University of South Wales Working Paper Series*, no 56, October 1983.
Pattison, J. and Quelch, J., 'Problems of Eurobond Underwriting', *The Banker*, October 1978, pp 68–75.
Porter, R., National Westminster Bank plc. Speaker's notes: seminar for academics, *The London Commodity Exchange Co Ltd*, 5 November 1984.
Queck, J., 'Will Simex Become the Missing Link?', *Euromoney*, October 1984, pp 346–7.
Redhead, K., 'The Use of Financial Futures for Hedging Foreign Exchange Risk – An Exposition', *Coventry (Lanchester) Polytechnic Staff Seminar Discussion Paper*, July 1984.

Revell, J.R.S. and Gardener, E.P.M. (eds), *World Banking Abstracts*, vol 1, nos 1–5, vol 2, nos 1–3, 1984–5.

Shafer, J.R. and Loopesko, B.E., 'Floating Exchange Rates After Ten Years', *The Brookings Papers on Economic Activity*, The Brookings Institution, 1983.

Shaw, E.R., Howcroft, J.B. and Gill, C.P., 'Identifying International Lending Risk. Part I', *The World of Banking*, March/April 1982, pp 27–31.

Shaw, E.R., Howcroft, J.B. and Gill, C.P., 'Identifying International Lending Risk. Part II', *The World of Banking*, May/June 1982, pp 31–8.

Stonham, P., 'Reforming the Paris Stockmarket', *The Investment Analyst*, no 60, April 1981, pp 4–11.

Stonham, P., 'Revolution in the Euromarkets', *Paper presented at the Haute École Commercial*, Paris, May 1985.

Volkskas Bank, South Africa 'The Free-Market System in South Africa', *Volkskas Economic Spotlight*, February 1984.

Watson, J., 'A Study of Possible Gains from International Investment', *Journal of Business Finance and Accounting*, vol 5, no 2, 1978, pp 195–205

Watson, J., 'The Stationarity of Inter-country Correlation Coefficients: A Note', *Journal of Business Finance and Accounting*, vol 7, no 2, 1980, pp 297–303.

Wicks, J., 'Boom in the Swiss Franc Capital Market', *The Banker*, July 1984.

Winder, R., 'The Final Days of the Trading Floor', *Euromoney*, October 1984, pp 86–91.

Wise, W., 'The Mending Wall: The Rise of the Universal Financial Market', *The World of Banking*, March/April 1984, pp 16– 19.

Wolf, M.S., 'The Private Use of the European Currency Unit (ECU), *Economic and Financial Prospects* (Swiss Bank Corporation), no 3, June/July 1984, pp 1–5.

World Bank, *The World Bank Annual Report 1983*, Washington DC.

Yallup, Peter J., 'A Study of Possible Gains from International Investment and the Stationarity of Inter-Country Correlation Coefficients: A Comment', *Journal of Business Finance and Accounting*, vol 9, no 1, 1982.

Yamey, B.S., 'The Economic Performance of Futures Trading', *The Three Banks Review*, no 141, March 1983, pp 33–43.

**Newspapers**

*Financial Times* (London) from June 1984 to June 1985.

# Index

African Development Bank, 80
Agency for International Development Aid (AID), 79
American Depository Receipts (ADRs), 123
arbitrage,
  in foreign exchange markets, 173–4
  interest, 174
  space, 174
  swap, 93, 109–10
  triangular, 174
Asian Development Bank, 80
Asia–Pacific region,
  financial development of, 48
  stockmarkets, 125–30
Association of International Bond Dealers (AIBD), 49, 102
auditing and accounting standards,
  of listed companies, 29
  harmonisation of, 198
Australian Associated Stock Exchanges (AASE), 126
automatic teller machines (ATMs), 186–7
balance of payments reports, 15–16
Bank of England, 44
Bank for International Settlements (BIS), 6, 79
banks,
  central
    activities in foreign exchange markets, 20, 145
    in LDCs, 85
    open market operations, 34, 68, 140
    regulatory activities, 20, 68–9
  commercial, 69
    in currency markets, 19
    in interbank market, 143–4
    in LDCs, 85
    in swap market, 111
  foreign, 83, 87
  information for, 184–7
  international, 4, 80–2, 106–7
  Lombard, 44
  merchant, 44, 69
  multinational, 82–5
  operations in foreign exchange

markets, 20
regional development, 80
restrictions on, 34–6
beta risk, 156–7, 162–3
'Big Bang', 118
black markets, 39, 146
bonds,
droplock, 108
Euro
advantages of, 101
convertible, 108
future of, 201–2
issue procedure, 102–4
market for, 100–6, 201–2
multi-currency, 107
with warrants, 108
*see also* foreign bonds
Euroyen, 105, 129
foreign, 97–100
international, 97–104, 106–9
multi-currency, 107
parallel, 109
Samurai, 98–100
Swiss market for, 98–9
West German market for, 100
Yankee, 98
Zero-coupon, 107
Bretton Woods system, 47, 50–1, 70–1

Capital asset pricing model (CAPM), 157–8, 160–3
Capital market line (CML), 26–7
capital markets,
deregulation of, 5–9
largest, 9
overview of, 3–4
Cedel, 49, 189–90
ceilings on purchases of securities, 32
Chicago Board Options Exchange (CBOE), 121
Clearing House Automated Payments System (CHAPS), 185
Clearing House Interbank Payments System (CHIPS), 185
closed-circuit markets, 36
co-financing, 78, 86
colonial system, 45
Commissaire du Controle des Banks, 123
communications systems, 30
comparative advantage, 24–5
Computer Assisted Executive System (CAES), 188
Computer Assisted Order Routing and Executive System (CORES), 188
cost of capital, 160–3
cross-border financial flows,
demand for, 24–8
discouragement of, 31–6
encouragement of, 28–31
restricted *vs* free, 23–41
currencies,
'cocktail', 107, 146, 200, 206–7
types of, 145–6
currency markets,
parallel, 121
restrictions on, 36–7
two-tiered, 36
*see also* foreign exchange markets

debt crisis, 54–5, 84, 86, 204–5
depository receipts, 129
deposit requirements,
in foreign currencies, 35
on purchases of securities, 32–3
Depository Institutions Deregulation and Monetary Control Act, 65, 83
deregulation,
influence of Euromarkets on, 8, 202
in Australia, 83
of banking, 82–4
of currency markets, 96
of London market, 117–8
trend in the 1980s, 54–6, 197
Development Assistance Committee (DAC), 79
Development Bank of Japan, 80
development cycle, 40–1
diversification, 2
by pension funds, 158–9
gains from, 27–8, 156–9
international, 155–60
Markowitz, 27–8
naive, 27
restrictions on, 159–60
dollar crisis, 50

East India Company, 44
efficiency of markets, 8–9, 181–2
electronic funds transfer and payments systems (EFTPOS), 184
Employment Retirement Act (ERISA), 158
EPIC, 190
EUCLID, 189
Eurocheques, 81
Euroclear, 49, 189
Eurocurrencies,

Eurodollars, 9, 93–5
financing with, 95–7
for denominating Eurobonds, 98, 100, 102
origins of, 93–5
time value of, 142
Euromarkets,
borrowing in, 92–7
controls on, 37
developments in, 52–3
geographical scope of, 4
influence of, 6, 208–9
links with other markets, 16, 18–19
multinational banks in, 84
origins of, 48–9
Euronotes, 97
European Composite Units (Eurcos), 107
European Currency Unit (ECU),
composition of, 146–8
for denominating bonds, 104–5, 107, 112
origins of, 52
popularity of, 200
European Economic Community (EEC),
Code of Conduct Relating to Transactions in Transferable Securities, 7, 53, 116
Code of Liberalisation, 7
political system, 116–7
Treaty of Rome, 116
European integration, 48–9
European Investment Bank (EIB), 78–9
European Monetary System (EMS),
future of, 205–10
origins of, 52
role of IMF, 70–6
European Options Exchange (EOE), 121
European Payments Union (EPU), 47
European Unit of Account (EUA), 107, 146
exchange rates,
determinants of, 19
equilibrium theories of, 168–70
fixed, 138
floating, 52, 140
forecasting, 167–70
of currencies against the dollar, 72
pegged, 139
exchange risk, 19, 165–75
expectations theory, 168–70

Federal Reserve System, 46
fiduciary certificates, 119
financial markets,
anonymity in, 13
characteristics of, 28–31
chronology of events in, 58–60
domestic, 16–18
innovations in, 8–9
morphology, 13–22
regulation of, 5–6, 25
world, 16
Financial Services in the United Kingdom (White Paper), 118
First World War, 45–6
Fisher's theory, 168–9
floating rate notes (FRNs), 53, 106–8, 148
forecasting,
cash flows, 163–4
exchange rates, 167–70
foreign exchange markets,
currency options, 8, 142
forward, 141–2
futures, 8, 142
innovation in, 52
interbank, 143–4
links with other markets, 16
nature of, 19–21, 137–52
Foreign Investments Review Board (FIRB), 126
free market system, 3, 159–60, 182

General Agreement on Tariffs and Trade (GATT), 6
General Agreement to Borrow (GAB), 54
Glass–Steagall Act, 60
gold standard, 45–6, 139
government restrictions,
arguments against, 38–40
arguments for, 38
during the 1930s, 46–7
on currency markets, 36–7, 95
on securities markets, 32–4
via the banking system, 34–6

hedging,
basics of, 170–1
exchange risk, 166, 171–2
in forward markets, 171–3
in futures markets, 172–3
in inefficient markets, 170

industrial revolution, 45
information,
and market efficiency, 181
for banks, 184–7
for markets, 187–92
systems, 30
technology industry, 183–93
insider trading, 30
INSTINET, 188
Institute of International Finance (IIF), 186
Inter-American Development Bank, 80
interbank market, 20, 143–4
Interest Equalisation Tax (IET), 32, 33, 42, 52, 124, 201–2
interest rate risk, 172
International Accounting Standards Committee (IASC), 127
international asset pricing model (IAPM), 158
International Bank for Reconstruction and Development (IBRD), 6, 47, 76–7
International Banking Act, 64, 83
International Dealers Association (IDA), 46, 124
International Development Agency, 77
international equity, 4, 53, 82, 116
International Finance Corporation (IFC), 77–8
International Money Market (IMM), 53, 124, 149–50
International Monetary Fund (IMF),
and the monetary system, 70–4, 145, 200, 205–8
Articles of Agreement, 70–1, 73, 74
co-operation between multinational banks and, 84
development role of, 6, 54
introduction of SDR, 51–2
meeting in Jamaica, 51
meeting in Rio de Janeiro, 74
origins of, 47
*see also* World Bank
INTEX, 191
investment currency pools, 36

Japan
liberalisation of financial markets, 4, 9, 55–6, 128–31
Japanese Post Office Bank, 55

Kuponsteur tax, 61

law of one price, 168–9
loss developed countries (LDCs), 2
debt crisis and, 9, 54, 79
financial restrictions in, 7
future for, 202–5
institutional developments in, 85–7
links between markets, 6–7, 12–22
London Business School Risk Measurement Service, 162, 183
London gold pool, 48
London inter-bank offered rate (LIBOR), 95, 97
London International Financial Futures Exchange (LIFFE), 149–50

margin trading, 149
Marshall Plan, 47
Mexico, 54, 84
monetary system, *see* International Monetary Fund (IMF)
money,
nature of, 200
future of, 205–6
multi-currency capital budgeting, 163–4
multinational companies, 2, 19, 28
multiple discriminant analysis (MDA), 186

NASDAQ, 124, 188
National Association of Security Dealers and Investment Managers (NASDIM), 65
National Companies and Securities Commission (NCSC), 126
National Financiera of Mexico, 80
National Market System (NMS), 188
new issues (controls on), 32
note issuance facilities (NIFs), 84–5, 96, 112, 119

offshore markets, *see* Euromarkets
options,
currency, 81, 148–52, 175–7
Financial Times Stock Exchange (FTSE) index, 150
markets, 148–52
Organisation for Economic Cooperation and Development (OECD), 6, 49, 79
Organisation for Petroleum Exporting Countries (OPEC), 39, 50, 52–4, 80
overseas investment (motives for), 2, 24–8

over-the-counter markets, 17, 29
  for Eurobonds, 123
  US, 124

pension funds, 158–9
Perouse Commission, 53, 65, 120
personal finance computer links, 192–3
petrodollars, 53
political risk, 31, 164–5
Prevention of Fraud (Investments) Act, 61
protectionism, 3
  motives for, 38, 49

Regulation Q, 94
revolving underwriting facilities (RUFs), 84–5, 96, 112, 148, 199
risk and return, 2, 5, 31
  concept for financial managers, 200
  differences between markets, 25–7
  facilities for dealing with, 13
  for Eurosecurities, 97
risk premium, 165
rollover credits, 96
Roman Law, 44

satellites, 21, 184
Saudi Arabian Monetary Agency (SAMA), 65
Second World War, 3, 47–8
Secrecy Laws, 193
Securities Exchange Commission (SEC), 47
Securities Investors Protection Corporation, 124
Securities Research Institute of Singapore, 127
SICOVAM, 187–8
Singapore inter-bank offered rate (SIBOR), 106, 108
Singapore International Monetary Exchange (SIMEX), 128, 149, 151
Smithsonian Agreement, 50
'snake-in-the-tunnel', 51–2
Society for Worldwide Interbank Telecommunications (SWIFT), 185
sole placing agency revolving underwriting facility (SPARUF), 96
Special Drawing Rights (SDRs),
  as a composite currency, 146, 207
  as an international reserve asset, 200
  at the IMF, 74–5
  composition, 52
  for denominating Eurobonds, 107
speculating,
  with currency options, 175–6
  with stock index options, 177
Stock Exchange Assisted Quotation System (SEAQ), 190–1
Stock Exchange Commission (SEC), 124
stock exchanges,
  American, 123
  Amsterdam, 121
  Antwerp, 121
  Basle, 122
  Berlin, 118
  Bologna, 122
  Boston, 123
  Bremen, 118
  Brussels, 120
  Cincinnati, 123
  Dusseldorf, 118
  Florence, 122
  Frankfurt, 44, 118
  Geneva, 45, 122
  Genoa, 122
  Ghent, 120
  Hamburg, 118
  Hanover, 118
  Hong Kong, 45
  Liege, 120
  London, 82, 102, 117–18
  Mexico, 77
  Midwest, 123
  Milan, 122
  Montreal, 124
  Munich, 118
  Nairobi, 61
  Naples, 122
  New York, 33, 46, 82, 102, 123
  Pacific, 123
  Palmero, 122
  Paris, 53, 119
  Philadelphia, 123–4, 149
  Rome, 122
  Singapore, 127–8
  South Korea, 77
  Stuttgart, 118
  Sydney, 48, 126
  Tokyo, 45, 53, 129
  Toronto, 124–5
  Trieste, 122
  Turin, 122
  Vancouver, 124
  Venice, 122

Winnipeg, 124
Zurich, 82, 122
stockmarkets,
Asia–Pacific, 125–30
Australia, 125–6
Belgium, 120–1
Canada, 124–5
characteristics of, 28–32, 115
Europe, 9, 116–23
France, 53, 116, 119–20
Hong Kong, 126–7
Italy, 116, 122–3
listing standards, 29
Luxembourg, 102, 104, 123
Malaysia, 48, 127
Japan, 3, 4, 9, 128–30
Netherlands, 9, 116, 121
Singapore, 127–8
supply of stocks, 31
Switzerland, 9, 102, 121–2
trading floor supervision, 30
UK, 9, 32, 116–8
USA, 3, 9, 31–2, 46, 123–4
W. German, 9, 118–9
world, 115–36
supply and demand, 4, 13, 21, 34, 96, 97
swaps, 93, 109–13, 199
currency, 81, 111
interest rate, 110–1
markets, 111–2
Sydney Futures Exchange (SFE), 126
syndicated loans, 84

TALISMAN, 190
technical revolution, 45–6
techniques for financial managers, 154–80
tender panel (TP), 96
topic, 90
trading techniques, 170–7
two-tiered markets, 36

underwriting,
by banks, 82, 84–5, 97, 98
Eurobonds, 102–4
safe procedures for, 102–4
universal capital market, 4–6, 11, 208

Wall Street Crash, 46–7
weighted average cost of capital (WACC), 160–2
Wise, W., 5
withholding taxes, 33, 105, 117, 119, 121, 122, 125, 126
World Bank, 2, 76–8, 84
and IMF, 75
projects, 86
Special Action Program, 54
World markets,
chronology of, 58–67
overview of, 3–5